Educating Deaf Children Bilingually

by

Shawn Neal Mahshie

With Insights and Applications
from Sweden and Denmark

Support for this project was received from The World Institute on Disability IDEAS Project (U.S. National Institute for Disability and Rehabilitation Research [Grant #H133D00005]), The Swedish National Board of Education, The Swedish-American Women's Club, The Gallaudet Research Institute, and Gallaudet University Pre-College Programs.

*Persons who wish to obtain additional copies of this document
may contact the Gallaudet Bookstore, 800 Florida Ave, N.E., Washinton, DC 20002
202-651-5380 (TTY/Voice), 202-651-5489 (Fax).*

To receive a complete listing of other Pre-College Publications, please write to:
*Pre-College Outreach Services
Kendall Demonstration Elementary School,
800 Florida Avenue, N.E.,
Washington, D.C. 20002-3695*

Cover design by Shawn Mahshie

*Our deaf children are part of a rich cultural and linguistic heritage.
They are part of a deaf community that values their deafness,
while at the same time recognizes the importance of their
taking their place in the larger, hearing community.
Our children use two languages—sign language and English—
and will make a mark on two communities,
the deaf community and the larger, hearing community.*

Congressional Testimony of
the American Society for Deaf Children,
Barbara Raimondo, parent and board member.
April 28, 1994

Table of Contents

ix . . . . Acknowledgements

xii . . . . Review of this Work

xiii . . . . Prologue

xvii . . . . Introduction

xvii . . . . Optimal Models

xix . . . . About this Book

xix . . . . Organization

xx . . . . Terms Used in this Book

xxi . . . . Background

xxi . . . . Bilingual Education in Sweden and
Denmark: What Does it Look Like?

xxiii . . . . A Decade of Transition: What Have They Learned?

xxv . . . . Other Sources of Information

xxvii . . . . Sweden and Denmark: A Brief Overview

xxvii . . . . Identification and Early Services

xxviii . . . . School Placement

xxx . . . . Support for Home Languages

xxx . . . . Sign Language as an Academic Subject

xxxi . . . . Sign Language Instruction for Parents and Teachers

xxxii . . . . Factors Leading to Change

xxxiv . . . . Experimental Classes

xxxiv . . . . Transition

1 . . . . **Chapter One: A Closer Look: Developing Literacy**

3 . . . . *Adam's Book*

15 . . . . Trusting the Children's Process

16 . . . . Outcomes

16 . . . . Reading Achievement

20 . . . . Overall Achievement

23 . . . . Developing Literacy: Theory

27 . . . . Comprehensible Input

28 . . . . Grammar Teaching

32 . . . . Literacy and Developing Skills in the Spoken Language

33 . . . . One Basic Prerequisite

36 . . . . Timing is Critical: First Things First

38 . . . . Writing

40 . . . . The Role of Errors

43 . . . . The Pay-Offs of Patience

46 . . . . At Their Own Pace

48 . . . . Expression in Either Language "Counts"

50 . . . . Process Writing/Signing

51 . . . . Applying Second Language Research and Resources
51 . . . . "Home Language" and "Mother Tongue"
52 . . . . Sorting Out the Differences
52 . . . . W- and S-Languages
54 . . . . More than Just a Luxury
56 . . . . A Measure of the Need for Change

57 . . . Chapter Two: Let Deaf Children Be Children

61 . . . Chapter Three: Let the Parents Be Parents

63 . . . . The Impact is on the Family
64 . . . . Acceptance and Support
64 . . . . Grieving
67 . . . . Parents in Transition
67 . . . . A Soft Start
71 . . . . Differing Needs
73 . . . . Respect
75 . . . . A First Language: Whose Choice is It?
75 . . . . A Win-Win Situation
75 . . . . Different Paths to Bilingualism
78 . . . . The Whole Child
80 . . . . The Opportunity to See for Themsleves
82 . . . . Cognitive Academic Language Proficiency
84 . . . . Keeping Expectations High
85 . . . . Emphasis on Speech Skills
86 . . . . A Cost-Benefit Perspective
89 . . . . Residual Hearing
91 . . . . Hearing or Feeling?
92 . . . . Ramifications
94 . . . . Critical Period and Spoken Language
94 . . . . Acquisition vs. Learning
97 . . . . Access Is the Key
99 . . . . A Hard Reality
101 . . . . Critical Period and Sign Language
102 . . . . Early Amplification
103 . . . . If and When
105 . . . . Cochlear Implants
109 . . . . Making Decisions
111 . . . . The Importance of Natural Language
111 . . . . The Significance of a Community of Language Users
114 . . . . Early Natural Language Input and the Brain
115 . . . . Beyond Modality

117 . . . . Use of Simultaneous Communication and Sign-based Codes
for the Majority Language
117 . . . . The Rise and Fall of Sign-based Codes
120 . . . . Sign-based Codes as Input for the Acquisition
of a First Language
120 . . . . The Signed Portion of the Input
123 . . . . Further Research Support
125 . . . . The Spoken Portion of the Input:
A Child-Centered View
128 . . . . Input in Two Modes
129 . . . . Use of Signed Codes by Older Students Whose First
Language is Sign Language
131 . . . . Sheltered Subject Matter Teaching
133 . . . . The Learning of Sign Language by Parents
134 . . . . Choices
137 . . . . The Parents' Own Language
137 . . . . Something In-Between
139 . . . . Sign Language Teaching
140 . . . . Minority Parents
141 . . . . Whatever it Takes
143 . . . . Placement Decisions
143 . . . . Integration of Deaf Children into Classes with Hearing Children
147 . . . . 'Segregated' Placements
151 . . . . Placement of Hard of Hearing Children
151 . . . . Integration into Classrooms with Hearing Children
153 . . . . Placement in Schools for the Deaf
155 . . . . Deaf, Hard of Hearing, and Hearing
Children Together
156 . . . . Placement with Other Hard of Hearing Children

157. . Chapter Four: Let the Teachers Be Teachers

157 . . . . Trust
158 . . . . Deaf Teachers
161 . . . . Sign Language as an Academic Subject/Deaf Studies
163 . . . . Expertise
163 . . . . Knowledge of the Structure of Both Languages
166 . . . . Knowledge of the Language of the Deaf Community
169 . . . . Training for Teachers of Sign Language/Deaf Studies
as an Academic Subject
170 . . . . Respect for Both Languages
171 . . . . Good News
172 . . . . Commitment to Individualization
173 . . . . Larger Class Size: An Important Strategy for Individualizing
176 . . . . A Team Effort

179.. Chapter Five: Change the System, Not the Children

179 . . . . Meeting Deaf Children "Where They Live"

182 . . . . "Yes, but....

182 . . . . Cost-effectiveness

185 . . . . Socioeconomic status of parents

187 . . . . Cultural diverstiy

189 . . . . The impact of bilingual education for minority Deaf children

190 . . . . Deaf/Hearing dynamics

193 . . . . Sharing Sign Language and Deaf culture

194 . . . . Hearing and Deaf parents connecting

200 . . . . Lack of expertise

200 . . . . Making changes in a large, diverse nation

204 . . . . Turning the World Upside Down

204 . . . . Making a Transition

209.. Appendices

209 . . . . Appendix A: Author's Note: Terms Used in this Book

209 . . . . Rationale

210 . . . . Conventions

214 . . . . Appendix B: Procedure and Limitations of this Study

216 . . . . Appendix C: Addresses of Organizations Named in Text

219 . . . . Appendix D: Diagram of the Swedish School System

220 . . . . Appendix E: Swedish National Curriculum

235 . . . . Appendix F: Bonaventura Parents' Organization Advice to "New" Parents

239.. References

Acknowledgements

Help from a number of individuals and organizations in Sweden, Denmark, and the United States was critical to the implementation of my studies and the writing of this book. Significant help demands significant thanks.

I would first like to thank the World Institute on Disability (WID), for making my first study possible through their timely support and recognition of the significance of such a research endeavor. Special thanks go to **Judith Heumann**, then vice-president of the WID and principal investigator of the IDEAS (International Disabilities Exchanges And Studies) project, and **Mark Conly**, IDEAS project director, for their help, sustained enthusiasm, and interest in the complex issues surrounding the education of deaf children here and abroad. I wish also to acknowledge The American Women's Club in Sweden for its assistance at a critical time. I applaud the Club's support of academic cooperation between the two countries. I thank **Robbin Battison** in particular for his role as liaison with this group, for his help in loaning me a computer, and for the friendship he and his family so graciously extended. I greatly appreciate the support of the Gallaudet Research Institute and Dean **Michael Karchmer** in giving me release time to conduct the first study, publishing my earlier occasional paper on this topic (Davies, 1991), and providing editorial support for the current book. Finally, thank you to the Swedish National Board of Education and Gallaudet University Pre-College Programs and for the continued support needed to complete this work. I extend very special gratitude to **Margaret Hallau,** Director of Pre-College Programs' Center for Curriculum Development, Research, and Evaluation, who acknowledged—through support of this project—the significance of these countries' experiences and insights in shaping current innovations in the United States. Margaret offered immeasurable wisdom, support, and flexibility during the writing of this book.

Each individual I interviewed, each class I observed, each home I visited added shape, color, texture, and detail to the gradually unfolding picture I was forming about efforts to provide a bilingual education for deaf children in Sweden and Denmark. I wish to thank all the individuals I interviewed or observed for their openness to my questions, their willingness to share (sometimes very candidly), and their time in meeting with me.

My primary contacts in each country spent many hours helping to conceptualize the study, guiding me to the people who became important sources of information, offering their perspectives on issues that needed further illumination, providing feedback concerning the accuracy or inaccuracy of my perceptions, and generously sharing with me their warm hospitality. To the following people in the following countries, I wish to say "Tack" [Swedish/Danish for "Thank You"]:

In Sweden:

...to **Brita Bergman** (Head Professor at the Stockholm University Department of Sign Language), my primary contact in Sweden, who accepted the responsibility of supervising me as I conducted the study and who has continued to generously offer her time and expertise in so many ways. ...to **Christina Edenås** (assistant principal at the Manilla School for the Deaf), who provided logistical support and information regarding the inner workings of the Swedish schools for deaf students, and who went the extra mile to help me feel at home in Stockholm by sharing valuable insights about Swedish culture (deaf and hearing), and opening her home to me on many occasions. ...to **Inger Ahlgren** (Docent in Linguistics at the Stockholm University Department of Sign Language), who became a primary contact because of her seminal contributions and pioneering thinking on the subject of bilingual education of deaf children, and who is best remembered by me for her outspoken common sense about language learning. ...to **Lars Åke Wikström** (now President of the Swedish National Association of the Deaf), who not only shared his consumer/teacher/researcher point of view on the historical underpinnings of the important turns of events I was studying, but was a major player in the politics that actually *turned* those events. (As a result of the thoughtfulness of this "deaf radical," including his periodic interpreting—for my benefit—I experienced less deaf/hearing separation than I had previously known.) ...to **Lars Wallin** (first person in the world to receive a Ph.D. in Sign Language), for the many observations he shared with me during his six months as a visiting scholar at Gallaudet. ...to **Arne Risberg**, then Head Professor of Hearing Technologies in the Royal Institute of Technology, who welcomed me into his home and into the Department of Speech Communication, and who spent time sharing his views about the past, present, and future state of affairs in the field of speech research and teaching in Sweden, ...to **Sten Ulfsparre** (first deaf teacher to utilize translations of Swedish Sign Language in teaching written Swedish and now a trainer of teachers), who provided generous accommodations in his home on my second visit. ...to **Kristina Svartholm** (Docent at the Stockholm University Department of Nordic Languages), for her ongoing enthusiasm for my work and sharing with me her theoretical perspectives on the teaching of Swedish as a second language. ...to **Kerstin Heiling** (Psychologist at the University of Lund Department of Educational Research) for providing information about reading skills and achievement, ...to **Gunilla Christersson** (teacher and developer of curriculum materials at Manilla School for the Deaf), for her forward thinking about language learning and her trust in the capabilities of deaf children.

In Denmark:

...to **Britta Hansen** (Director of the Centre for Total Communication in Copenhagen), my primary contact in Denmark, whose realism, insights, and humor translate into great wisdom. Britta taught me much about tolerance of diverse situations in the homes and classrooms of deaf students. Britta also helped arrange both visits to Denmark, opened her home to me, and provided comments on pieces I have written about Denmark. ...to **Elisabeth Engberg-Pedersen** (linguist who has analyzed and written about Danish Sign

Language), who so generously invited me into her home for two weeks, filled in information gaps during late-night sessions, and challenged me to get all I could out of my first visit in Denmark. ...to **Ritva** and **Asger Bergmann** (who are parents, officials in the Danish National Association of the Deaf, and teachers/researchers/interpreter trainers at Copenhagen's Centre for Total Communication) for sharing valuable information about their many areas of experience and expertise, for welcoming me into their home, and for opening my eyes with their fluency in so many signed and spoken languages. ...to **Bent Neilsen,** psychologist at the Kastelsvej school, who wrote up his test results for me in English. ...to **Wendy Lewis** (teacher in the first bilingual project in Copenhagen), who had so little free time at school that she invited me to spend the night in her home to interview the ground-breaking team of teachers of which she is a part. ...to **Tové Ravn,** (also a teacher in the same class) who provided lodging in her home on my second visit and shared with me hours of insights from her experiences learning (often through trial and error) about bilingual teaching.

In the United States:

...to my earlier teachers about deaf people and language: **Joseph Schmitz, Marina McIntire, Dennis Cokely, Rick Zimmer, MJ Bienvenu, Gary Malkowski, Matt Glottfelter, Ceil Lucas, Betty Colonomos, Diane Kerner, Ramy Bustamante, Susan Karchmer,** and **Pam Rush,** who each helped me in a different way to clarify the issues in my mind. ...to **Bill Stokoe** and **Bob Johnson**, for all they taught me, and for their concrete and tacit support of this project and many of my other academic and vocational pursuits since 1982. ...to my current teachers about Deaf children, parents, and language-learning: **Marie Philip, Lon Kuntze, Judith Treesberg, James Mahshie, Lynne Erting, Nancy Topoloski, Janet Weinstock, Dave Schleper, Melvia Miller-Nomeland, Laura Petitto, Laurene Gallimore, Susan Dyer, Barbara Gerner de Garcia, Steve Nover, James Cummins, Virginia Collier,** and **Beti Leone,** each providing a taste of their own world of information and experience.

...to **Robert Clover Johnson**, who pulled time out of a hat to do the final editing of this book, and who has always been the best cheerleader in encouraging me to trust my intuitions about the importance of this line of study. ...to **Sara Gillespie** for assistance in the final stages of production of this book and moral support throughout. ...and to the team of people in Pre-College Programs who assisted in proofreading.

...to my parents, **Lee** and **Dorothy Neal,** and my entire family, for surrounding me with the belief that there were no limits to what I could do.

And finally, to my dear husband, *Jim.* Thank you for challenging me in a way that has forced me to clarify and better articulate my ideas about the learning of both spoken and signed language, for your patience with this all-consuming process, and for sharing this memorable journey with me.

Review of this Work

This book touches on a number of disciplines needed to discuss issues that are of interest or concern to parents and educators of deaf children. My treatment of each area and review of the literature could not, within the limits of this study, be comprehensive. Rather, the aim was to suggest to the reader the broad scope of research, theory, and experience that support the model described. I have relied heavily on various experts to confirm that the premises described here were in line with their experience or their specific area of expertise. I am greatly indebted to the following parents, teachers, researchers, speech and hearing professionals, administrators, and consumers for reviewing all or part of this manuscript, and for generously offering helpful commentary and thought-provoking questions:

Dr. Brita Bergman
Ritva Bergmann
Gunilla Christersson
Dr. Harvey Corson
Siv Dahlen
Jacqueline Dickey
Dr. Linda Delk
Dr. Carol Erting
Lynne Erting
Dr. Carolyn Ewoldt
Dr. Barbara Gerner de Garcia
Sara Gillespie
Sharon Graney
Dr. Margaret Hallau
Britta Hansen
Robert C. Johnson
Marlon Kuntze
Dr. Beti Leone
Dr. James Mahshie

Dr. Susan Mather
Carolyn McCaskill-Emerson
Jennifer McMillan
Dr. Steven Neal
Dr. Laura Petitto
Marie Jean Philip
Deborah Nussbaum
Leslie Proctor
Barbara Raimondo
Nancy B. Rarus
Tové Ravn
Julia Robertson
David Schleper
Dr. Irene Serna
Dr. Patricia Spencer
Nancy Topoloski
Judith Treesberg
Bettie Waddy-Smith
Janet Weinstock

Prologue

At first, people refuse to believe that a strange new thing can be done, then they begin to hope it can be done, then it is done and all the world wonders why it was not done centuries ago (Frances Hodgson Burnett).

In 1981, after years of grassroots activism by Deaf adults and parents of deaf children, the Swedish Parliament passed a law stating that deaf people need to be bilingual in order to function successfully in the family, in school, and in society. The result of this legislation[1] was that deaf children acquired the right to be educated in a way that fosters proficiency in both Swedish Sign Language and Swedish, with a focus on literacy. Since that time, schools have been charged with the responsibility of educating deaf children bilingually. In 1983, major changes in national curriculum policy governing deaf children's education were released in response to the new law.

While no similar legislation was passed in Denmark[2], it is reported that, "Today, the idea of bilingual education is widely accepted and bilingualism in Danish Sign Language and Danish is the official aim of all schools for deaf children" (Engberg-Pedersen, 1993, p. 15). Furthermore, Danish Sign Language as an academic subject is now part of the curriculum for all deaf children in Denmark, based on a regulation issued by the Danish Ministry of Education.

In the United States today, a large percentage of children who are deaf or hard of hearing are educated *mono*lingually, through English-based, speech-centered approaches. From its most recent Annual Survey of Hearing Impaired Children and Youth[3] Gallaudet University's Center for Assessment and Demographic Studies reports the following figures about current modes of communication used in the education of deaf and hard of hearing children in the United States:

- 41.1% of the children are addressed using "auditory/aural methods" (spoken English only).

---

1   Proposition 1980/81:100, supplement 12.

2   No language is given official recognition in Denmark, (Engberg-Pedersen, 1993, p. 16).

3   For this survey, conducted during the 1992-93 school year, CADS gathered information about 48,300 children, which represents approximately 60-65% of deaf and hard of hearing children receiving special education in the U.S. Schools and programs filled out one form for each child. Words in quotes above reflect the actual choices on the survey. No response was given by the schools to this question about communication modes for 587 children (Schildroth, 1994).

- 56.1% are addressed in "both speech and sign" (spoken English accompanied by signs in English word order).

- 1.9% are addressed primarily in "sign only" (includes American Sign Language).

- .5% are addressed using "cued speech" (spoken English accompanied by hand signals intended to aid in lipreading).

- .4% are addressed using "other."

Despite the fact that deaf people *can* become extremely proficient readers and writers, educators of deaf children have generally been at a loss to find an approach that consistently brings about this result. The past 20 years have witnessed new approaches for teaching English to students who are deaf or hard of hearing, greatly improved amplification technology, earlier intervention in the teaching of speech, increased focus on placing deaf children in the mainstream, and widespread use of English-based sign systems in educational settings. In spite of intensified efforts to provide deaf children with more English, earlier English, better audition of English, visual access to English through manual symbols, and more immersion in English through classes with hearing children; patterns of depressed English skills and school achievement of deaf children in the United States persist.[4]

At the same time, advances in research about deaf infants, sign language linguistics, bilingualism, and language learning have provided a new framework for understanding the causes of traditional problems in educating deaf children. In 1989, faculty of the York University Department of Education (Toronto) and Boston University Center for the Study of Communication and Deafness released an extensive review of the literature surrounding the issue of native sign language acquisition and its relation to proficiency in the majority language, as well as to academic achievement and social development (Israelite, Ewoldt, Hoffmeister, 1989).[5] Their final report to the Canadian Ministry of Education summarizes three decades of evidence that deaf [6]children who acquire sign language early function cognitively, linguistically, and socially at levels that are developmentally appropriate; and that early acquisition of sign language as a first language facilitates learning of the language of the majority.

---

4   Allen, 1986; Gentile, 1972; Goodstein, 1988; Lucas, 1989; and Paul, 1987.

5   Copies of this report may be obtained by writing to MGS Publication Services, 880 Bay Street, 5th Floor, Toronto, Ontario, M7A1N8, Canada.

6   Different use of terminology to refer to deaf children and sign language will be applied when discussing this bilingual model, beginning with the Introduction. See Appendix A for further explanation.

Consistent with this view is the fact, long recognized by researchers, that deaf children of Deaf parents who do have early access to sign language on average score higher than deaf children from hearing families in most measures of academic and reading achievement.[7] However, those deaf children born to Deaf parents are clearly in the minority. Over 90% of deaf children are born to hearing parents and have no older Deaf relative.[8]

Recognition of a chronic cycle of poor English skills and low achievement of deaf children in America,[9] coupled with the strong recommendations of scholars in a variety of disciplines,[10] has led to growing interest in the concept of educating deaf children *bilingually*, acknowledging the value of both American Sign Language (ASL) and English in the classroom. Proponents of a model in which both English and ASL are considered crucial to deaf children's successful functioning claim that the system must be re-structured to provide very young deaf children (and their parents) opportunities for extensive interaction with Deaf adults who use a natural sign language. It is argued that in this way, deaf children of hearing parents—like the small percentage of deaf children who have Deaf parents—can gain access to the following: 1) a first language they can acquire through natural processes during the same developmental period in which language begins to flourish among hearing children, 2) the kinds of knowledge, cognitive development, and emerging literacy that children can attain well before starting school, and 3) the normal social-emotional development that accompanies interacting with children of all ages and adults who are accepting of their deafness and of their language(s).

Policy makers in the United States and countries around the world are beginning to acknowledge the cultural significance of native sign languages, and their educational role in deaf students' acquisition of majority languages. The United Nations Educational Scientific and Cultural Organization (UNESCO) has stated that the sign languages of the world should be "afforded the same status as other linguistic systems" and that they must play a major role in educational programs for deaf children. As of the writing of this manuscript, a number of schools in the U.S. and Canada have made formal changes in policy and practice (Strong, in press) to begin approaching deaf and hard of hearing children's education from a more bilingual perspective.

7   Corson, 1973; Kampfe & Turecheck, 1987; Meadow, 1967, 1968; Moores, 1987; Stuckless and Birch, 1966.

8   Meadow, 1972: Rawlings & Jensema, 1977; Trybus and Jensema, 1978.

9   COED (U.S. Commission on Education of the Deaf), 1988; Johnson, Liddell, & Erting, 1989; Liddell & Johnson, 1992; Trybus & Karchmer, 1977; Schildroth & Karchmer, 1986; Schildroth & Karchmer, 1986.

10   Ahlgren, 1982; Barnum, 1984; Bergman, 1978; Bouvet, 1990; Corson, 1973; Cummins, 1984; Davies, 1991b, 1994; Erting, 1978; Grosjean, 1992; Hansen, 1987, 1989; Johnson, et al, 1989; Kannapell 1974, 1978; Kuntze, 1992; Lane, 1992a, 1992b; Mahshie, S. 1995; McIntire and Groode, 1982; Paul 1988; Quigley and Paul 1984; Ramsey, 1993; Stevens 1980; Stewart, 1982; Strong, 1988; Svartholm, 1993; Woodward 1978, and others.

Introduction

This book is about the perspectives and practices of those who have, for some time now, been making an effort to educate *Deaf*[1] children bilingually, with three basic goals in mind: grade-level academic achievement, full participation in society, and fluency in both the language of the majority and the language of the Deaf community (as well as the language of the home—if different from the above). It is about what the parents, teachers, researchers, and students involved in such efforts have learned, and what we can learn from them.

While there is some mention in this book of how these bilingual educational environments came about and how they are being made to work, the common ingredients for making a real change in the lives of Deaf children and their parents seem to run deeper than practical strategies or "how-to"s. More important, at this point, are the attitudes and insights that result from observing Deaf children as they grow up in an environment where early language can be acquired naturally. Such attitudes and insights, which continue to evolve as a result of experience and research, are the primary focus of this book.

Optimal Models

There has been discussion at a number of major conferences for parents and educators in the U.S. about using both American Sign Language and English in the education of Deaf children, and American research has provided strong theoretical support for educating Deaf children bilingually. Yet, as the figures shown in the Prologue indicate, the language of the Deaf community (American Sign Language) is not yet being utilized to any significant degree in educating Deaf children in this country. Widespread implementation of a model that promotes fluency in both the language of the majority and of

---

1   For the remainder of the book, which focuses on a model that views deaf children and their language differently from the current monolingual model, conventions are applied in labeling deaf and hard of hearing children that tend to differ from current usage in the U.S. In general, a *Deaf* child or adult is, in this context, considered to be *"one for whom the primary receptive channel of communication is visual."* The reader is encouraged to turn to Appendix A, which describes the rationale for the terms chosen. Appendix A also discusses more *specific* references to "Deaf," "deaf," and "hard of hearing" children.

the Deaf community would represent a significant departure from current practices in the United States.

My contact with programs that have committed themselves to implementing bilingual education for Deaf children in the U.S., Canada, and France indicates that they have arrived at conclusions and developed strategies that are, in many ways, consistent with those that will be presented here. The nucleus for discussion in this book, however, is centered around classrooms and homes in Sweden and Denmark, where there has simply been *more* time and external support for developing a bilingual model. Clearly, not all of the obstacles have been overcome, but the transition to bilingual education of Deaf children is well under way in many areas of these countries, with growing political and financial support for implementation over the past 15 years.

When practices in both Sweden and Denmark are compared to those of other countries, some important differences exist in the following areas:

- Early services and approaches to *deaf*[2] children and their parents

- Approaches to teaching *Sign Language*[3] and the language of the majority

- Attitudes of educators and medical professionals toward Sign Language, the Deaf community, and minority languages in general.

For example, many early services (which are provided in Sweden and Denmark through a cooperative effort of medical professionals, social workers, preschools, parent organizations, and the Deaf community) are considered to be crucial ingredients in the successful implementation of a bilingual model for Deaf children. Such early and extensive support for families with deaf babies may currently seem out of reach in some countries. *Nevertheless, it is extremely important to study environments where such attributes are already in place when outlining models toward which to strive.* Drawing conclusions based on environments that do not provide these early services can contribute to a less-than-optimal picture of the real possibilities for Deaf children.

---

2   Please see Appendix A regarding use of the term "deaf."

3   This book will follow the convention used by educators and linguists in Denmark of capitalizing the term, "Sign Language" when it is used to refer to the natural language used for interaction within a Deaf community. Please see Appendix A, "Author's Note: Terms Used" for further explanation.

About this Book

Information shared about attitudes, practices, and events in Sweden and Denmark seems to have been of value to parents and educators in the U.S. Many strategies for parental support, for example, have already been borrowed from the Swedish or Danish models and put into practice in certain areas in the U.S.[4] This book will share in greater detail the experiences and perspectives of individuals in Sweden and Denmark, with a focus on *insights* (what they have learned from their experience conducting bilingual education) and *applications* (some of the practices that seem to be working). The book also discusses some of the theoretical underpinnings for the model described, and looks briefly at how these theories and practices might—or might not—apply to our situation in the United States.

Organization

The remainder of this *Introduction* gives some background about the nature of the inquiry in Sweden and Denmark, and a brief description of services there. *Chapter One* provides a glimpse into one aspect of theory and practice in educating Deaf children bilingually— the teaching of reading and writing. The three central chapters, starting with *Let Deaf Children be Children,* focus on some of the most important insights of those involved in concentrated, long-term efforts to educate Deaf children bilingually. Among other things, these chapters look at issues surrounding first language acquisition, placement, support for parents, and training for teachers. The book concludes by outlining some important considerations and potential problems in the transition toward a new model.

The final chapter also includes a discussion of some of the real and perceived obstacles to implementation. There appear to be a number of stumbling blocks or *"Yes, but...."*s to implementation of a model like that used in Sweden and Denmark in a large, culturally-diverse nation like the United States. For example, when I have described this bilingual model to individuals in the U.S., some tend to minimize or disqualify its applicability, stating that Sweden and Denmark do not have the cultural diversity we have in the U.S. Many of these same people are clearly dissatisfied with the biases inherent in our current monolingual model. They *are* interested in alternatives, but have trouble relating our situation to countries where the people are often characterized as more homogenous than people in the U.S.

While it is true that the percentage of individuals of minority cultures in Sweden and Denmark is not as high as it is in the U.S., there is a great deal of cultural and linguistic

---

4   M. Kuntze, California; L. Roberts, Michigan; N. Topoloski, Washington, DC; personal communication.

diversity in these countries. Many residents have recently emigrated or have been in Sweden or Denmark for a generation or two but are not of Swedish/Danish descent (for instance, many individuals and groups from the Middle East have migrated to Sweden, as it is considered a politically-safe refuge).

More importantly, it is asserted by many minority Deaf individuals in the U.S. that full access to education, information, and opportunities would go a long way toward promoting equality. Many have argued that discrimination against them because they are Deaf—and denial of their right to an accessible language—are issues that far supersede other forms of cultural discrimination they have faced (Gallimore, 1994). This is one of the topics discussed under the "Yes, but..." section in the last chapter. Readers who find themselves asking a lot of questions or harboring many doubts about the feasibility of Deaf-hearing cooperation or the cost-effectiveness of implementing such a model in the U.S. may wish to refer to the last chapter, which includes further discussion of these and other difficult issues.

Terms Used in this Book

In many cases the terms used in this book differ from current usage in the United States and other countries. Appendix A, "Author's Note: Terms Used in this Book," should therefore be read early, as it describes terms used throughout the book and the reasons for choosing them. This is especially important for readers who find themselves having difficulty accepting or understanding the conventions used here to describe Deaf children and Sign Language.

Background

Bilingual Education in Sweden and Denmark:
What Does it Look Like?

During discussions sponsored by the Gallaudet Research Institute in 1988, various individuals referred to Sweden and Denmark as potential models for educating Deaf children. While these countries face the same basic challenges in educating Deaf children as the United States and most other countries around the world,[5] it was reported that they had initiated an approach to those challenges that appeared different in some very fundamental ways from current practices worldwide.

Word of the 1981 Swedish law and changes in the educational practices of both Sweden and Denmark had begun to circulate in the Deaf community and among some educators in the United States; however, there was little information published in English about the extent and nature of the activity. The make-up of the Swedish and Danish systems for educating Deaf children had been largely the object of conjecture in the U.S., making it difficult to assess the importance and applicability of their experience. Major gaps existed in our knowledge of these countries' long-term, nationally-supported efforts to implement their goal of educating Deaf children to become bilingual or multilingual[6] adults. At a time when re-shaping of policy in the direction of bilingual education was being seriously considered by some schools in the U.S., many questions remained:

- What theoretical evidence, societal factors, and political events led to this change in attitudes and practices in educating Deaf children in Sweden and Denmark?

- To what extent has bilingual education of Deaf children been implemented and accepted in these countries?

- How is it being implemented? What problems have been encountered?

---

5 See last chapter for discussion of socioeconomic, multi-cultural, political, and fiscal differences.

6 There is an emphasis on supporting development of the home language of multicultural Deaf children, therefore these children would learn at least three languages. Deaf children in Sweden and Denmark also study English, and sometimes German. Furthermore, it is considered important for Deaf children to gain opportunities for exposure to the Sign Languages of English-speaking countries (see Swedish Curriculum, Appendix E).

- How have these educational systems dealt with the many practical, economic, and attitudinal obstacles that are seen in the U.S. as major stumbling blocks to implementing an education based on Sign Language and extensive involvement of Deaf adults?

- At what stages in the education of Deaf children are signed, written, and spoken language introduced? How is each being taught?

- How is the success of programs being evaluated?

These and other questions were the focus of the first study, supported by the World Institute on Disability IDEAS project,[7] the Swedish-American Women's Club, and the Gallaudet Research Institute. The aim was to provide a descriptive overview of this new approach to educating Deaf children in Sweden and Denmark, in the hope that educators, policy makers, and ultimately Deaf children in the United States might in some way benefit from the Scandinavians' experiences.[8]

This four-month study, conducted in Sweden and Denmark in early 1990, consisted of 99 interviews and 27 classroom or home observations. Teachers, support staff, principals, assistant principals, and a retired principal were interviewed from all five schools for the Deaf in Sweden, two of the four schools in Denmark, and from the upper-secondary school where older Deaf teenagers are educated on the same campus with hearing students. Preschool teachers and administrators, parents, children, school psychologists, speech therapists and audiologists, teacher trainers, children's clinic staff, and social workers also provided information during both interviews and observations. Key individuals in the government were interviewed, as well as leaders in each country's National Association of the Deaf, the Deaf Clubs in two cities in Sweden, national and local parents' organizations, and in the fields of Sign Language teaching, Sign Language and speech research, interpreter training, and curriculum development. I met with two

---

7   IDEAS stands for International Disabilities Exchanges And Studies, a program administered by the World Institute on Disability in collaboration with Rehabilitation International, funded by the U.S. National Institute for Disability and Rehabilitation Research (Grant #H133D00005).

8   A portion of the information gathered during this study has been discussed in earlier works under the author's former name: Davies, 1990, 1991a, 1991b, 1992a, 1992b, 1993, 1994a, 1994b. For those seeking more information, copies of Davies, 1991b, *The Transition Toward Bilingual Education of Deaf Children in Sweden and Denmark: Perspectives on Language* may be obtained from the Gallaudet Research Institute, 800 Florida Ave, N.E., Washington, D.C. 20002. Much of the information in the other publications has been incorporated into the current book, with two exceptions: Davies 1990 contains 1) lists of contacts' names and addresses and of some relevant works published in Swedish and Danish and 2) a summary of research studies that led to the changes in each country.

parents' groups and two groups of teachers, and observed classes in almost every grade from preschool through high school.

I am neither Swedish nor Danish; more importantly, I am not Deaf. It is important, therefore, to keep in mind that this book is written from the perspective of an outsider. While the description obtained was qualitative (not quantitative) in nature, procedures resembled investigative reporting rather than ethnography. The purpose of the first study was neither to establish statistics as a basis for comparison nor to survey large groups of people. Rather, the aim of this World Institute on Disabilities IDEAS project was to gather some first-hand information about bilingual education in both countries based on interviews, observations, and available publications. Hence, much of the analysis phase consisted of noting consensus and difference in interviewee's perceptions on an ongoing basis, confirming as much information as possible through observation (especially where discrepancies in policy and practice were noted), and reviewing publications collected. Where applicable, direct quotes from taped interviews or notes are used throughout this book.[9] The reader is encouraged to be mindful that these quotes are primarily personal observations and anecdotes. They are shared because of the perspective they represent, and cannot necessarily be generalized to all Deaf children or their parents.

One of the main goals of the first study was to identify Swedish and Danish individuals who could be good sources of information for further inquiry. I found many of these individuals willing to act as contacts for researchers who wish to undertake future studies to look more closely at various aspects of Deaf children's development/achievement or parents' adjustment in these countries. It is hoped that information from this overview will be a catalyst for scientific studies to follow.

A Decade of Transition: What Have They Learned?

Beyond this general description, I began to wonder: *What insights have been gained over the past 10+ years in this ongoing transition toward educating Deaf children bilingually? What can we in the United States learn from looking at a system that is structured to address Deaf children, their parents, and their education in a different way?* The second study, in March 1992, was undertaken in an attempt to capitalize on the experiences and insights of those individuals who had been identified during the first visit as the experts: those with the most knowledge, experience, or success in the area of educating Deaf children bilingually.

---

9   See Appendix B, "Procedure and Limitations of this Study."

The goal of this study was to seek out some of the people who have worked in or studied preschools, homes, and classrooms in Sweden and Denmark where the most concerted efforts have been made to raise Deaf children in a way that yields well-educated, bilingual or multilingual adults. Since the first of the children in such classes were just completing their compulsory school education (tenth grade) and moving on to upper-secondary education,[10] it seemed like a good time to gather the reflections of these parents, teachers, researchers, and students.

- What have these individuals learned from their experience? What aspects of educating Deaf children bilingually were unlike what they had expected? What had they learned from observing the children?

- What do the teachers plan to do differently when they start over with a new group of students?[11] (Or what would they have done differently the first time around?)

- What has been learned about the following: 1) the teaching of *signed*,[12] spoken, and written languages to Deaf children, 2) the teaching of Sign Language to parents, 3) the training of teachers?

- Where do hard of hearing children fit in?

- What are some of the current challenges or difficulties these individuals (and these countries) face in educating Deaf children bilingually?

- What vision do these individuals hold for the future?

The transition in Sweden and Denmark to a fully-functioning bilingual education is not complete. As with any overview of educational settings, it is clear that some locales have better services, some teachers apply more sophisticated techniques, and some parents are more invested and actively involved (which can have a significant effect on outcomes in any approach).

---

10   See Appendix D for diagram of levels of schooling in Sweden (also similar in Denmark).

11   Teachers for both hearing and Deaf children in these countries often stay with the same group of children for many years.

12   Use of the term "signed language(s)" throughout this book is meant to be parallel to "spoken language(s)" and should not be confused with signed codes or invented sign systems. See Appendix A, "Author's Note: Terms Used" for further explanation.

It is important to note that the observations and attitudes shared in this book[13] do not represent a cross section of interviewees, but are intended to reveal the stories and sentiments of those involved with environments that are considered successful. While the focus was on optimal settings, the students in the bilingual classes of which I speak were not "hand-picked," nor were they educated in private schools. The model discussed here is fully supported in public education. The first bilingual project in Copenhagen, for example, was comprised of all the Deaf children in the Copenhagen area who were ready to start school in 1982.

Other Sources of Information

In addition to the information gathered in Sweden and Denmark, important perspectives have also been gained through interactions with teachers at the Kendall Demonstration Elementary School (KDES) and the Model Secondary School for the Deaf (MSSD) (both on Gallaudet's campus), and by talking with individuals from The Learning Center in Framingham, Massachusetts; the Indiana School for the Deaf; the California School for the Deaf in Fremont; and the Cleary School in Long Island, New York. The Sign Talk Children's Centre in Winnipeg, Canada has also provided an enlightening glimpse into a two-way bilingual preschool where Deaf and hearing children are educated together using American Sign Language and English (Evans, Zimmer, Murray, 1994). While many changes have taken place in the policies of schools for the Deaf over the past few years, these are among the programs in the United States and Canada[14] that have been moving in the direction of bilingual, and in many cases, bicultural, education for some time. As of the writing of this book, a number of schools for the Deaf and other programs in the U.S., Canada, and other countries have declared the bilingual education of their Deaf students to be one of their goals, and are in various stages of transition toward meeting that goal. Repeated encounters with perspectives and practices common to each of these settings yields an ever-clearer picture of the elements that promote early natural language competency and high-level bilingualism or multilingualism in Deaf children. It also sheds light on the elements that are likely to cause such efforts to fail, or to be greatly slowed.

Finally, information has come from individuals all over the United States and from other countries who have written or called to learn more about Sweden and Denmark, at the same time sharing with me their own experiences and obstacles. I have learned a great

---

13   Permission has been granted from interviewees to use the quotations that appear throughout this work. Some of the quotations found in this book were also incorporated, with permission, into a talk given at the International Conference on Bilingualism in Deaf Education in Stockholm, Sweden (Davies, 1994b).

14   Addresses of the schools and organizations in the United States, Canada, Sweden, and Denmark that are cited throughout this book are listed in Appendix C.

deal through one such association with a group of parents, the Oakland Society for Deaf Children in Livonia, Michigan. Some of the parents in this group had experienced early exposure to Deaf adults, excellent Sign Language instruction through nearby Madonna University, and a positive orientation very soon after learning the child was deaf. They seemed very much like parents in Sweden and Denmark in their attitude, their Sign Language skill, their relationship with the Deaf community, and the high reading levels of their Deaf children upon entering kindergarten.

These families, and others I have met at Kendall Demonstration Elementary School and in various locations around the United States, send a clear message that such successes are not just a Scandinavian phenomenon, but a question of having systems in place to give parents and children the early support they need.

Sweden and Denmark:
A Brief Overview

Before taking a closer look, it may be helpful for the reader to be familiar with the basic configuration of service provision in Sweden and Denmark. On the next few pages appears a brief description of the infrastructure of the Swedish and Danish systems for educating Deaf children, including some of the circumstances surrounding the move toward bilingual education. This description will provide a frame of reference for the information presented throughout the book, highlighting some aspects of implementation that differ from our system in the United States.

Identification and Early Services

The discovery that a child is deaf usually takes place early in Sweden and Denmark due to post-natal visits to the homes of most infants. Under the auspices of local "hospital (health care) districts," home visitors conduct a very simple screening called the BOEL test, intended to alert health workers to a variety of differences that can be detected when children are 6 to 10 months of age. If further testing is indicated, children are sent to a designated hospital (or—in Denmark—a children's hearing clinic). If, after three episodes of testing, it is determined that the child has a hearing loss, the doctor, ideally, contacts a psychologist, social worker, or home visitor/teacher who is affiliated with the preschool in the child's area before informing the parents. The intent is that one of these professionals be available to counsel the parents almost immediately upon notification of the diagnosis by the medical doctor.

Services vary in rural areas; however, the hospital districts nationwide have funding and inservice training for professionals who provide early services to parents and deaf infants. In both countries, these professionals receive information through their training networks or by the outreach efforts of the respective National Associations of the Deaf and local or national parents organizations. In general, they have been made aware of the following:

1) Parents need the support of other parents with Deaf children.

2) It is extremely important that the children (and their parents) interact with other Deaf children who know Sign Language and with Deaf adults.

These goals for very young Deaf children and their parents seem singularly clear in Sweden and Denmark. To achieve these goals, there has been widespread restructuring of the system of early intervention and re-educating of medical professionals, social workers, and preschool personnel. In addition, parent groups, Deaf clubs, and communities also go to great lengths to ensure that these two things do indeed happen. Benefits gained through attention to the early needs of both parents and children are considered well worth the expenditure of time and resources.

The high priority placed on early services is perhaps the most important reason why Deaf children in the many small towns and remote rural areas of Sweden are not as isolated as would be expected. The health care districts, which have jurisdiction over children before they enter school, transfer funds to make possible the crossing of traditional district boundaries to bring Deaf children to the same preschool. Here every effort is made to hire at least one Deaf preschool teacher and, ideally, some Deaf support staff, who may later train to be teachers.

For those children who can't reach the designated site daily, attendance once a week (even once a month) is considered essential for the opportunities it can provide: support and example for the parents, and the experience for both parent and child of being with Deaf adults and attentive, inquisitive Deaf children. Other possibilities involve the child (or family) staying with a Deaf family for limited time intervals, hiring a Deaf babysitter, or in some cases, the family relocating to be closer to services, support, and socialization. Depending on the location, Denmark provides parents support to go once a week, once every two weeks, or—if they live too far away to reach the site regularly—for extended live-in visits (one or two weeks at a time) to a childrens' clinic at the school for the Deaf. Here the parents (and siblings) receive Sign Language training, advice, and the opportunities to build relationships with other parents. During this time, the children are cared for and evaluated by specialized preschool teachers.

School Placement

These countries are known for their excellent services for individuals with a variety of disabilities, including their efforts to fully integrate the children into schools with non-disabled children. However, due to the strong focus on language, providing an adequate public education for Deaf children is seen as a very different undertaking. The priority is to ensure Deaf students full participation in society through multilingualism, and an excellent education through two fully accessible languages: Sign Language and well-developed literacy in the majority language.

Policies regarding Deaf children relate to the necessity of ensuring their bilingual status, which is thought to be the best insurance for success in school and in society. Practice in education of Deaf children increasingly reflects the premise that linguistic, cognitive, and social competence are best achieved in environments that provide unencumbered communicative access to curricular content and expanded opportunities for socialization. While most Deaf children work to develop intelligible speech, their success or failure as students and their ability to fully integrate into society as productive, well-educated citizens is not based on their speech skills.

Because of the commitment to placing Deaf children in environments where they can be full participants who communicate freely with children of all ages and all adult staff, mainstreaming in both countries is primarily limited to *hard of hearing children*[15]—and only those who are considered able to function in a classroom with hearing children without an interpreter (see section on placement).

While placement in public schools with all hearing children *is* an option for Deaf children, reports are that almost no parents choose it, having seen during preschool the educational and social benefits of placing their children with Deaf peers and adults. There are five schools for the Deaf in Sweden, a country approximately the size of California, with a much smaller population (see "Yes, but..." section for more discussion). Denmark has four schools for the Deaf, which includes a "center school" where a significant number of Deaf children are brought together on the campus of a school for hearing children.

When children reach school age, there are a variety of options. In Denmark, which is a very small country, the majority of children are within commuting distance to one of the four main state schools for the Deaf. In both countries, the state provides transportation, starting with taxis for very young children and utilizing buses, trains, and other forms of public transportation as children get older. (After a certain age, it is common for all children in both countries to use public transportation for travel to and from school). While this may, at first glance, appear expensive, it is considered more cost-effective than housing a large number of Deaf children and paying overnight and weekend caretakers.

Children whose commute is much more than 1 1/2 hours stay in foster homes with Deaf families or schoolmates during the week, or in lodging provided by the schools—often staffed by Deaf adults. This lodging is often in the form of houses located in neighborhoods where there are other children. Attempts are made to approximate normal family life by placing children of both sexes and varying ages in the same household, and by providing bedrooms—sometimes private—rather than dorms. The children who stay during the week and are sent home (occasionally by plane in the northern areas in Sweden) on weekends. (Again, sending these few children home is considered more cost-effective than housing and caring for them over the weekend.) It is felt to be very important that all Deaf children maintain regular contact with their families. Even though these residential options exist, distant families sometimes choose to move closer to their children's school and to a broader range of contacts and services.

---

15   Please see Appendix A regarding use of the term "hard of hearing" in this book.

Support for Home Languages

In Sweden, all children whose parents speak a native language other than Swedish are provided instruction in their home language once a week, and may be taught some other subjects through that language, as explained in the following quote from the Swedish Compulsory School Curriculum. (Currently, work is being conducted to expand this law to include Sign Language instruction to siblings of Deaf children.):

> *Home language as a teaching subject is offered to pupils whose parents use a language other than Swedish or Sign Language. The same pupils must also be offered study guidance in their home language for one or more other subjects if this is found to be necessary. Schools must also arrange special instruction in Swedish as a foreign language for these pupils. This type of instruction is obligatory. (Supplement to the Swedish Compulsory School Curriculum, 1983, p.23).*

In Sweden and Denmark, a multicultural home is seen as an asset to children's education, not a liability. Strong family ties and clear communication between parents and children are considered important enough to require the extra investment of providing educational support for the home language. In one medium-sized city in 1990, this meant providing teachers for 42 different languages. These countries do have diverse cultural groups, as well as historical patterns of oppression of some groups or languages.

Sign Language as an Academic Subject

Both countries have incorporated instruction in Sign Language as an academic subject into the curriculum for Deaf children. According to a regulation by the Danish Ministry of Education, Danish Sign Language, starting in 1992, must be a part of the curriculum for all Deaf students—including those hard of hearing children placed in public schools. The Swedish Special Schools curriculum, (published in response to the 1981 law) specifies Sign Language grammar, public presentation skills in Sign Language, and other aspects of Sign Language as required parts of the language block (see Appendix E). In the same way students in Sweden and Denmark learn about the culture of English-speaking peoples while they are learning English, instruction about Sign Language also includes study of the history, accomplishments, and culture of Deaf people, as well as information about TTYs and alerting devices, and discussion of options for successful functioning in a variety of societal and emergency settings (Bergmann, 1994). This broader interpretation of the concept of Sign Language as an academic subject is roughly equivalent to the Deaf Studies curricula being implemented in some schools in the United States.[16]

Sign Language Instruction for Parents and Teachers

Both countries have undertaken the practice—now almost universal—of offering Sign Language courses in intensive one- or two-week blocks. Where that is not possible, even intensive weekend workshops for Sign Language study are considered far more effective than periodic shorter classes. The support and socialization of other parents or teachers learning together in these classes is also said to be very important, and learners comment that they come away with a large enough growth spurt that they can see the difference when they return to their homes or classrooms. Those I interviewed (both teachers and learners) reported to me that the students in such classes were able to concentrate much more fully on learning Sign Language and utilizing what they have learned, because this structure allows them to leave their jobs and homes behind all day (sometimes all weekend or week, if the course is in another town). Parents can generally get release time and coverage of lost wages by petitioning their respective communities for financial support from a special fund designated for people in challenging circumstances.

These intensive Sign Language teaching blocks ("steps," as they are called) are hosted by the schools, the Deaf clubs, the parent organizations, and the University—the usual host organization varying in different parts of each country. Most of the courses in Sweden were reported to be taught by Deaf teachers, some of whom have studied Sign Language at the University level. In Denmark, the primary group responsible for teaching parents and teachers has concluded that highly qualified Deaf and hearing teachers working as a team seems to be very successful for teaching these block courses (Hansen, 1994). In either case, teachers work in teams to be able to handle these workshop-type courses and to stay abreast of discoveries in Sign Language research and in adult second-language teaching.

While the goal of these classes is to teach parents the language of the Deaf community, (not sign-based codes to represent the majority language) the fact that these parents have studied Sign Language structure and usage provides them with the knowledge and flexiblity to make informed choices about how best to communicate with their Deaf child in various situations in the home, school, and community. (See Chapter Three on the learning of SignLanguage by hearing parents.)

---

16 *The KDES Deaf Studies Curriculum Guide*, (Miller-Nomeland & Gillespie, 1993) likewise presents a course of study for grades 1-9 that includes lessons in the following areas: Identity, Communication, American Sign Language, American Deaf Culture, History, and Social Change. Information on how to obtain this guide appears on the title page of this book.

The SDR (Swedish National Association of the Deaf) has impressed upon its well-organized network of Deaf clubs and local chapters that they have a responsibility to ensure a better future for Deaf children. To this end, many local Deaf clubs host parents' association meetings and Sign Language steps. They also plan regular activities varying from potluck dinners to weekend outings and camping trips to provide for reciprocal interaction between hearing families with a Deaf child and Deaf families with both hearing and Deaf children. Such events contribute to parents' level of comfort and skill with Sign Language.

In 1989, the Stockholm University Department of Sign Language was given a 5-year grant by the Swedish Board of Education to develop and implement Sign Language training for teachers who had already been working in the schools before bilingual education was mandated. Some had been using a form of signed Swedish; some used very little manual communication of any kind. In addition to hiring more Deaf teachers (see Chapter 4), major changes in coursework and entrance requirements have been implemented for new teachers. It also became clear to education officials that real change would be greatly delayed unless there was a better system for giving *current* teachers instruction in Swedish Sign Language. Therefore, every spring, a total of twenty teachers from the various schools for the Deaf in Sweden were given one semester of release time during the spring to take full-time coursework at the University of Stockholm in a concentrated program designed especially for them. Improvement in both skills and knowledge of the language have been reported among the teachers attending that the program. Therefore, the funding has been extended so that all teachers will have an opportunity to attend, and the course is now also being conducted in an additional location.

Factors Leading to Change

The respective evolution of these and other changes in the education of Deaf children in both Sweden and Denmark both have fascinating histories. In both cases, the common element in bringing about change was the consumer. While Swedish federal policy and support have yielded a major reorganization in a relatively short period of time, it is important to note that years of grassroots activism and political networking preceded each new government mandate. Close cooperation between the Swedish National Association of the Deaf (and its affiliated local chapters and Deaf clubs); the National Association of the Hard of Hearing; the National Association of Parents of Deaf, Hard of Hearing, and Speech Impaired Children; and linguists at the University of Stockholm has made possible the efficient dissemination of information and a remarkable sense of unity of political goals. These groups have formed a strong network that is now consulted regularly by policy-makers in matters that concern Deaf and hard of hearing children and adults.

No government mandates were passed in Denmark. On the contrary, each teacher's right to decide what is best behind his/her own classroom doors is heralded. Such differences in attitudes, perceptions, and funding sources are apparent in the two countries' approaches. Nevertheless, education of Deaf children in both countries has moved in a similar direction through somewhat parallel, but separate activity.[17] There has also been sharing of information through periodic meetings where educators of Deaf children in all of Scandinavia gather to discuss current challenges and share research findings.

One of the major turning points for the schools in Denmark began with the analysis of deaf children's sign language. What was previously thought to be an ungrammatical, incoherent series of gestures that could not be understood by hearing teachers was described by the researchers as a comprehensive, systematic, and sophisticated language that the children and other Deaf adults comprehended fully in conversations with one another (Sörensen, 1975; Sörensen and Hansen, 1976).

Copenhagen's Center for Total Communication (also known as Kastelsvej Center or KC), a self-supporting corporation that provides most of the Sign Language teaching, research, and interpreter training services in Denmark, has been a powerful force for change. This group, which is located adjacent to the Kastelsvej School for the Deaf in Copenhagen, has worked closely with the school, with the parent organizations, and with the Danish Association of the Deaf since 1972. Schools and organizations regularly contract with KC to conduct workshops and courses. The specialized staff at KC also conduct research and develop materials on Sign Language linguistics and teaching, interpreter training, Sign Language/Deaf Studies as an academic subject, bilingual teaching of Deaf children, teaching speech, and parental support. They have been extremely effective over the years in making this information readily available to consumers, parents, and schools in Denmark (and internationally). While this group does not receive public funding, their staff has almost doubled since 1990.

Linguists and developmental psychologists at the University of Stockholm were likewise instrumental in the changes in Sweden. After their early research about Sign Language and Deaf children's language learning pointed to the need for major educational change, faculty at the University began working closely with the Deaf community and later the parents' organizations to disseminate information about their findings. The first studies were in the early '70s, conducted by linguists (who had no prior knowledge of Sign Language) and the Deaf consultants they hired. Originating as a couple of small projects under the department of linguistics, the work has now expanded into a full-fledged academic Department of Sign Language whose findings in both theoretical and applied linguistics are recognized internationally. In addition to conducting research, the

---

17   See Svartholm, 1993, or Davies, 1990, 1991b for background leading to changes in the Swedish law.

department works closely with the Department of Scandinavian Languages, offering various level degrees in Sign Language, Interpreting, and Bilingual Teaching of Swedish/Swedish Sign Language (a major available only to Deaf students). They also offer the only Ph.D. level degree in Sign Language in the world.

Experimental Classes

In the early 1980's, parents' wish that their Deaf children's education should be on a par with the education of hearing children resulted in each country starting their own form of bilingual education through experimental classes. The goal of these classes was to capitalize on both Sign Language and the language of the majority in supporting a higher level of literacy and academic achievement (see Davies, 1990 & 1991b for details).

In both cases, these classes were periodically evaluated by researchers. In addition, the team of teachers in the experimental project in Copenhagen wrote four books about their methods, results, and insights—books that were disseminated through the producers of Danish educational materials to other schools and teachers (Lewis, 1994 [English version]; Lewis, et al, 1992; Sörensen, et al, 1983, 1984, 1988). Their open sharing of ideas, attitudes, and discoveries about their Deaf students' language and learning processes was at least partially responsible for the widespread change in perspective of educators in Denmark.

In each country, parents and teachers involved in experimental classes were among the earliest activists in their efforts to share their successful experiences with other parents and to continue to demand a high quality education for Deaf children

Transition

The transition toward educating Deaf children bilingually has been under way in both Sweden and Denmark for a number of years, but is by no means considered complete. Those involved agree that the implementation of this model—which involves putting in place personnel, practices, expertise, and other attributes that have not not typically been present in either the educational or the healthcare system—requires both time and broad-based support (see Chapter Five; also Davies, 1991b).

Despite the long term nature of such a transition, it is important to note that the theoretical soundness and validity of the model described in this book no longer seem to be topics of dispute in either country. Educational outcomes of students taught bilingually surpass those of previous generations of deaf children in both countries (see section on Outcomes), bolstering widespread commitment to this major change in philosophy and approach.

CHAPTER ONE

A
Closer Look:
Developing Literacy

Please take a moment and try to picture a second grade class. The children are at the *Manillaskolan* (the Manilla School for the Deaf) in Stockholm, Sweden. They're a little excited today because they have visitors all the way from Estonia....

The visitors are observing one reading group as the teacher gives the children an unfamiliar text to read. They read it silently. Then they take turns—each focusing on a page or so—telling the visitors in Sign Language what the text says. There is more going on here than just reading. There is also translation into Sign Language—in a way that accurately reflects the meaning of the passages each has read.

During our interview, the teacher described that visit—which she said was typical of what they do daily. Some of her comments follow:

> *We had some foreign visitors at our second grade reading lesson. I gave my students quite a difficult text. It was an old fairy tale, big old-fashioned language. It wasn't easy at all. They read it, and they had no problem with it the first time they saw it. It is a good group. The five kids in this group (8-9 years old)[1] are really readers. Otherwise I would not have given them that sort of text. They were standing there and really looking at the text, thinking about it, translating it—and then signing its meaning for us.*
>
> *The teachers who were visiting were amazed, not only because the kids read this text independently, but because they were commenting on each other's Sign*

---

[1] Swedish children would typically start second grade at age 8, but it was springtime; therefore some of the students had turned nine. The traditional age for all children to start first grade in Sweden has been 7, but recent legislation now allows parents the option of starting their child in school at age 6.

Language production in translating it. They would say to each other things like "I think that is a bit too Swedish, it's not really good Sign Language—we have to find a much better way to sign this part." They were discussing the grammar of both languages with each other, and I think that is the goal. They know what they are doing. They know there are two languages and that those languages can communicate the same meaning—but in very different ways (G. Christersson, personal communication, March 12, 1992).

Many Deaf children in Sweden and Denmark, like the children in this class, acquire their first language naturally. They are not *taught*, but rather, learn through interaction with their peers, caretakers, and parents. In the case of this second grade class, many of the children had Swedish Sign Language as their first language, although a couple of the children acquired quite a bit of spoken Swedish naturally (without special teaching) as their first language.

When they were in preschool, these children played, made friends, went on field trips, and learned to sit still long enough to talk about those field trips—just like many other children do. Their Deaf and hearing teachers listened to them, explained things to them, consoled them when they were upset, and mediated arguments between peers—just like many other preschool teachers do. When they are at home, their parents play with them, feed them, read to them, discipline them, comfort them, love them, and answer their questions—just like many other parents do.

From a very early age, many of these Deaf children's parents and teachers read to them as often as possible from books, translating the stories into Sign Language and talking about the pictures, the characters, the words, and whatever else the children wanted to know, much the way Deaf parents have traditionally done with their children (Akamatsu & Andrews, 1993; Mather, 1989).

The children soon begin reading the words for some of the things that interest them, translating words on cereal boxes and public restrooms for their parents, and telling their own outrageous tales in Sign Language. They learn to write their names, copy letters and words, scribble make-believe letters and notes, and make labels for their drawings—just like hearing children who are in an environment where reading and writing is part of their everyday experience. While most preschool teachers said they did not "teach" reading in the preschools, the teacher quoted earlier noted:

Some of the kids in this group were already readers when they came to school. They had a good start in life: A lot of books around them at home and their parents were signing stories to them every night before they went to bed....Yes, well I think there are different sorts of parents and different kinds of family settings....

These kids, I don't think anyone has forced them; no—they're just curious. Like hearing kids. "What's that?" "What's this?" "Mommy, what's that?"

Ideally, no one pushes them to read, write, or speak, or engages them in a lot of tedious or repetitious activity they do not comprehend. When they are ready, their natural curiosity—and the fact that they have come to recognize that the written word holds lots of information and fun—gets them interested in reading. From blocks to books to TV captions, the written word is so much a part of their lives that there is no discreet starting point for learning Swedish/Danish (or English as a third language). The same seems to be true for the spoken word, in the case of children who have adequate access to it through their hearing (see "A First Language: Whose Choice Is It?" in Chapter 3).

Many Deaf children also begin well before they enter first grade to fingerspell Swedish/Danish words as part of their Sign Language conversations and to type words to 'grandma' on the *text telephone* (TTY). Whether they have Deaf or hearing parents, the two languages in their lives are all just a natural and inseparable part of everyday communication. Based on comments of teachers and administrators, a typical class profile of today's Deaf students in Sweden and Denmark includes a number of children who are already reading when they enter first grade at age 7. Others are drawing, building, playing outdoors—they could care less about books right now. Depending on their hearing levels and aptitude for/interest in speech, some of the children at this age utilize quite a bit of speech; others less; others not at all. Some like to wear hearing aids; some don't; others wear them only for certain activities (M. Dahlquist, personal communication, May 15, 1990).

Adam's Book

When these children start first grade, they begin to learn about Swedish through children's literature (classic children's stories as opposed to basal readers) and Sign Language. Many teachers in Sweden now use *Adam's Bøk* (Christersson, 1990). The *Adam's Bøk* set is a text and videotapes developed by a teacher to formally introduce written Swedish by utilizing parallel Swedish text and videotapes with Sign Language translations of the same stories. Both the book and videotape tell a series of engaging stories about a Deaf child and his classmates and family. The book is very compelling because of its colorful illustrations and the nature of the subject matter, one of the only books of its kind (Hudelson, 1984; Wilding-Daez, 1994) about healthy, happy Deaf children and their everyday struggles and triumphs. It has full sentences with diverse grammatical constructions; not repetitive, primer-type Swedish. The book and videotape tell the same stories. Many are reflective of mainstream Swedish culture, as well as some of the other cultures that are prevalent in Sweden, and of the ways of life of Deaf people there. Selected pages from *Adam's Bøk*, shown on the following pages, are meant to be representative of different aspects of the book. Each story, part of a story, or single page is translated below in English. Simply by studying the pictures and translations, one can pick up a great deal about the Swedish language.

Min familj

Min pappa
Anders Blom

Min mamma
Birgitta Blom

Min lillasyster
Hanna Blom

Jag
Adam Blom

4

Alla i min familj är döva.
Vi bor i ett gult radhus
på Hallonvägen 5.

5

My father. My mother. My little sister. Me. / All in my family are deaf. We live in a yellow townhouse at 5 Raspberry Street.

Min klass

Min fröken heter
Eva Andersson.
Hon är jättesnäll.

Nesrin Toprak

Nesrin har långt
svart hår. Hon är
jättesöt.

Calle Lundström

Calle är min bästis.
Han är starkast i
klassen.

6

Emma Larsson

Emma har gult hår
och blå ögon. Hon
älskar djur.

Per Öman

Per är längst i klassen.
Han älskar böcker.

7

My teacher is named Eva Andersson. She's really nice. / Ema Larsson. Ema has blonde hair and blue eyes. She loves animals. / Nesrin Toprak. Nesrin has long black hair. She is very cute. / Calle Lundström. Calle is my best friend. He is the strongest in our class. / Per Oman. Per is the tallest in the class. He loves books.

Nesrins mamma öppnar.
— Men hej Adam! tecknar hon.
— Hej! tecknar jag. Jag kommer med Nesrins mattebok.
— Det var snällt. Vill du komma in?
— Ja tack, svarar jag.

20

Nesrin's mother opens the door. "Oh, Hello Adam," she signs slowly. "Hi," I sign. "I'm bringing Nesrin's map book." "How kind of you." "Do you want to come in?" "Yes, please," I answer.

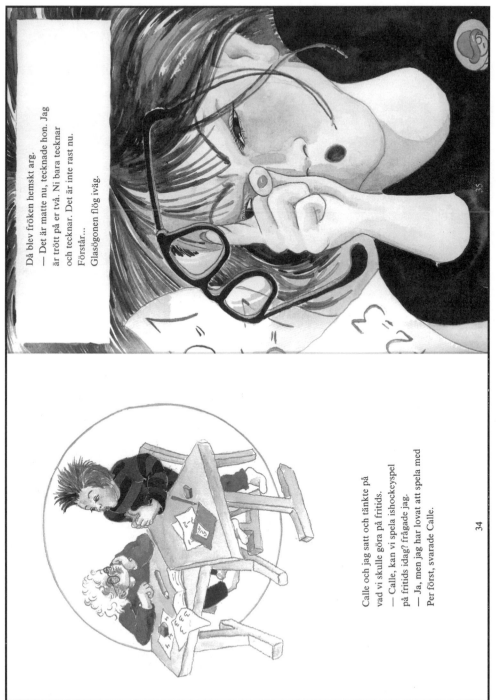

Calle and I were sitting and thinking about what we were going to do at fritids [supervised after-school activities on school premises]. "Calle, can we play table hockey at fritids today?" I asked. "Yes, but I promised Per I'd play with him first," Calle answered. / Then the teacher became very angry. / "I'm tired of both of you. You're just signing and signing and signing. It's not recess now. Understand...?" and her glasses flew off her head.

Då kommer mamma.

— Vad bråkar ni om? frågar hon.

— Ludde har tagit min hörapparat,
tecknar Emma.

— Nej, det har jag inte alls! skriker Ludde.

— Lugna er! tecknar mamma.

— Emma, minns du var du la hörapparaten?
frågar mamma.

— På skrivbordet, där jag alltid lägger
den, svarar Emma.

47

Then mother comes in. "What are you arguing about?" she asks. "Ludde has taken my hearing aid," Ema signs.
"No, I have not!" Ludde shouts. "Calm down," mother signs. "Ema, do you remember where you put your hearing
aid?" mother asks. "On my desk, where I always put it," Ema answered.

Hos mormor och morfar

Min mormor och morfar är döva. Jag älskar
att vara hos dem. De har alltid gott om tid.
Vi kan sitta och teckna i flera timmar.

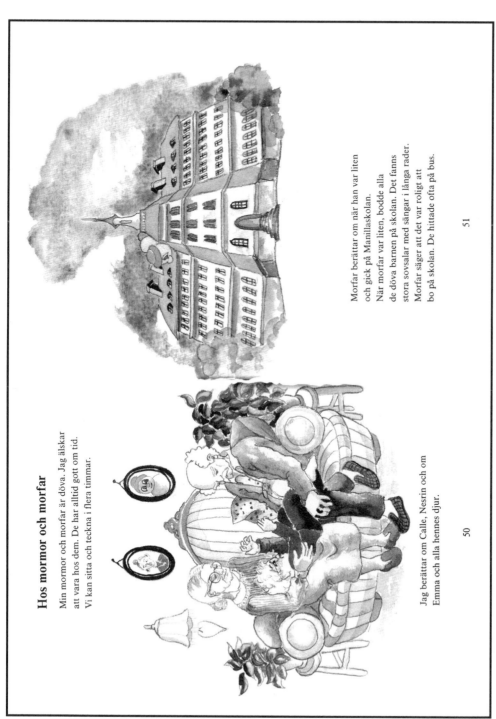

Jag berättar om Calle, Nesrin och om
Emma och alla hennes djur.

50

Morfar berättar om när han var liten
och gick på Manillaskolan.
När morfar var liten, bodde alla
de döva barnen på skolan. Det fanns
stora sovsalar med sängar i långa rader.
Morfar säger att det var roligt att
bo på skolan. De hittade ofta på bus.

51

"At Grandma's and Grandpa's." My grandmother and grandfather are deaf. I love to go to their house. They always have plenty of time. We can sit and sign for hours. I tell them about Calle, Nesrin, and about Ema and all her animals. / And grandfather tells about when he was little and went to the Manilla School. When grandfather was little, all the deaf children lived at the school. There were big dormitories with beds in long rows. Grandfather says that it was fun to live at the school. Often they did mischievous things they weren't allowed to do.

Textis

Både jag och Hanna gillar att skriva på texttelefonen.
När det ringer, rusar Hanna till telefonen för att
svara. Hon skriver bara: HANNA HÄR *.

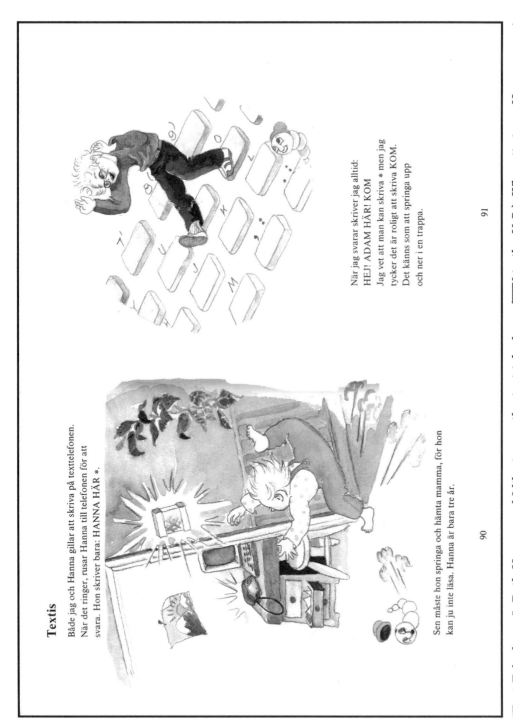

Sen måste hon springa och hämta mamma, för hon
kan ju inte läsa. Hanna är bara tre år.

När jag svarar skriver jag alltid:
HEJ! ADAM HÄR! KOM
Jag vet att man kan skriva * men jag
tycker det är roligt att skriva KOM.
Det känns som att springa upp
och ner i en trappa.

"Text Telephone." Both Hanna and I like to use the text telephone (TTY in the U.S.). When it rings, Hanna runs to the telephone to answer. And she writes just: HANNA HERE * . Then she must run and get mother because she cannot read. Hanna is only three years old. / When I answer, I always write: Hi, Adam here, ga. I know that you can write * [same as GA] but I think its fun to write KOM [same as *]. It feels like running up and down the stairs.

Så här skrev vi igår:

ADAM HÄR. KOM
Hej min lille vän. Det är mormor. *
HEJSAN MORMOR! KOM
Hur är det med dig? *
BRA!!!!!!! KOM
Trivs du bra i skolan? *
JAAAAAAAAAAAA,
FÅR JAG SOVA HOS DIG PÅ LÖRDAG? KOM
Ja visst får du det. Det skulle vara
roligt. Har du frågat mamma och pappa? *
NEJ, VÄNTA.......
PAPPA SÄGER OK. KOM
Bra då ses vi på lördag. Du kan komma
och äta middag, Pannkaka!
Hälsa mamma, pappa och Hanna. Morfar hälsar.
Kram o k.l.s.l. *
HEJ DÅ! KRAM KLSL

COMPUTER 80

Jag älskar min mormor och hennes
pannkakor.

93

Sen väntar jag och ser vem som ringer.
Det brukar vara mammas kusin Ylva
eller pappas kompis Bengt. De vill
nästan aldrig prata med mig.

Men ibland är det mormor och hon vill
prata med mig. "Hej min lille vän. Det
är mormor." brukar hon skriva och sen
pratar vi länge.

92

Then I wait and see who is calling. Usually it is mother's cousin Ylea or daddy's pal Bengt. They almost never want to talk with me. But sometimes, its Grandma and she wants to talk with me. "Hi, my little friend. It's grandma," she will write, and then we talk for a long while. / This is what we wrote yesterday: Adam here* Hi, my little friend. It's grandma* Hi there, grandma. How are you?* Goooood.* Is everything going OK at school?* Yeeeees! Can I sleep at your house on Saturday?* Yes, sure you may do that--that would be fun. Have you asked your mom and dad?* No, hold on.* Daddy says OK. Good, then we will see each other on Saturday. You can come and have dinner--pancakes. Say Hi to mother, father, and Hanna. Grandfather says Hi. Hugs and kls (sk) Bye Bye (kls). / I love my grandmother and her pancakes.

En gång, när vi var hos doktorn, tolkade Anna åt mamma och mig. Vi var där för att jag hade ont i halsen.

Doktorn tittade mig i halsen och så pratade han. Anna tolkade:
— Gör det ont i halsen när du sväljer? Jag berättade att det gjorde hemskt ont när jag åt hårt bröd. Och då sa Anna det till doktorn. Han funderade en stund.

112

Sen pratade mamma och doktorn länge. Anna tolkade hela tiden. När doktorn pratade, tecknade Anna till mamma. Och när mamma tecknade, pratade Anna.

113

One time, when we were at the doctor's, Anna was interpreting for mother and me. We were there because I had a sore throat. / The doctor looked in my throat and he was speaking. Anna interpreted: "Does it hurt your throat when you swallow?" I said that it really hurt when I eat crackers. And then Anna told that to the doctor. He was thinking for a while. / And then mother and the doctor spoke for a long time. Anna was interpreting all the time. When the doctor was speaking, Anna signed to my mother, and when mother signed, Anna spoke. When we were finished and were about to leave, Anna signed, "I have to hurry because I need to interpret at another place." "Who are you going to interpret for now?" I asked curiously. "I'm not supposed to say," Anna answered and hurried off.

Each week or so, the children are asked to focus on a different story,[1] starting with the videotape. They first view the tape, then review to make sure everyone understands it, then talk about some aspect of Swedish Sign Language. For all the children, but especially those children who have had less exposure to Sign Language, this is a time for them to improve their comprehension of various aspects of Sign Language. Like all children, these children love to see the story told over and over again. The teacher rewinds the tape to various points and focuses more closely on the signer, facilitating the children's discovery of some aspect of the grammar that is like what they themselves use; in much the same way hearing children begin learning in first grade about the grammar of their own language, which they also speak with relative fluency by that age. The focus, however, is not so much on *teaching* grammar in either language at this stage, but on developing literacy in both languages by providing comprehensible input.

The teachers' manual is structured to help the teacher raise children's awareness of aspects of Sign Language or Swedish grammar[2] that the children are developmentally ready to handle. But much of the discussion of grammar comes only as clarification of parts of the story the children didn't understand, or in response to their questions.

The teachers' manual also shows pictures and translations of every sign as it is used in context on the videotape. While teachers less skilled in the language can learn something about grammar and vocabulary from these lessons, successful use of the materials is largely predicated on sensitive instruction by teachers with high levels of fluency in and grammatical knowledge of both languages. After studying the videotaped story on the first day, the class reads the same 3-4 page story in Swedish the next day. The teacher translates it into Swedish Sign Language while the children look at the text and pictures. They discuss some aspect of Swedish grammar that shows up in the story and may discuss how it is like—or different from—their own grammar in Sign Language. Again, the teaching of grammar is not the goal so much as providing the children with comprehensible input in the language, a familiar context for learning how to get meaning from those "squiggles" on the page, and confidence in their abilities.

[1]   Pages from *Adam's Bøk* were reprinted with permission from Gunilla Christersson, SIH läromedel, Stockholm.

[2]   The Sign Languages used by Deaf people have richly complex 'phonological,' morphological, syntactic, discourse, and semantic structures that are equal in linguistic sophistication to those found in any spoken (or signed) language, yet each has grammatical structures that are distinct from the spoken language in the country where they are used, and distinct from the Sign Languages used in other countries.

Gradually, the children start to read well enough on their own that the text is presented the first day, then they view the videotape afterwards to confirm what they read. They also read in the same way from many other story books and their own grade-level textbooks. Subject matter teaching relies heavily, at first, on the teacher's translation of materials, since many of these materials have no videotaped translation. Through translation and building experiences around the material in their textbooks, the children become intensely aware that the printed word holds information of great interest to them.

Emphasis is also on making sure there is mastery of grade level subject in the early grades, even if the children are not ready to independently comprehend the texts. As children become independent readers, more and more of their subject matter is communicated to them through written texts. And of course, reading for fun and pleasure is one of the biggest contributors to their developing literacy. Many children become avid readers outside of class (H. Björneheim, G. Christersson, personal communication, May, 1990).

In the first printing of *Adam's Bøk* for first graders, the text was written first, then Sign Language translations were produced to reflect the meaning. While every effort was made to use full, descriptive, Swedish sentences, the Sign Language version on videotape happened to come out with a greater level of detail. It has become clear to the teachers who use the book that Deaf children do not have a problem with the full Swedish text when presented systematically in this way. Therefore, the next printing of *Adam's Bøk* will include expanded text which represents an exact translation of the more detailed videotape.

Widespread use of *Adam's Bøk* indicated that Deaf children and their teachers had been much in need of a book/videotape like this from both a self-esteem and a linguistic point of view: reading about Deaf children and their lives in a positive context, learning about the grammar of their own language, and learning about Swedish from a second language perspective as contrasted with their own language. As word of these materials spread, classrooms all the way up to 9th and 10th grade began working through these entertaining and informative lessons. As a result, the teacher who wrote the first book has now been given more release time to prepare similar materials for older students. This time, the stories—about Deaf high school students—were created and told on the videotape by high school students. The Swedish text for the book is composed as a direct translation of these students' videotaped stories.

Trusting the Children's Process

I wanted to learn more about this emerging literacy, about this lack of word-for-word teaching of reading and writing in Swedish. I was curious to see if there was one piece of the language the children first grasp when they make that switch from just looking at whole texts and pictures to actually READING. Do they first learn to associate the written vocabulary with the pictures? Is it the grammatical items they were discussing in class? What is it that defines each child's path to literacy? When I asked the teacher who wrote *Adam's Bøk* if she had any clues about Deaf children's transition from being non-readers to being readers, she replied:

> *Every teacher would like to know the answer to that question. I think it is something even scientists truly do not understand. I think you have to trust the process going on in every child. I think you have to trust the childrens' ability to*
>
> *learn language. You have to provide the best input possible, but I don't think you can* **teach** *them to read. You really have to have so much trust in the kids — in each child. You have to believe that this is a whole person and he is able to learn.*

The kind of trust this teacher exhibits is the same unique kind of trust we bestow on all small children. We trust that they will learn to roll over and sit up and walk and—yes, learn to read—at their own pace. Sometimes we may be impatient, but we learn to trust our children to tackle each challenge when they are ready. We celebrate their triumphs as they achieve them; but we are forced to accept the fact that no amount of coaxing, training, or modeling will force a child to take her first steps, say her first word, or read her first word before she is ready. Children simply do not do things unless they are developmentally ready. And, unless something is terribly wrong, they *will* do them when they *are* ready—given the tools they need.

This teachers' attitude about learning to read is not just a leap of faith. It is theoretically sound, based on what we know about emerging literacy in very young children. Her transition to this level of trust seems based on acceptance of her own responsibility as a teacher to give her Deaf students the tools they need to move through school in much the same way other children do. Having studied the grammar of both Swedish and Swedish Sign Language, this teacher sought ways to present Swedish that would capitalize on what the children already know about language and about their world (which researchers have identified as natural, crucial factors in the development of literacy in all children). The methods she employs are theoretically sound, but beyond that, she has a healthy level of confidence in the children's abilities.

Outcomes

Reading Achievement

Regarding her own first attempts to use translations in person and on videotape with a variety of books, the teacher who wrote *Adam's Bøk* explained to me during the first visit in 1990:

> *We often tried to be very distinct in telling them, "This is Sign Language, this is Swedish," all the time. And it seems to work. That class—they are now 5th grade—we had them for four years, and the two first years, we worked with the videotapes and parallels in the two languages, with different books once a week. And then in the third grade, it wasn't needed any more because they were good readers. So, we just kicked out this part and we used ordinary stories and textbooks without videotapes, and they could do it the other way around—start with the Swedish and translate back into Sign Language. And in the end of the fourth grade, they read by themselves and you didn't have to check them that closely. I knew they could read and if they didn't understand something, they asked me. I think they get very aware of the differences between the two languages and that's the main part (G. Christersson, personal communication, May 22, 1990).*

In the first experimental bilingual class in Sweden (starting in 1982), a Deaf and hearing teacher began, when the children were in second grade, to use "parallel" Swedish Sign Language and Swedish in a similar way, but without videotapes. The Deaf teacher told the story in Sign Language first (often a story from classic children's literature). After discussing it, the class read the same story from a book and spent time discussing parts of it to see how the message came across in Swedish. (These children all had early Sign Language and interaction with other Deaf children and adults before starting school.)

Given an unfamiliar Swedish text (designed for hearing 12-year-olds) these children, when tested by linguists at Stockholm University, demonstrated that they had attained threshold reading levels by fourth grade. In other words, they could read well enough to accurately comprehend the meaning of the text, and had the skill to estimate the meaning, based on context alone, of most of the words they hadn't previously encountered. This was a task their Deaf agemates in other classes at the same school could not accomplish. This threshold reading level now seems to be attained at a younger age in many children (for example, the group described earlier who were reading quite independently in second grade).

Back in 1989, Britta Hansen discussed test results of a group of 12-year old Deaf children in Copenhagen while they were in the process of being educated bilingually:

The reading skills of the children have improved tremendously compared to what we used to see in the education of the Deaf generally. Whereas 10-15% of deaf children used to learn to read for meaning, we now see 55% of them being able to do this at the age of 12. That means 55% read Danish at an age-appropriate level.

22% can read at a transitional stage, where they search for meaning of individual words, idioms, and certain grammatical structures. This group is expected to develop their reading skills to an age appropriate level before leaving school.

The remaining 23% read as signal readers [at age 12], and they tend to grasp one word out of several and through that, try to understand the whole message. Before the bilingual approach, more than 56% of the deaf children left school as signal readers. The radical improvement of the children's reading skills is one very important result of the bilingual teaching programme (p. 6-7).

The first Deaf students in bilingual classes in Sweden and Denmark graduated with reading and math levels considered comparable to hearing children.[3] In her presentation at an international conference in Luxembourg, Swedish psychologist Kerstin Heiling (Lund University Department of Educational Research) summarizes this progress as follows:

A number of deaf children whose hearing parents started to use signs when the children were two years old or younger, last spring performed just as well as hearing age-mates on a standardized reading achievement test given in all final classes of compulsory schools in Sweden (Heiling, 1993b, p. 77).

Two teachers at the Österväng School for the Deaf in Lund, Sweden, recently published the results of a standardized reading achievement test (designed for 10th grade hearing students) that was administered to their 10th grade Deaf students (Salander & Svenden-fors, 1993). These students, while not in an experimental class, had been exposed to Sign Language during their preschool years and had been, during some of their school years, taught from the viewpoint that Swedish was, for them, a second language. Of the nine students, results were as follows (compared to norms for hearing students):

---

3   B. Nielsen, School Psychologist, Kastelsvej School, Copenhagen, personal communication, March 9, 1992; L. Henning, Assistant Principal, Lund School, Sweden, personal communication, August 19, 1993; H. Björneheim, teacher, Manilla School, Stockholm, personal communication, August 20, 1993.

READING:

> - 3 students above average
> - 5 students average
> - 1 slightly below average

WRITING:

> - 3 students above average
> - 1 student average
> - 5 students below average.[4]

In addition to comparing favorably with hearing graduates, students in the two main experimental bilingual classes in each country also tested higher in reading than their Deaf agemates during periodic evaluations[5] throughout their school career, as well as when compared with a sample of Deaf adults from the previous generation. Svartholm (1994) relates the results of a test conducted on 23 students who were graduating from their compulsory school education (10th grade) at the Manilla School in Stockholm. These students, who all finished in the same class, had very different early orientations to their first and second language. Six of the 23 students had been part of the "Saturday School" project, (Ahlgren, 1994; Davies, 1991b) in which their parents were given a solid orientation to raising a Deaf child and to Sign Language through interaction with a group of Deaf parents whose children were the same age. These children were also taught Swedish as a second language through translations.

In one study, all the children were tested on various measures of reading comprehension. One of the tests of reading skills was designed for hearing immigrants; comprehension of this test was correlated with a very high level of competence in Swedish—equivalent to native proficiency (Svartholm, 1994). This test was also presented to Deaf adults enrolled in adult education courses all over Sweden (Deaf immigrants were excluded). Of the 57 adults who took this reading comprehension test, only two could answer all the questions, 5 gave roughly acceptable answers, but "*The great majority,*" Svartholm relates, "*did not even try to answer them. The test was clearly too difficult for them*" (1994, p. 69).

The tenth-graders' responses to the questions were signed and videotaped, so that the test would measure reading comprehension separate from writing skills. Answers were

---

4 Based on the time it takes to fully acquires one's second language, these results would most likely be expected to continue to improve if the students continue in the next level of education (Collier, 1994).

5 I. Ahlgren, Stockholm University, personal communication, April 12, 1990; Nielsen, 1991.

translated into written Swedish by individuals who did not know the students (to prevent the investigators from recognizing any of the students on tape), analyzed, and placed into three groupings: 1) full comprehension, 2) partial or incomplete understanding of the text, and 3) little or no comprehension. Half the group, who had been educated in traditional classes, fell into the 'no comprehension' group. Those that fell into the top group comprised all of the students from the bilingual "project" class, and two others. (One of the others had lost her hearing at age four and had been with the project class for much of her schooling; the other girl had always been considered exceptional by her teachers) (Svartholm, personal correspondence, September 5, 1994). Svartholm (1994) notes that this full-comprehension group not only showed an advanced level of knowledge about written language, but that their comments about the text revealed a clear awareness of how to tackle a new and difficult written text in their second language.

Looking back, the results of a study in 1973 by Palle Vestberg Rasmussen, a Danish psychologist, showed the reading levels of students in Denmark to be consistently low. His results were much like Furth (1966) and other researchers in the United States, Sweden, England, and other countries who have noted a plateau in Deaf children's average ability to achieve greater than a fourth grade reading level. Vestberg Rasmussen found that only a minority of the Danish Deaf children tested at that time, who were in grades 3-9, progressed beyond a third grade reading level. In seeking to establish a developmental trend, he also concluded that the reading skills development of Deaf pupils followed neither a course like the normally-reading hearing child nor a course like that of the slow-learning hearing reader. Ironically, he observed, the teaching of reading was "at the center of the curriculum," which he felt was cause for great concern; in other words, it was not the amount of time spent teaching reading, but the methods that must be deficient.

In contrast to these former low standards of both European and American deaf children, psychologist Kerstin Heiling, who has spent many years testing children's progress, remarked during our interview, "*It is now easily possible for deaf children in Sweden to get past the 'fourth grade plateau'*" (personal communication, March 16, 1992).

Bent Neilsen, the psychologist that followed the reading progress of the first bilingual project in Denmark, notes that a later group of students being taught bilingually (those who entered school five years later in 1987), showed still earlier reading progress than the original 1982 group (Neilsen, 1991). Much like in Sweden, teachers and administrators felt this increasingly earlier proficiency in reading was not the result of earlier formal teaching, since there is no teaching of reading or grammar, per se, in the preschools. Instead, they felt it could be explained by the growing emphasis in both countries on early access to language for Deaf infants and toddlers, and early services for their parents. There seemed to be general consensus among those who worked with young children that the earlier the children's Sign Language and ability to understand their surroundings is in place, the earlier they move naturally into discovering the meaning in text. Parents and teachers I spoke to reported that many students approach reading and writing with confidence, both as a source of information and for pleasure.

Overall Achievement

In the classrooms where bilingual education has been implemented, much of the focus is on academic achievement. From the first grade on, many children work through grade-level texts—the same texts used by public schools for hearing children in Sweden and Denmark. During the early school years, much of the subject matter in books is communicated to Deaf children through Sign Language, in the same way teachers impart knowledge to hearing children through spoken language before they can read. As the children's command of the written word improves, dependency on text as a source of information increases. In other words, the goal is that school achievement not be allowed to suffer while children are in the process of learning the language of their textbooks. To this end, more content is communicated, at first, in other ways.

Historically, teachers of Deaf students in many countries have used simplified texts (Ewoldt, 1983), not necessarily those used by children in public schools. Moreover, Deaf children in many countries have traditionally been given 2-4 extra years (depending on level of attainment) to complete their compulsory school education. The extra years built into the system have often been considered a means of accommodating Deaf children's learning needs; however, linguists have for years argued that this strategy only accommodates ineffective communication practices (Bergman, 1978; Johnson, et al, 1989; Svartholm, 1994; Woodward, 1978). They claim that Deaf children, given full access to subject matter and comprehensible input in the majority language through literacy, can perform on an academic par with hearing children.

Knowing that lowered expectations for Deaf children were the norm rather than the exception, the *primary* demand of parents that prompted the first official bilingual class in Copenhagen was: *We want our children to be accountable for the same knowledge as hearing children in Denmark and to adhere as much as possible to the same course of study as is offered to hearing children.* At that time, these parents did not know anything about bilingual education. It just seemed like common sense to them that, in order to gain knowledge in a timely way, their children would need to get it through face-to-face communication in Sign Language, and through reading in Danish. (Hansen [1989, p. 4] relates how the parents at first thought both languages should be given equal time in the very early stages, then came to realize—along with the teachers—that the children simply had to build a strong foundation in Sign Language before they could easily learn about Danish and their other subjects. Later, when Sign Language competence was no longer a pressing issue, the focus began to shift to Danish literacy.)

In addition to this group, many other classes throughout the two countries have reportedly been working from grade-level texts in most subjects. (This does not include

Swedish texts, which are designed for children who grew up speaking Swedish). Except for the compulsory school exit exam, ongoing standardized testing and comparison of student achievement is rare in Europe, even for hearing children (Vestberg-Rassmussen, 1973).[6] However, teachers and administrators feel this mastery of grade-level material serves as one measure of achievement that far outpaces past outcomes in Sweden and Denmark and current outcomes in many other countries.

Looking at results of past deaf students, Norden, Tvingstedt, & Heiling (1989) compared the norms of tests administered in the 60's with a test program administered to all Deaf eighth graders at the Lund School for the Deaf from 1985-1989. The focus of these tests was primarily on Swedish language and mathematical and numerical ability. Results are summarized as follows by Heiling:

> I have found that the average level of theoretical knowledge has risen dramatically in deaf children who have had access to visual/gestural communication in their preschool years compared to the achievement of orally-trained age-mates in the sixties (Heiling, 1993b, p. 77).

> The subjects from the eighties were superior to their deaf age-mates from twenty years earlier in all tests measuring ability to understand and use written Swedish. They also performed significantly better on tests of mathematical and numerical ability. The differences between the two decades were more pronounced, however, in the texts measuring language proficiency (Heiling, 1990, p. 8).

Upon graduation, achievement of the students in the bilingual class in Copenhagen was at or above grade level, and all the students passed their exit exams "on time"—tests that had previously been considered unattainable for Deaf students. I recently received a letter from one of the teachers of this bilingual class, accompanying some photos I had requested for the cover. This "project"—the first in Copenhagen—included all Deaf students who entered first grade in Copenhagen in 1982. In other words, the children were not "hand-picked." The teacher who wrote me was among two who stayed with the students for the entire ten years (not unusual in these countries. She discussed their students' exit exams and plans to attend *gymnaseum* or upper-secondary school (also referred to as 'high school' in the quote below)[7], the level of non-compulsory education that students in Europe can enter after 10th grade if they pass a compulsory exam. The teacher's letter reads:

6   More discussion about attitudes and practices in regard to evaluation and standardized testing in both countries appears in Davies, 1990, as well as summaries of selected studies that were cited as having an impact on current directions in Deaf education.

7   This form of upper secondary school would be somewhere between 11th grade and the first 2 years of college in the U.S. See Appendix D.

As you might know from Tové or Britta, our project finished last June. All the pupils left with their exam results equal to the requirements of hearing pupils' school-leaving. The eleven children all passed Danish oral and written, English oral and written, Physics, and Math. Only because their teacher of German was never there did they not pass German, which is required here at that level after 10 years of schooling.

Of course the written exams were straightforward. For the oral (spoken) exams, we used moderators from the normal school system, combined with the necessary interpreters, and the pupils used Sign Language—naturally—to answer questions about Danish. English exams (oral) were carried through with writing on the computers in dialogue with the teacher (me) and with the moderators checking our conversation via the screen—by reading behind our backs. Great success.

I'm in contact with the pupils now that they are at Nyborg with other Deaf students from all parts of Denmark.... Usually children from Deaf schools will have to pass their exams at Nyborg, but as our class had already fulfilled these demands, they have mainly worked on social, political, and psychological areas which are not required but still a great advantage to know about when entering 'high school.'

Seven will now return after one year to Copenhagen in order to go to high school [the same as hearing students do] for the next three years and then will be able to go to University or any higher education they wish. We are sure they academically will all be O.K., and we the teachers and the parents feel we did the right thing in the proper way with these students!! (W. Lewis, personal correspondence, May 20, 1994).

Developing Literacy: Theory

Stephen Krashen, researcher in first and second language acquisition, uses the following example, "The Paris Argument," to clarify the concept behind bilingual education:

> *Pretend that you have just received, and accepted, an attractive job offer in Paris. Your French, however, is limited (you have two years of French in high school and one semester in college, and it was quite a while ago). Before your departure, the company that is hiring you will send you the following information, in English: what to do when you arrive in Paris, how to get to your hotel, where and how to find a place to live, where to shop, what kinds of schools are available for your children, how French companies function (how people dress in the office, what time work starts and ends, etc.), and specific information about the functioning of the company and your responsibilities.*
>
> *It would be very useful to get this information right away in English, rather than getting it gradually as you acquire French. If you get it right away, the world around you will be much more comprehensible, and you will thus acquire French more quickly.*
>
> *Anyone who agrees with this, in my opinion, agrees with the philosophy underlying bilingual education (Krashen, 1991, pp. 2-3).*

By giving Deaf children information in a language they can understand, they feel at ease, have a way to comprehend their surroundings, and can readily build their knowledge and establish contexts for the situations about which they will be reading. They have a language through which to learn about their world and with which to discuss the language they are learning, whether it is the spoken or written form of Swedish/Danish. This approach, of course, relies on the children having a sufficiently developed first language base to express their thoughts and comprehend classroom discussion when they enter school. Hence, the emphasis in the preschools in Sweden and Denmark is on early exposure to a language that is completely accessible to them visually.

Early acquisition of Sign Language and its use in education is not considered to be a threat to development of competency in written or spoken Swedish/Danish, but rather the best way to ensure such competency. This view is well-supported in the literature on bilingualism and biliteracy. In a comprehensive review of three decades of research on the characteristics and effects of bilingualism, findings indicate that the native language and the second language are complementary rather than mutually exclusive, and that native language proficiency is a consistent and powerful predictor of second language development (Hakuta, 1990). Rather than having separate areas in the brain for the first and the second language, theorists now generally agree that there is a form of common underlying proficiency that contributes to competence in more than one language. In other words, once that underlying proficiency is developed in one language, it serves as the foundation for acquiring a second language, or many other languages (Cummins & Swain, 1986).

Both research and practice in first language acquisition, second language acquisition, and bilingual education hold clear implications for Deaf children, as do studies in child development, literacy, bi- and multilingualism, and biliteracy. There are a wealth of resources available to professionals who consider ASL on an equal par with other languages of the world, and Deaf language learners on an equal par with hearing language learners. When educators begin to read in this area, they notice striking parallels between the acquisition and use of signed and spoken languages. But they are more than just parallels. Language is language, and children are children.

When I describe the video/text approach discussed above, some people's reaction has been, "Well, of course the kids can understand what they read. You've already told them what the story was about." Or, "Don't they get bored and want to skip doing the story the second time?" As background, it is important to look past this one activity at the larger context. The educational goals for Deaf children in these countries include: well-developed first language and sense of self-esteem, grade level academic achievement, high levels of literacy in the majority language (and in many cases other languages, as well), and full participation in society.

Therefore, teaching is largely focused on imparting grade-level information about math, science, history, etc. In other words, at the same time Deaf children are learning to read and write the majority language, they are receiving comprehensive instruction in all their subjects—including learning *about* their own Sign Language and Swedish or Danish—through Sign Language. Grade-level texts are used for all subjects except Swedish/Danish (which must be approached as children's second language), translating where necessary; with a focus on concept-building activity and work in groups so that students can reinforce and learn from each other.

But the specific goal of this teaching—the teaching of another language—is somewhat different. It is important to distinguish the *ultimate* goal of this second language teaching—to be able to receive and express information in written Swedish—from the immediate goal. One immediate goal of this parallel teaching is not simply that the students get the information in the stories, but that they learn *how* to get information—and ultimately *how* to express information—in this target language. The other immediate goal is to develop a level of comfort, familiarity, and confidence with this new language in an environment where there is little pressure, where they feel in control of the content. This building of comfort, confidence, and context may be among the most important ingredients in this model.

In the early stages, language learners can figure out much more of a text by themselves (and let the exercise be *about* language learning—not about struggling for crucial information) if they are given some context clues. These clues can come through pictures accompanying the text, through telling the story or imparting the information first in their own language, by hands-on experience, taking field trips, or having discussions to set up expectations for what the text might say. A fundamental principle in reading instruction is that the child must have a "schema," some prior frame of reference for comprehending what is in the text.[8] It is important to predispose new readers (especially those learning a second language), through a variety of context cues, to be confident that the information itself will not elude them because of their lack of skills in the language. This is basically how the parallel video/text approach works.

I was fortunate to have personal experience with this process on my last trip to Sweden. I had stopped over in Iceland and had time to take a bus tour. The tour guide gave long explanations in English about Icelandic geographical sites, then summarized her comments in French for a few people on the bus. While I still had to work hard to comprehend, I was able to understand more of this guide's French than I had ever understood in my French class or on visits to France. This fairly rapid, fairly technical discussion was one that normally would have "flowed" right over me with no comprehension. Knowing in advance some of the topics the guide would be discussing gave me enough context to identify many of the key words that carried the meaning. I was able to notice some of what she was doing with grammar and syntax to show the relationships between those words. Hearing the information first in my own language gave me the luxury to do more than just struggle for meaning. I could also notice HOW she was developing meaning. My confidence increased, and I realized that I actually know a lot of French. It became clear that what I typically lack in listening to French conversations are ongoing clues about context (to pull me back on track when I get lost or to help me guess the meaning of words I don't know.) A similar principle is at work in the parallel approach used with Deaf first graders in Sweden.

Cummins and Swain (1986) expand on this notion, claiming that meaning is primary, and that the primary work of extracting meaning in many communicative exchanges would overshadow a first or second language learners' ability to focus on the form of the language. They claim:

---

8   The importance of context and of drawing on prior knowledge, are discussed in Schleper, D. (1992) *PreReading Strategies*. Exercises designed to facilitate Deaf students' readiness to approach a text are also presented (see title page for ordering information).

*The first assumption, that the exchanges themselves are facilitative to
grammatical acquisition, rests on the possibility that the learner can pay
attention to meaning and form simultaneously. However, this seems unlikely.
It seems much more likely that only when the substance of the message is
understood can the learner pay attention to the means of expression—the form
of the message being conveyed (p. 131).*

They use, as an example, the repetitive nature of mothers' communication with babies,
where the mother tries to match and echo back the child's communicative intent. If this
match exists, the baby does not have to work to understand her meaning, but can
concentrate on some aspect of the *form* of her expression. Claiming that the same
underlying principle is at work for second language learners, they continue:

*In other words, it would seem that negotiating meaning—coming to a
communicative consensus—is a necessary first step to grammatical acquisition.
It paves the way for future exchanges, where, because the message is understood,
the learner is free to pay attention to form. Thus comprehensible input is crucial
to grammatical acquisition, **not** because the focus is on meaning, **nor** because a
two-way exchange is occurring, but because by being understood—by its match
with the learners' ongoing intentions and cognitions—it permits the learner to focus
on form (p. 131).*

Take a moment and study the first few pages from *Adam's Bøk*. Having a translation in
a language you already know makes for an interesting and very independent learning
process. No one teaches you that "*Min mormor och morfar ar döva*," means "My
grandmother and grandfather are deaf." You arrive at that conclusion by yourself. The
next time you see "*och*" in a sentence, you may pause a minute, then remember that it
means "and." After a few times, there will be no thinking or translation; "*och*" will actually
become for you the concept of a connector, independent of the English word, "and." You
also learned that *döva* means "deaf." Later, when you see that "*Dövas Hus*" is the name
of the Deaf club in Stockholm, you will wonder if adding the "s" makes the word "*döva*"
plural or possessive. (You know about plural and possessive functions because you use
them in your own language.) At that point, you may either ask the teacher, or keep
looking for patterns in the print matter you see until you are sure enough of this usage
to incorporate it into your own expression. You may at first think that *Hus* means, "club,"
but through exposure, will soon figure out that it means "house." There will be other
aspects of Swedish that really don't have any parallels in English structure. You will
learn to pay attention to them, partly because they are so different.

This is roughly how the process works. Whether it is grammar or vocabulary, much of
what you learned is retained—because you figured it out yourself. Or you asked—when
you were ready. No one "fed" it to you. Your discovery process had meaning because it
was based on what you were interested in, and what you could figure out from what you

already understand about how language works. Having translations in their own language, whether they are on videotape or the story is read and translated in person— allows Deaf children to focus their energy on figuring out *where* in those squiggles on the page the meaning lies. And how it was constructed.

Rather than focusing on single words, or implying that there is a one-word-one-sign correspondence between Sign Language and Swedish, the focus of the video/text introduction to written Swedish is on meaningful units. The goal is to help the children gradually discover *for themselves* the contrasts and similarities in how meaning is produced in the two languages. In signed languages, for example, a single verb which incorporates information about subject, object, number, and location—and is accompanied by non-manual grammatical markers—can easily communicate the meaning of a ten-word sentence in Swedish or English text. Teachers using *Adam's Bøk* begin to raise children's awareness of both languages by helping children notice such interesting comparisons. (For example, "Wow! Hans just noticed that this sign holds the meaning of many Swedish words! And did you know that sometimes it works the other way around?") The fact that children have the internal cognitive and linguistic competence to *produce* meaning through such structures is the real basis for their learning a second language—not their ability to explain or describe those structures. Beginning to point out differences and similarities at this age is largely done with the goal of making it very clear that there are two *different* languages, and of familiarizing the children with the different ways these languages can communicate things.

The process also instills pride and confidence in the children about their grasp of their own language, which they grow up recognizing is just as complex and sophisticated as the majority language. This, alone, is a major change in approach from the days when Sign Language was forbidden, shunned, or simply considered to be "bad grammar" in the majority language.

Comprehensible Input

It is clear to see that their progress has gone on quickly since you were here last. Not only are all the children reading, but some of them have the possibility of talking [using spoken Danish] more also as they know the language better. I am teaching Danish in the middle group. I can give them any sort of text and there seems to be actually hardly any problems. Many of the texts we are working on are 200-year old Danish; they are reading old literature because they are going to try to pass the exam here in June....

And we really saw like a 'boom' in writing. That was four years ago now that it happened. The boom I believe was because now they were reading so many different subjects, hard subjects with difficult language, such as physics and biology and so on. They now meet so many different kinds of language through the books, and carry on discussions of so many different subjects that all link together. It broadens their Sign Language. And also broadens their Danish from being exposed to all these kinds of books. They're not being restricted to what they had when they were younger, where everything they learn comes to them through the teacher. (W, Lewis, Copenhagen bilingual project teacher, personal communication, March 11, 1992).

Language learning theorists, for the most part, agree that the actual learning of a language comes through interaction with input from that language and its users in many information-getting situations (Bruner, 1983; Krashen, 1981, 1982, 1994; Preisler, 1983; Vygotsky, 1962). Again, the most successful teachers seemed well aware that they didn't actually "teach" all the structures in the language; they knew the learning was really up to the children. They depended on each child's own process of searching for meaning in text and discussing that search for meaning with others. Hence, the other important ingredient in Deaf children's achievement of literacy in Swedish and Danish is simple: Deaf children must have a great deal of exposure to all kinds of texts that carry meaning for them.

There is a large body of data (summarized in Krashen, 1994) to support the "input hypothesis" for acquisition of languages and literacy. This premise basically states: All language (including the written form) is learned through a process that depends heavily on exposure to *comprehensible input* (Krashen, 1981, 1982). Input is considered comprehensible when it is understandable because it is clear and fully accessible and the learner has a prior frame of reference or is given enough context to assist in finding the meaning. Krashen claims that, in order to make a comprehensible contribution to language learning, input in a language must be just beyond the learner's current level of competence in the language, known as *interlanguage*.[9] Studies of students who received *non-comprehensible* input—input that is somehow inaccessible or is too far beyond their level of competence or experience—show very limited language development. As with the example above (Deaf students reading old Danish literature), what is comprehensible to a reader of a language changes over time, with increasingly less need for familiar words, structures, context cues, or pictures.

Grammar Teaching

While we can illuminate children's understanding of a linguistic rule or decrease confusion about certain usages through explanation, Krashen and others systematically discount theories that we actually "teach" grammar, spelling, or vocabulary. In other words, if we were to compare a child's performance in spoken, signed, or written language

---

9   Krashen's formula for comprehensible input = i + 1 (interlanguage + a degree more difficult).

with the time we have to formally teach each structure that they know, it is clear there simply are not enough hours in the day to account for that child's competence. Children's ongoing generation of unique sentences—many of them never before uttered—is clear evidence that language competence is not simply imitation, and goes much deeper than the structures children can explain or have consciously memorized.

According to the preschool teachers I interviewed, there is little or no formal teaching of Swedish in the preschools, but there is a great deal of reading to the children and storybook sharing and building context for reading through experiences. And even in school, reading is not *taught* at first; the best teachers approach it in the most natural way possible—using what we know as "whole language" principles (Freeman & Freeman, 1992; Goodman, 1986; Weaver, 1990), which seem to be captured in the following quote by a teacher from the first bilingual class in Copenhagen:

> *In the first place, the children must be interested in the subject. The text must relate to something they already know in themselves. Of course, they are just looking for meaning. Worrying about the sequence of the words will come gradually along with some formal teaching in making them conscious of the formation of sentences. But learning to read is really not about the teaching of grammar.*
>
> *It is just about having the meaning jump out of the paper. That is going to be the big 'Ah-Ha:' "Oh, lovely…I'm getting information!" That is the most important thing. That is the great leap. As soon as you get any sort of information out of these little fly-legs on the piece of white paper, then it starts being interesting. You find something that links up with your whole social life—or gives meaning to the picture next to the text—and you are on your way (W. Lewis, teacher in Copenhagen bilingual classroom, personal communication, March 11, 1992).*

In this learner-centered process, information about grammar is primarily incorporated as it relates to the comprehension of meaning in the text, in much the same way you (the reader) would learn a great deal about Swedish grammar if you worked your way through *Adam's Bøk*. Later, when the students become aware of the societal benefits of their polishing and perfecting their production of the majority language, formal study of grammar "takes off."

Linguist Kristina Svartholm comments:

> *The main idea behind the role of grammar teaching can be summarized as follows: Children have a right to get parts of grammar explained to them, not for the sake of learning grammar as such, but for developing deeper understanding of texts. Later on, knowledge about grammatical rules may be useful to them as a tool for expressing meaning in an understandable way in texts. But the principle purpose*

of teaching grammar to young Deaf children is to show them how grammar can be a tool for understanding text; i.e., grasping content.

In this kind of teaching it is of the utmost importance that the focus on texts include an awareness of input quantity. No second language learner can be expected to gain proficiency in the language from a very restricted input. Thus, the size and number of texts to go through with the children must be given priority over any attempts to explain details in the texts, no matter how important such details and training in them may seem from a traditional point of view (Svartholm, 1993, p. 327).

According to linguist Ahlgren (personal communication, April 22, 1990), as well as many of the teachers and speech therapists I interviewed, young Deaf children become intensely interested in the signed, spoken, and written languages in their environment if their natural curiosity—that wish to learn "everything"—is nurtured. In other words, their education is structured to make encounters with each form enjoyable, developmentally appropriate, and without excessive pressure or meaningless repetition. Like other bilingual or multilingual children, Deaf children also become very intuitive about which language forms to use in which contexts, including use of Sign Language that incorporates features of the grammar of the majority language, sometimes known as "contact varieties" (Lucas and Valli, 1988, 1992) in the presence of hearing signers whose production contains influence from the majority language (Grosjean, 1992; Johnson, 1994; Johnson and Erting, 1989; Philip, 1994).

Later, as the children become more aware of the existence of two *separate* languages and develop necessary cognitive sophistication, they start to discover the differences (Cummins & Swain, 1986). They become able to engage in "metalanguage," the ability to think and talk about one's own language processes. I interviewed each of the teachers who worked in the first Deaf-hearing team in 1983 where the goal was to teach Swedish by using Sign Language translations of children's literature. One teacher reminisces about their first encounter with this awareness in the children:

And we took ordinary children's books that were suitable for their age. Sten signed and they had their books in front of them and they could just look down if they wanted to. But very often, they just forgot the book because it was so exciting—what he was telling. And so they had some pages to try to read at home. They came back and we asked if there were some questions and they always had plenty. So we could work very hard on these five pages.

Sten and I were looking at some videotapes of one of these sessions, and it is interesting to see how the children began discussing words and the meaning of words among themselves. They were talking about two Swedish words that are spelled the same way but they mean very different things. Then one of them said,

"Well, you have to look at the context. You have to see what is before and after and then you understand the meaning of the word." And we thought that was really good that they had got that insight so early (Harriet Björneheim, May 10, 1990).

Every effort is made in the early years to give Deaf children in Sweden and Denmark early exposure to whole languages: the natural signed language used by the Deaf community, as well as the spoken/written language that is prevalent in society. It is accepted that the Sign Language children acquire when they are young has a grammatical structure distinct from that of the majority language. In other words, educators and parents do not view the children's language as being based on Swedish word order or having a one-word-one-sign match with the spoken language.

The second grade teacher quoted earlier illustrates potential problems in her description of one child in her reading group who seemed to be having trouble with the notion that the two languages had different ways of handling concepts:

One boy's parents are very efficient. They want to teach their son to be a good reader. I am sure they've been working with him a lot. And he is one that has the most problems mixing Sign Language and Swedish. He has a hard time separating the two languages, I think because his parents have taught him that way—to sign one sign for each word. So we've had to say, "Please, can you try to explain what that is in Sign Language? Can you translate what it says into Sign Language?" And now he is coming on (G. Christersson, personal communication, March 20, 1992).

Based on this understanding of the separateness of the two languages, parents and teachers, would not, for example, be likely to correct children's Sign Language grammar in the direction of Swedish/Danish grammar. In fact, only once did an interviewee suggest early attempts to impart Danish grammar through simultaneous communication (talking and signing at the same time). As a result, it seems, there are fewer assumptions among parents or teachers that the children already possess competence in Swedish grammar before learning to read (see section on simultaneous communication and sign-based codes for more discussion). One problem with not separating the two in schools in the U.S. has been that, since ASL structure was not acknowledged, children sometimes believed that what they were signing *was* English grammar. If this was true, they should merely have to write the way they sign and would have grammatical English sentences. Yet this rarely happened, which resulted in many children thinking that their own language was simply ungrammatical English.

It was explained to me (by Swedish teachers who had been teaching before the transition to bilingual education) that their current efforts *not* to "mix" spoken Swedish and Sign Language (not to use both at the same time), have made it much easier to point out to the children that there are two languages. The children become aware that Swedish is a *separate* language and that this language is the same in some ways—and different in some ways—from their own language. This not only frees them to really attend to the differences as such, but also allows them to feel good about having a perfectly grammatical first language, acknowledging that they are *in the process* of learning their second language.

Literacy and Developing Skills in the Spoken Language

This emerging literacy and metalinguistic awareness of both languages is also seen as having the potential to contribute to emerging speech development in some children. Over time, developing competence in language, through Sign Language and literacy, can reinforce some students' ongoing work on speech production and lipreading by providing a solid internal knowledge of the language, as well as a grasp of the written form of the words they are learning to pronounce. This knowledge can bring meaning to the task for students who are developing skills in the spoken form of the language.

Hansen (1980b) comments that developing literacy especially seems to contribute to improved lipreading (speechreading) skills. Whether in single words or connected speech, there is a great deal that can't be seen on the lips and face, and there is significant ambiguity in the forms that *are* visible on the lips. Clearly, good speechreaders must do a lot of "filling in the blanks." This information is not new. Studies conducted almost forty years before the writing of this book (Woodward, M., 1957) documented that a high percentage of sounds are not noticeable through visual observation, and that if speechreaders are to distinguish the ambiguities among the sounds that can be seen on the lips—but look alike—they must rely on phonetic, lexical, or grammatical redundancy (See O'Neill & Oyer [1981] for summaries of other early studies). In other words, clues from the rest of the word, the context in which a word appears, or the arrangement of other words around it are important. Yet the other words in the sentence may provide little information, as they stand to be equally hard to distinguish through lipreading. Furthermore, in a conversation, one cannot take time to isolate and examine a single sentence or ask for a repetition. The speaker simply keeps on talking.

Such intense ongoing analysis of what can be seen when looking at the lips and how it contributes to the construction of meaning is at least in part based on well-developed knowledge of how sounds (a very abstract concept for one who has never heard), morphemes (parts of words), and words connect in a given language. For this reason, much of today's current teaching of speechreading is more of a top-down process, looking at the whole picture, spending less time memorizing single facial configurations and more time on how they work together. This process is most productive for those who lost their hearing later in life. Clearly, knowledge of the language is an indispensable part of the guesswork needed to reconstruct the missing pieces when viewing connected speech. (See section on sign-based codes and simultaneous communication for more discussion.)

During my second study, I had dinner with a Deaf family in Denmark. The mother knew ASL and English, and therefore translated my comments for the children. While the young girl clearly relied on her mother as interpreter, it soon became clear to me that the boy (about 14 years old) understood much of what I said. When I asked where he had been exposed to ASL, he said he hadn't, but he was mostly reading my lips. (Clearly, I was mouthing a lot of English!) This boy has little comprehensible speech. However, his teachers report that his excellent command of Danish through literacy and study of spoken phonology seem to have contributed to his being a good lipreader. They also felt that this knowledge of how language/phonology work through his study of Sign Language and Danish not only made it relatively easy for him to pick up English as a third language (starting around age 11), but also to utilize that knowledge in lipreading English.

One Basic Prerequisite

The methods described earlier for the teaching of reading are built on principles used by teachers of second languages:

- continue development of context, knowledge, and academic skills through the first language,

- rely heavily on pictures, interactional context, and life experience in introducing the second language at an appropriate level of difficulty,

- use the students' own language to discuss features of the second language,

- capitalize on the students' competence in their own language as a foundation for understanding structures in the second language.

Clearly, success with the methods described here is heavily predicated on the child having a fairly well-developed first language. When Deaf first graders, like hearing first graders, have already had a number of years of meaningful interaction in their first language, they know how to exercise various acts of communication (questioning, inflection, referencing, asserting, scolding, joking, turn-taking, word-play, etc.). They start school with a solid base of internal competence in language and how language works, as well as the ability to comprehend discussion of age-appropriate subject-matter.

Almost all hearing children have a fairly well-developed first language upon entering school, even if their language is different from that spoken by the majority. This basic competence, *so* crucial to the success of bilingual and second-language teaching methods, is taken for granted in schools for hearing children. Hearing children, for the most part, naturally acquire the language of their parents and peers before entering school, despite linguistic, ethnic, or socioeconomic differences. As Axelsson states, *"Even if rate of development varies a lot among first language learners, it is beyond doubt that all normal children, given a reasonably normal upbringing, successfully acquire their first language "*(1994. p. 249). The same is true for Deaf children of Deaf parents. (For an overview of the extensive research on the first language development of Deaf children exposed early to Sign Language, see Newport & Meier [1986].)

Until recently, the *only* settings where deaf children have consistently received early and adequate exposure to Sign Language for the acquisition of a first language is in homes where the parents are Deaf. This early exposure seems to have clear payoffs in linguistic competence and cognitive abilities. As Ewoldt (1993) notes:

> *Widely acknowledged among professionals working with the deaf and strongly supported by the literature worldwide is the finding that, in comparison with deaf children of hearing parents, deaf children with deaf parents are generally superior in language-related endeavors such as speechreading (popularly called lipreading), reading, writing, and speaking, as well as signing (Israelite, Ewoldt & Hoffmeister, 1989). The generally accepted reason for this finding is that these children have access to Sign Language from birth. Thus, native Sign Languages are, in fact, true languages upon which deaf children can build and learn other languages, and signing deaf children are no different from other children for whom English is a second language [Cummins & Danesi, 1990] (Ewoldt, 1993, p. 3).*

Rather than dismissing these results as desirable, but unattainable, phenomena—restricted to Deaf children growing up in homes with Deaf family members—Deaf families have now became *models* for the early childhood components of the Swedish and Danish support for hearing families. Researchers in these countries and the U.S. have made it clear that the closer the system could come to creating an environment full of visual language and acceptance for Deaf children of hearing parents, the more likely it would be that these children's language and cognitive development would, likewise, improve (Ahlgren, 1978, 1980, 1994; Corson, 1973; Erting, C., 1992b, 1994; Spencer, Bodner-Johnson, & Gutfreund, 1992).

Efforts to give Deaf children of hearing parents in Sweden and Denmark solid early exposure to Sign Language seem to be making a difference (see Chapter 3 on support for parents and first language acquisition for children). First grade teachers I interviewed consistently reported that Deaf children entering school—with the exception of children who were fairly recent immigrants—possessed the linguistic competence to understand their first-grade lessons and express themselves appropriately. School psychologist Bent Nielsen, who tests children entering the Kastelsvej School in Copenhagen summarizes his observations as follows:

> *...such a big change has occurred in the attitude to sign language that by far the greatest number of children today have completely different qualifications when*

*starting school. Many have a fully functional age-correspondent sign language,
while others are well on the way. It is now an exception to meet infant school
[preschool] children without some form of language. However, in the pupil group
from 1969-1975, it was an exception for a pupil to master sign language. On the
whole, this only applied to children of deaf parents, which was why most school
starters were disappointed and intellectually starved, on top of having behind them
countless experiences of inadequacy during the oral stimulation and learning
process (Nielsen, 1991, p. 3).*

Long-held stereotypes about Deaf children of hearing parents—and their level of linguistic, cognitive, and social readiness upon entering school—*have changed* in settings where resources are devoted to building early language competence. Deaf adults in Sweden sometimes claimed they could not readily tell which of the children in a group of Deaf preschoolers had Deaf parents, a distinction that was always easy to make in former times: children with Deaf parents have traditionally possessed a level of confidence and fluency in language that made them stand out. Similar observations of more confident, fluent, Deaf children of hearing parents have been made in settings in the U.S. where Deaf children of hearing parents had early and sufficient exposure to Deaf peers and adults (Bienvenu, 1994; also K. Rust, personal communication, 1994).

When the Swedish children start first grade (age 6-7), it is important that they have a strong first language; are comfortable with their identity; already know a great deal about their world; and have the linguistic, cognitive, and social readiness to attend to the lessons being presented. With this competence and plenty of active exposure to written language, many of the children develop an interest in written Swedish well before entering first grade without formal instruction.

In Denmark, evaluations of the Danish Sign Language competence of today's Deaf students of hearing parents entering first grade are much higher than for the early bilingual class (S. Toft, R. Bergmann, personal communication, March 11, 1992). Because so much rests on Sign Language competence, work is continuing in both countries to improve methods for testing each child's skills in signed language. Attending to Deaf children's early linguistic and cognitive competence by testing their abilities in Sign Language (and cognitive abilities *through* Sign Language) can help to identify problems in language development. More importantly, such evaluation is part of recognizing the primary role of the first language in the child's life, as well as in academic achievement and in acquisition of the majority language (Evans, et al, 1994; Kelly, Bloechle, Esp, Van Hove, Ingrassia, Morseon, 1994). It is not assumed that the children are somehow magically fluent in Sign Language simply because they are deaf and are *communicating*. Requirements that Deaf children be taught Sign Language as an academic subject (and that their competence in that language be regularly tested) are recognized as an important component in the education of all Deaf children.

Teachers who work with younger students could not seem to stress enough the importance of these early factors in paving the way for academic success. A major conclusion gleaned from experience in Sweden and Denmark is as follows: *If resources in a country or program are limited, their most efficient use would be toward 1) setting up strong parent-infant programs and preschools staffed by Deaf and hearing teachers and aides fluent in Sign Language, 2) providing the best possible Sign Language training for parents, and 3) facilitating the child's starting school with a strong first language—spoken or signed.* (This approach is not intended to preclude the early natural acquisition of speech for those who have adequate access to spoken interactions through their hearing.) Early readiness, and a variety of experiences that build a strong framework for relating what is in print to the world around them, seems to contribute more toward emerging literacy—towards children's readiness to gradually become readers through regular exposure to text and pictures—than any educational techniques used at later ages.

Timing is Critical: First Things First

The first principle, that of first things first, establishes the central role of the child's first language in all aspects of his or her educational development. It says: ensure that the child's home [first] language is adequately developed before worrying about progress in the second language. It implies that the first language is so instrumental to the emotional and academic well-being of the child, that its development must be seen as a high, if not the highest, priority (Cummins and Swain, 1986, p. 101).

In their book, *Bilingualism in Education: Aspects of Theory, Research, and Practice*, Cummins and Swain (1986) explain this most basic principle for success in educating children who have a first language other than the language of the majority. Many theorists in bilingual education agree that, not only must there be a strong first language, but that the best way to ensure academic success is to support the first language in school; to continue to cultivate concept-development and literacy in that language (Collier, 1989; Cummins, 1980). Cummins has described knowledge of a first language as providing an underlying competence that applies to language in general—in other words, competence in a first language clearly contributes to one's ability to learn other languages.

If all is well in the development of a first language in young children, development of a signed or spoken second language—if it is fully accessible—can take place almost in tandem (Petitto, 1994b). If there are no impediments to the timely acquisition of a first language, Deaf children also seem to move quickly into acquiring the written form of majority language, if they are exposed to it through storybook sharing and environmental print (G. Christersson, personal communication, 1990/92; Erting, L. & Pfau, 1994; Ewoldt, 1985; Weinstock & Erting, L., 1994). Nevertheless, the learning of written language is a less interactive and more cognitively demanding process (Svartholm, 1993) than the learning of spoken language. Expectations for parallel development of both Sign Language and the written form of the spoken language are not reasonable at the earliest stages. Literacy, however, does emerge rapidly in circumstances where the child is developmentally ready and the written form is steeped in interactive and environmental contexts that are, in some ways, like face-to-face use of language. Preschool teachers working with both languages in the U.S., Sweden, and Denmark have often volunteered their own observations which seem to reiterate the gist of the quote above: If the first language is not solid-—growth in the second language and academic achievement are not likely to come up to par. Almost all of the teachers of younger children I met on the first visit mentioned to me their observation that if students' own language, sense of themselves, and ability to understand classroom discussions about many different things were not in place, efforts to teach Danish (or Swedish) were largely lost on them.

None of the teachers claimed that all exposure to the second language needs to be put on hold while the children master a first language; rather, they suggested that *the priority* must be on giving children what they need to acquire "the basics" before they can proceed. If children do have those attributes in place when they start school, the rest seems to go much more according to schedule. Skipping the basics altogether is likely to keep grade-level mastery of subject matter permanently out of reach. Going back later and playing "catch-up" takes time and delays the child's school achievement, still jeopardizing children's ability ever to achieve on a par with hearing children (Collier, 1989; Cummins, 1979; Paulston, 1977).

Such delays have been reluctantly accepted around the world as an inevitable part of educating Deaf children. Yet, it seems that many of the difficulties students traditionally encounter are not results of an inability to perform learning tasks, but of inappropriate understanding and expectations in meeting each child's linguistic, cognitive, and developmental readiness for the tasks.

The conclusions about readiness and timing that teachers in the early bilingual classes arrived at through their own experience and observation are clearly supported by theories of child language learning and child development. Preschool teachers working with both languages are adamant about giving children opportunities for exposure to print and about the remarkable growth they see in literacy during these early years. Yet, they seem to agree that, for most Deaf children, approaching the majority language in its written form must be based on each child's level of interest and readiness. Formal *teaching* of that language or its structures cannot typically be given a central role until the first language is somewhat well-established, the child has a good command of world knowledge, and the child takes an interest in print. Anyone who observes very young children knows that first language, socialization, and *awareness* of text are "their job" during the early years. First things first.

Teachers in Sweden and Denmark communicated a sense that rushing in to compensate for perceived deficits by getting an early start on teaching the majority language is less effective than observing each child closely, keeping in mind that there are certain activities for which children are ready at different times in their cognitive, linguistic, and social development.

In the same way we can push a child "too soon," we might also miss critical periods of readiness if we *don't* work with what the children have learned for themselves and support any interest and growth that is emerging with regard to print. In a recent interview, Carolyn Ewoldt, researcher in Deaf children's literacy, expressed a similar perspective:

> *We found out that even children who hadn't been exposed to Sign Language had remarkable awareness of environmental print well before starting school—age 3 or before. Even if they didn't have a firm language, they understood a lot about print and its functions. So I don't think we need to wait till they start school or even have a first language to start valuing what they DO know, what they've picked up on their own. It's really about how you look at what they already know.*

> *I think we're just not good, yet, at watching them and seeing what they know and letting them build on that. One of the very young children in our study recognized "McDonald's" in print. That word had meaning for him—a fun place to go get food. Another knew the word "Baby Powder"—something to sprinkle on my bottom. No one taught them to read these words; they learned them from how they function, and because they had significance for the child. That's good strategy for learning language—going from it's broadest context. It's not helpful to proclaim when we should teach or not teach something, but to look at what each child already has in place and let them know that what they're doing is the right kind of thing to be doing (C. Ewoldt, personal communication, August 25, 1994).*

In essence, if teachers and parents are watching closely, with open minds, the children will lead. If tasks are presented when a child is ready and interested, learning proceeds easily and comfortably.

Writing

> *"Learning by writing" must be preceded by some other kind of linguistic input; linguistic output must be preceded by comprehensible input....The input-output distinction...is important because of its impact on the actual work in the classroom. It ought to be reflected in the proportion of time given the two activities of "reading" and "writing." The former has the right of precedence and ought to be totally dominant in the first few years. Later on, when the child has a storage of linguistic knowledge from which to derive production, the proportions between the activities in the classroom may well be changed (Svartholm, 1993, p. 313-314).*

Deaf children in Sweden and Denmark are encouraged to write for fun, make notes, lists, labels, "write" letters, or dictate stories and reports for the teachers to write down (often illustrated by the children). But they are not expected to produce written matter that evidences correct Swedish/Danish grammar until they have had years of exposure to the Swedish language through reading. The early focus is on *input* in the language, mostly through frequent and enjoyable exposure to text. While creating *output* in the new language is a important part of a learner's process in acquiring high levels of proficiency (Cummins and Swain, 1986), how that output is viewed by the teacher seems to be an important component in children's success. Whenever the children do write, many teachers in Sweden and Denmark explained that they study the children's output, using both errors and correct productions as information about each child's learning process and level of mastery of certain forms. In first and second language acquisition theory, errors are seen as positive signs, evidence of a productive process of testing and refining hypotheses about how the language works. Svartholm notes:

> *Claims...about the deficient language learning in deaf children utterly lose their reliability as soon as you turn away from comparing deaf children to hearing children who are using their mother-tongue in reading and writing. If you instead look at hearing second-language learners and their language development in the second language, the picture becomes totally different.*

> *Such a comparison will clearly show that many of those grammatical errors, that have been described as peculiar to the deaf, are far from peculiar in reality. Whether hearing or deaf, the second language learner uses the information available about the new language, makes generalizations and other simplifications on the basis of this information, and constructs inner, mental hypotheses about the language. The outcome of this is often deviant from the language system in question, but it is nevertheless the result of an active and creative language learning device.*

> *In this perspective, the presumed 'deficits' found among deaf language learners deserve great interest. Instead of being taken as proofs of some kind of disability, they can be taken as perfect evidence of the language learning capacity (Svartholm, 1994).*

Teachers who have learned this come to see their Deaf students' writing as a window into their current understanding of the language. Errors help them peer into the child's process. Teachers are able to focus on what the children know about the language, as well as gain intelligence about what they don't yet know.

As two Swedish teachers note in their new book, it's the *process* that is important at this stage:

Language development is an ongoing process all through life, and we all learn differently and at different paces. Therefore, we have to choose a working method that allows for our students' different learning strategies. We feel that a process-oriented method gives us that flexibility....(p. 35).

A process-oriented method focuses the teachers' attention on skills that have been developed and not the lack of them. Right or wrong does not exist if you see the student in a phase of a process. ((Foss Ahldén & Lundin, draft version, p. 17).

In this way, Deaf children who have received solid early exposure to American Sign Language are no different from other children whose first language is not English. In *The Primary Language Record*, (Barrs, Ellis, Hester, & Thomas, 1989), many issues are addressed related to monitoring and recording progress in a child's writing. These issues relate to confidence and independence, experience, strategies, knowledge and under-standing, and reflectiveness. They note that teachers of second languages in particular need to know what they are looking for, what is reasonable to expect from a child at various points in the process. Hester (1990) notes that:

It is important to remember that children may move into English in very individual ways, and that the experience for an older child will be different from that of a young child. The stages (discussed later) emphasize the social aspects of learning as well as the linguistic. Obviously, attitudes in the school to children and the languages they speak will influence their confidence in using both their first and second languages.

Their methods of monitoring and evaluation of children's writing samples are based on:

- describing in positive ways what the child can do

- noting development along a continuum of growing fluency

- setting a framework for describing aspects of language development that take into account differences in the structure of the first language.

The Role of Errors

Many errors that had long been thought to be influence from the learners' first language are now seen as just a natural part of their own processing of the target (new) language. It is very helpful for teachers to understand some of the psychological processes that are basic to learners of first and second languages, among them simplification and overgen-eralization, which appear at all levels as new structures are being acquired. *Simplification* is somewhat like taking morphological or syntactic "short-cuts," largely because a learner does not yet know or cannot yet control some aspects of the language (for example, leaving out articles and other form words while concentrating on content words). *Overgenerali-*

zation means that a learner takes one rule he has acquired and applies it incorrectly in similar situations. Axelsson (1994) gives the example of over-use of the regular verb inflection in English, resulting in the learner saying "goed" instead of "went." She explains that learners may seem to have mastered a production, then regress, then finally produce it on a consistent basis. This is known as a "U-shaped" development, in which learners don't just learn and memorize a new structure, they restructure their whole system to accommodate it, which causes periodic downswings in progress (Lightbown, 1983).

Natural influences from the first language and the errors made as a normal part of the learning process have previously been viewed from a negative perspective: "interference" and "developmental errors." Errors are now viewed from a more cognitive, process-oriented perspective—as evidence of the learner's active contribution in acquiring the language. The nature of specific errors can give the teacher information about which errors originate from the learners' first language (*interlingual errors*) and are therefore somewhat predictable based on a contrastive analysis of the two languages; and which errors are within the realm of the students' developing picture of the new language (*intralingual errors*). Axelsson (1994) explains that consistent errors give clues to *lack of knowledge* of a part of the language system, whereas inconsistent productions (first right, then wrong) signal *insufficient control* of the what has already been learned (Corder, 1974). These are just a few examples of how second language teachers—trained to know what to look for and how to interpret the errors they see—gain information about each student's process in learning to read, write, or speak. This information can guide teachers in providing comprehensible input and relevant instruction.

It is vital not to assume that Deaf children will master production of this second language in its written form in the same time course and the same sequence as hearing children, who have had auditory access to the structures of the language since birth. By providing an accessible first language and acknowledging that written English is a second language, children are not deprived of content or self-expression; their first language is always available to them. It is then possible to acknowledge that, depending on experience, levels of hearing and speech, exposure to text, home support, etc., different children will be at different stages in getting acquainted with this new language and form of expression. Hester (1990) describes four stages learners of a second language (English, in this case) go through that can be helpful in setting reasonable expectations for each child:

- new to English

- becoming familiar with English

- becoming a confident user of English

- a very fluent user of English in most social and learning contexts

Despite traditional efforts to come up with new ways to fully immerse the children in one form of English or another over the years, many Deaf children in the U.S. never reach the third stage, where they become *confident* users of English, even as adults. They have not traditionally been given time to just "soak up" English in its full form through reading before being evaluated on their writing. Deaf children can enter school with a wealth of knowledge about English through print and fingerspelling and print (Blumenthal-Kelly, 1994; Erting & Pfau, 1994; Ewoldt & Saulnier, 1992; Padden & LeMaster, 1985), competence that has sometimes been overlooked because it didn't follow the progression expected. That language competence can be nurtured, supported, and viewed as a precious *resource*—rather than a liability or a problem (Nover & Ruiz, 1992).

Because learning other languages is not part of every American child's education, parents and teachers in the U.S. are likely to be unfamiliar with the lengthy, but natural, processes second language learners go through while acquiring fluency. As a result, Deaf children's writing has often been critiqued early, often prematurely. The children can get the message that "how" they say it in English is more important than "what" they say. There is a great deal of research to indicate that this negative cycle—which often accompanies immersion in the majority language and neglect of their own language competence in academic settings—is unnecessary. Moreover, immersion—the idea that children best learn a second language when totally surrounded by it and not encouraged to use their own language—has not been found to constitute the most efficient model for acquiring the second language while keeping the focus on achievement levels:

> *Recent research shows that when bilingual programs are set up correctly, they work very well. Krashen and Biber (1988) found that students in well-designed bilingual programs in California outperformed comparison students [those in English immersion or poorly-designed bilingual programs], and did very well compared to local and national norms....(p. 5).*

> *Several scholars have pointed out that when bilingual education is shown to be just as effective as all-English programs, this is a remarkable result since it means that the children have acquired just as much English with significantly less exposure to English. This confirms the underlying theory of bilingual education. Some of the critics...have missed this point entirely (Krashen, 1991, p.3).*

The programs Krashen and Biber determined to be "well-designed" always included continued subject matter teaching through the first language. When content can be communicated and literacy developed in the first language, teachers have the luxury of time in letting each child arrive at a comfort level with English. This practice also seems to foster a beneficial degree of patience in parents and teachers, as well as acceptance of other occurrences that are predictable phenomena in the learning of a second language.

This level of patience about grammatically correct writing may come more easily to parents and teachers of Deaf children in Sweden and Denmark, as *all* children there (who later become parents and teachers) learn English as a second language and become quite fluent due to reinforcement from English on T.V. and in movies. Most children in these countries learn English well enough for academic use by the time they leave high school, yet they do not start formal instruction until age 9 or later. So they have all had experience with what it means to learn a second language while continuing one's education in the first language. Such first-hand experience with the process is fairly rare in the U.S.

The Pay-Offs of Patience

Talk of "patience" in this context does not mean Deaf children's introduction to English should be purposely postponed. On the contrary, Deaf children should be surrounded very early with fun, meaningful, and comprehensible input in English that demands nothing more of them than to enjoy it. As Krashen (1994) states:

> *Those experiences that are good for language development are typically pleasant; those that are not good for language acquisition are perceived as painful. In other words, "No pain, no gain" does not apply to literacy development.*

When this enjoyable comprehensible exposure to text takes place, Deaf children cover basically the same ground as hearing children in emergent writing—going through stages of scribbling, writing the first letter of their name or another word to symbolize the whole word, etc. (Ewoldt, 1985; Ewoldt & Saulnier, 1992). Reliance on fingerspelling and environmental print is part of the everyday experience of many Deaf children from a very early age (Blumenthal-Kelly, 1994; Maxwell, 1984, 1988), and has been shown to eventually increase their awareness of the different attributes of their languages (Erting & Pfau, 1994; Padden and LeMaster, 1985).

The point is not to deprive Deaf children of writing experiences when they are ready; the point is to be careful about forcing them if they aren't ready. Addressing the question of how late is too late, Collier (1989), through an extensive review of research on academic achievement in a second language, concludes the following:

> *When the debate about the optimal age for beginning acquisition of a second language for schooling purposes takes this important intervening variable—L1 cognitive development[10]—into account, the arguments can be resolved fairly conclusively. Before puberty, it does not matter when one begins exposure to (or*

10   L1 refers to the first language, L2 to the second language.

---

instruction in) a second language, as long as cognitive development in the first language continues up through age 12 (the age by which first language acquisition is largely completed). Cummins (1981) refers to a common underlying proficiency, or interdependence, existing between a bilingual's two languages (even given widely varying surface features), with development of one language strongly aiding development of the second one (Collier, 1989, p. 511).

The implication of these findings are not that we should create unnecessary delays in teaching English as a second language to Deaf children, but that—when it comes to developing all-important competence in a first language—the studies Collier cites indicate that there *is* time for those who need it. In other words, if the first language is not strong when the child enters school, taking the time to develop competence and comfort in a fully accessible visual language is more important than rushing into teaching the spoken or written form of the majority language too soon.

The teachers I met in Sweden and Denmark who were most successful in teaching reading and writing were those who clearly understood through their own experience the benefits of taking time and letting the first language develop. One group expressed remorse that they had responded to external pressure to give both languages 'equal time' in the early years. They feel they pushed a few of the students in their bilingual class into expressing themselves in Danish before they were "settled" with their sense of themselves and Sign Language. These children had been in oral and signed Danish programs before entering first grade. Their skills in Danish Sign Language were not yet well developed (as determined both through their functioning and through formal evaluations) and the teachers report they did not evidence the same interest in or readiness for Danish as the others in the class. The others, whom the teachers felt were "ready" for more formal instruction in Danish at that time, later tested in reading at the same levels as their hearing peers and well above their Deaf agemates who were not educated bilingually (B. Nielsen, school psychologist, personal communication, March 10, 1992). Yet the children that the teachers feel they "pushed" always seemed to be struggling more with Danish. While these students experienced more difficulties and developed Danish competence much later, they still did pass their exit exams, including those in Danish. Nevertheless, the teachers found it difficult throughout their education to determine whether or not there was a possibility they had some other form of language learning disorder.

Consistent with these teachers' observations, recent findings suggest that:

The learning of a second language before the primary language is fully developed may result in arrested development or loss of proficiency in the first language. Therefore, the finding that a child is delayed in both the first and the second language does not necessarily mean that child has a language disorder (Schiff-Myers, Djukic, Lawler, & Perez, 1993, p. 237).[11]

The results of the single case study upon which this statement is based must not be overgeneralized; however, it is clear that the ramifications of incomplete development of the first language require more attention and study.

One teacher who had spent ten years with this bilingual class in Copenhagen (referred to on the previous page) spoke of how she hoped to approach her next class; that is, when she started again with a group of first graders:

> *I will start—absolutely start—with Sign Language. And of course with a deaf teacher. I would not do it without a deaf teacher or deaf teaching assistants. At least in some of the subjects. And then we would look at each child and watch what they are picking up in Danish, and after the first two or three years let them start off with actual teaching of Danish and learning with Danish materials, according to their interest, of course. Again, it depends on the children. Now so many enter school with much more signing than our class did in the beginning; so more children are ready and would not need to wait those years to start learning in Danish. But if some weren't ready, I would definitely let them take their time.*

> *I would let those who are not good in Sign Language wait, unless they really seemed interested in Danish and were coming along with both. That is what we wanted to do in the first place with some of the students in this class, but we had the pressure from the parents. They wanted us to begin both languages at the same time. But this time I would be more firm when it comes to these children; I would be more secure in what I am doing. I would say to the parents, "I know you want your youngsters to learn Danish. We think this is the best insurance that they will." I would explain that the children are just beginning to get a grasp on a lot of things; that if we wait until they are ready, they will be able to learn Danish in less time. I would feel free to say it and know I'm on safe ground; it would be a waste of time to use too much time on Danish too soon. (W. Lewis, personal communication, March 11, 1992).*

11 The child in this case study was first classified as communication disabled but seems to have suffered from language loss or arrested development of the primary language (Spanish) before attaining full competence in English. She experienced a temporary delay of development in both languages when formal instruction in English began, then eventually mastered English as well as her own Spanish. These authors describe indicators that may help teachers and psychologists sort out such delays from other language learning problems. They suggest that delays of this kind may be the result of immersion or too much formal teaching in the new language, and are less likely to occur with natural exposure in an environment where continued development in the child's first language is promoted.

At Their Own Pace

Irene Serna of the University of Arizona, who has been conducting research with hearing children in English/Spanish bilingual programs, relates that the best success in writing in the second language is seen when that writing is allowed to emerge at that child's own pace. Her observations are that, given a bilingual environment where a high value is placed on both languages, writing in the second language *will* emerge if there is sufficient development of literacy in the first language.

Research in bilingualism is almost unequivocal in its agreement that the best way to develop literacy in the second language is to foster and nurture literacy in the first language. Other variables that are cited as important (Barrs, et al, 1989) are:

- the need for positive attitudes and feelings (value of self and the worth of what one has to say/write)

- opportunities for social and cultural interactions

- importance of supporting the child's first language

- value of learning contexts for and through both languages across the curriculum

- the need for extra support during times of transition from one stage to the next and

- individuality in each child's acquisition process.

Looking at what the child is getting in each of these areas can give teachers important clues as to why a child may not have begun writing on his/her own.

By asking the children to perform too early in written English, we may miss the chance to consider the whole child, and the attributes (listed above) that will ultimately contribute to each child's successes or difficulties with writing. A Deaf child's gradually emergent writing in the second language is rarely approached as that, because English is rarely recognized as a language that may be—at first—quite unfamiliar to the child. When the adults in the child's environment allow written English skills to emerge at the child's own pace, they gain a great deal of information about that child's process and his or her relationship with each language.

Writing is such a tangible form of progress that parents, teachers, and students seem to depend on written papers and worksheets as evidence that something is happening. Yet these familiar ways of doing things inadvertently result in a higher value being placed on writing in English than on the clear expression of ideas in one's first language. (See Appendix E, Swedish National Curriculum, regarding expression in Sign Language.) English competency is often expected of Deaf children in the U.S. very early, simply because they live in a place where English is spoken.

At the 1994 TESOL[12] conference, Virginia Collier, whose studies have looked at the academic progress of bilingual children in a broad spectrum of environments, presented the following model in the form of a prism to emphasize the interrelationships among academic, cognitive, and linguistic development (Collier, 1994).[13] She stresses that growth in all these areas is necessary for academic achievement. It is important to note that every aspect of this growth is interdependent. In other words, an environment that allows for easy, unencumbered social interaction and supports the child's culture will have a positive impact on development in the other areas:

Language Acquisition for School

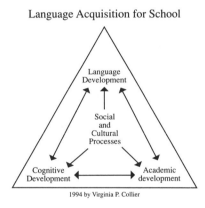

1994 by Virginia P. Collier

Olsen and Leone summarize Collier's comments as follows:

> *A program that emphasizes only one domain may inadvertently ignore or overlook the other two to the detriment of the individual's overall growth and future success. In other words, a program that emphasizes English only may neglect academic and cognitive development, which are equally important for future academic success and functioning in English.*

12   Teachers of English to Speakers of Other Languages
13   Permission was granted by Virginia Collier and TESOL Matters for use of this diagram.

Collier's prism tells us how it is possible to provide too much L2 [second language] instruction: if it interferes with academic and/or cognitive development....Children's cognition needs to be developed in the first language without interruption, for long-term cognitive and academic success in L2 (1994, p. 18).

Along these lines, the Spanish/English bilingual programs Serna describes as most successful are those that do not formally ask children to write in their second language until at least fourth grade. Only one of the ten case study children Serna worked with began writing in Spanish in kindergarten and by the end of that year wrote a letter to an English speaker—in English. This child continued to write in both languages through the primary grades.

The other children in the study wrote entirely in Spanish with increasing fluency and complexity through third grade. Beginning in fourth grade, they were provided opportunities to write in English and encouraged to continue to write in Spanish, the language in which they could express their ideas more competently. By this time, the children participating in the bilingual program had had enough exposure to written and spoken English to produce their own written English without much trouble, unless there was a delay in constructing knowledge of how to read and write in the first language, or another problem unrelated to linguistic competence. (In the past, Serna notes, bilingual children whose home language was other than English were often considered learning disabled if they weren't speaking, reading, and writing conventionally in English by the first or second grade.) It is important to monitor children's developmental progress with the first language, which may reveal learning disabilities; and not to base such judgments on lack of competence in the second language without adequate time for competence to develop.

Expression in Either Language "Counts"

Many of the Spanish-speaking children in the examples Serna (1994) describes became quite articulate in written Spanish, then began to make interesting transitions to gradually becoming literate in English. Some first wrote in Spanish, then translated texts orally to English. Serna notes that the children focused on translating meaningfully rather than word for word. Their translations are transcribed through dictation; teachers attempt to record children's language as dictated. These children seemed very motivated to produce their stories in both languages. They were convinced of the value of their own stories (through the strong emphasis on creating text in the first language) and wanted their English-speaking peers to be able to read them. Additionally, their school environment promoted the idea that expression in either language is equally valid.

As the children in Serna's study began to take risks writing in English themselves, some would write part of their composition in English, then switch to Spanish, then back again. Serna's analysis involved talking to the children about their writing. This questioning revealed that the children who did this switching were aware of the following: they could communicate almost any complex thought in Spanish, but knew they still had their limits with English. Therefore they might start writing in their second language, English, then switch to Spanish to write a paragraph that conveyed an idea they didn't know how to express in written English, then switch back again.

Efforts to acknowledge the expression of ideas through the first language and other mediums seem to have payoffs in allowing the child to develop a comfort-level with expression in the second language, an opportunity Deaf children have traditionally not had. Many Deaf adults clearly remember frustrating school experiences in which they had sophisticated, well-developed ideas, but did not have the skills to express them in English, which was the only language that "counted."

Two teachers in Sweden have written a book (soon to be published in both Swedish and English) about their methods using both process-oriented writing *and* process-oriented signing. They, too, have observed this natural "flow" between the languages, as long as both languages are valued as modes of academic expression:

> *Deaf students are able to use a process-oriented work method, using both their languages. When the children start school, we start them with process signing but in due course, they also start process writing. The students are able to "flow in and out" using the different models and choose for themselves which language they want to use to express their thoughts." (Foss Ahlden & Lundin, draft version, p. 14 (from rough translation).*[14]

It may be extremely important for schools to consider the validity of this concept: of developing Deaf children's expressive literacy in American Sign Language through face-to-face or video-taped expression for a variety of academic purposes and for the telling of stories (formal and informal). Bosso and Kuntze (1994) summarize their concept of literacy as follows:

> *For deaf students, the ultimate goal of literacy is to become literate in both ASL and English. ASL allows deaf students to become literate about their histories, experiences, and culture. And it is through a full command of English that deaf students find themselves linguistically empowered to engage in dialogue with the various sectors of the wider society (p. 43).*

In much the same way as these small, language-rich classrooms Serna described in the Spanish/English bilingual environment, a high value is placed on bi- or multi-lingualism

---

14   For more information, write SIH läromedel, Manillaskolan, Box 27 816, 115 93 Stockholm.

in small countries like Sweden and Denmark. Cummins and Swain (1986) in their chapter "Bilingualism without Tears," note how important it is for adults in the children's environment to celebrate the bonuses of being bilingual.

Those Deaf and hearing role models who have cultivated a positive attitude toward all languages and cultures present in the classroom, and who promote the benefits of being bilingual (or multilingual), can be a very powerful force in Deaf children's acquisition of English. The literature clearly indicates that if concept-building experiences and a high regard for their expression through their own language are coupled with a positive orientation to written text, Deaf children consistently move into English literacy quite early—on their own (Andrews & Taylor, 1987; Maxwell, 1983, 1984).

Process Writing/Signing

The demands of creating content and simultaneously thinking about how to convey it correctly in a second language are considered to affect children's ability to exercise their true competence in that language (see Mather, 1990). Hence, these countries' educational model stresses a long period of exposure to the language so that certain constructions become automatic, minimizing the need to move to a different part of the brain and think about or monitor *how* to say things (Krashen, 1981). Some teachers have also worked to help children build up a strong base of meaning in the text they create (before they have to focus on form) by using process-oriented techniques.

Some of the strategies used to keep the focus on expression of ideas are to let the children capture their thoughts through drawings, through building models, acting out plays, sharing them with a friend, signing to a video camera, or jotting them down in very rough draft or list-like form. Students then go back and expand of those ideas in written Swedish, then re-work their piece, continuing to clarify their meaning and apply what they have learned about Swedish grammar. Multiple revisions, conferencing with other students and the teacher, and "rough draft" videotaping or writing are all part of the process.[15] One teacher I spoke to lets her students choose the mode they prefer to use for their drafts. This seems to help children acknowledge that they can take responsibility for some of the difficulties inherent in writing in a second language by becoming familiar with the strategies that work for them. (G. Christersson, personal communication, March 12, 1992).

In addition to receiving information in their first language, literacy is promoted by placing a high value on developing inner thought processes and expression for academic

---

15   Many of these same approaches to writing are described in *The Writer's Workshop* (Fisher, 1994) and could be applied, likewise, to Sign Language. See title page for ordering information.

purposes (not just storytelling) in the *first* language. Some teachers employ a method they call *process signing*, which is similar to the *process writing* described above. They feel that encouraging the children to develop and improve the presentation of their ideas through their first language, Sign Language, carries over to the children's abilities to later get the most out of the writing process:

> *All human beings have a need for processing conscious and unconscious thoughts and making them visible. Often, this is done by writing in your first language. Deaf students must also have the chance to "write in their first language." As a written form of Sign Language doesn't exist, a videocamera must be used as a "pen." You should not have to give up writing because of the lack of "pens" at the school. Process signing, as we see it, should start in the first grade [with or without a camera]. The task of the teacher is to help the students to "catch" their own thoughts, which gives them a tool to use in their writing. Gradually, the students become "mature" enough to start writing in their second language and then process writing can start.*

> *The students will now have greater use of their experiences regarding process signing which will make the task of working with the second language much easier. When working with process writing, computers are invaluable as the revision stages become more fun. In this kind of work, it is not the end result that is the most important thing, but what goes on inside us when we formulate the message (Foss-Ahlden & Lundin, draft version, p. 35).*

Applying Second Language Research and Resources

Lack of understanding and first-hand experience in the U.S. with the gradual stages second language learners go through has been discussed as an obstacle in configuring Deaf children's education to meet their linguistic needs. But a more important prerequisite to capitalizing on these second language learning processes is the recognition that English must—for many Deaf children—be approached as a *second* language. Once this premise is truly accepted, there is an abundance of literature about how children learn first and second languages that can serve as a resource for developing strategies that facilitate Deaf children in becoming confident, competent users of the majority language.

"Home Language" and "Mother Tongue"

Some critics are quick to dismiss the relevance of research on bilingualism and ESL (teaching English as a second language) because the authors so frequently use the terms "home language" and "mother tongue." Sign Language is *not* the language of many deaf infants' homes, nor is it the native "tongue" of hearing mothers. However, if one is willing to substitute the terms "home language" and "mother tongue" with "first language" or "L1" whenever these terms come up, the literature becomes extremely applicable—that is, *in a system that ensures that all Deaf children have regular exposure to an accessible first language.*

Ironically, under such a system, the term "home language" once again takes on meaning for Deaf children of hearing parents. Given sufficient early support for parents in Sweden and Denmark, Sign Language *has become* one of the languages of many Deaf children's homes well before they start school. In Sweden, for example, many siblings become extremely fluent; grandparents or close family friends often know enough Sign Language to interact easily and comfortably with the children (Beret Meyer, personal communication, August, 1990). Moreover, this approach reconciles the concept of home language for Deaf children born into hearing families, by *expanding* the concept of family. Members of the close-knit Deaf community become, for many Deaf children and their families in Sweden and Denmark, a kind of extended family. By the time these Deaf children start school, they are similar to other "L2" children (children for whom the language of the school or the majority culture is a second language). Given these circumstances, methodology in "additive" bilingual education (where the first language is maintained and supported while the second language is added) is clearly applicable for Deaf children.

Sorting Out the Differences

While the literature on developing literacy in a second language is, in many ways, consistent for Deaf children who have a strong first language, the situation nevertheless differs. Most of the hearing children discussed in the literature who are learning to read and write in a second language are also learning to speak that language through daily interaction with peers. In addition to applying findings from L2 (second-language learning) literature, it will also be important to sort out how these processes *differ* for Deaf children who have little or no auditory access to the spoken form.

W- and S-Languages

There is plenty of evidence that the challenges in acquiring the majority language as a second language through the process of reading are not as great as the challenges involved for Deaf children in acquiring the spoken form as a first language. Nevertheless, linguists at Stockholm University have stressed to educators of Deaf children the importance of recognizing the differences between written vs. spoken/signed forms of language—*W-languages* vs. *S-languages* (Ahlgren, 1992). In a recent article in *Sign Language Studies*, Svartholm (1993) refers to Cummins and Swains' distinction between 1) face-to-face use of a language that is imbedded in activity and interaction ("context-imbedded") and 2) written language or language used for academic purposes

---

("context-reduced") (Cummins, 1980, Cummins and Swain, 1986). She compares the initial learning of Swedish by a Deaf child to other situations involving context-reduced language. In other words, as Ahlgren points out, because Deaf children do not have access (or complete access) to the spoken form, the learning of written Swedish is like other language situations in which children learn to read and write without having a strong command of the underlying spoken form—Chinese characters, for example, for speakers of some dialects. (Ahlgren, 1992; J. Woodward, personal communication, July 7, 1994).

Svartholm asserts that written language forms, as opposed to language which is learned naturally, through face-to-face interaction, "...impose different cognitive demands on the learner, and their learning implies different levels of maturity." This is also why the text Deaf children encounter early must be steeped in context that is meaningful to the children. In referring to written language for which the child does not know a spoken form, Svartholm continues, "Without context, such language has no perceivable meaning at all. It cannot even be described as a language from the child's point of view, since it communicates nothing in and of itself." While Svartholm emphasizes the enjoyable, rich experiences in which Sign Language is used to bring the written words alive from an early age, she feels efforts to *explain* written structures before children are ready "will presumably be more or less a waste of time, since what is actually learned by the child can be learned much faster later on" (Svartholm, 1993, p. 324). In much the same way, speech teachers in Sweden and Denmark seem to be capitalizing on familiar context by trying to "dovetail" work on pronunciation with what the children have learned to read.

One American teacher recently presented a paper that included discussion of her own revelations about the nature of teaching written language to Deaf children. This teacher, who had been teaching in a total communication environment, recently spent a one-year internship observing and assisting a Deaf-hearing team in a preschool research class that utilized both ASL and English.[16] She kept a journal of observations and strategies that she, as a hearing teacher, and hearing parents might employ to better support the cognitive and linguistic development of young bilingual Deaf children. One of her most significant "ah-ha"s in observing a Deaf teacher support emerging literacy was about the nature of print:

> *Another very important thing I had to learn was that printed English is not spoken English. It's just lying there on the page. It has absolutely nothing to do with this (points to her mouth as she is talking) as far as the kids are concerned. Even though I've been teaching for years, I'm just now learning how important it is to*

---

16 The class, one of the preschool research classes at Kendall Demonstration Elementary School, had primarily 3-4 year olds.

teach reading in a way that's not based on sound. It has to be context-based, not sound-based (Wischmeyer, 1994).

Ahlgren (1982) referred to a similar notion, reminding us that, for Deaf children, the written form was like "Silent Swedish"—not connected, as it is for hearing children, to the already familiar sounds, words, and strings of words that make up the spoken language. (See more discussion under section on teacher expertise.) In promoting bilingualism in Deaf children, it is imperative that we continue to develop our understanding of the differences in process between learning static, *W-languages* and dynamic, interactive *S-languages* (Ahlgren, 1992). While approaching the learning of the majority language from a second language perspective is beginning to solve some of the problems in Deaf children's development of literacy, there is still a great deal to learn about the unique aspects of bilingual teaching for Deaf students.

More than Just a Luxury

Research about children whose first language is not English clearly indicates that communicating academic material through the first language is more than just a luxury, it is a necessity. One major study indicates that it requires 5-7 years for students in the most effective types of programs to compete on an equal footing academically with native-English-speaking students (Collier, 1994). Students in the study who reached this level were typically those who had at least 2-3 years of schooling in their first language (L1) in their home country. Students with no schooling in L1 took 7-10 years or more (Collier, 1987, 1989, 1994; Cummins, 1981).

The fact that L2 students take longer to achieve this level with English does not mean they will fall behind, as long as their academic growth is maintained through their first language. In fact, those students in late-exit and two-way bilingual programs (both of which support cognitive/academic development in the first language)[17] not only tend to catch up, but often surpass their English-only peers in measures of academic achievement (Collier, 1989). But this takes time. Collier found that students with the greatest amount of academic and cognitive development in their first language demonstrate the greatest academic gains in English after their sixth year. After that point, students in strong L1 development programs achieve, on the average, above the national norm set

---

17 "Late-exit" bilingual programs are those in which the students are allowed to communicate and study in their own language for a large part of their education before approaching all academic material in English. "Two-way" bilingual programs are those in which there are speakers of both languages learning together. Ideally, efforts are made to continue cognitive and academic development in the minority children's first language (as they are less likely to encounter their own language in mainstream society), as well as their emerging second language, throughout their school career.

for English-only students; whereas it has been found that students with 0-2 years of L1 instruction may never, on the average, reach the national norm.

The literature indicates that even if a strong first language is acquired, but cognitive development in that language is not fostered during acquisition of a second language, the result is what Cummins (1984) refers to as limited bilingualism (a lower threshold of competence in the first language that is associated with other negative cognitive effects). The reason for this is that first language acquisition is believed to take a minimum of 12 years. Collier (1989) explains that children—from birth to age 5—acquire enormous amounts of L1 phonology, vocabulary, grammar, semantics, and pragmatics, but the process is far from complete by the time children reach school age. From ages 6 to 12, children continue acquisition of more complex rules of morphology and syntax, elaboration of communication acts, expansion of vocabulary (which she notes continues throughout a person's lifetime), semantic development, and some aspects of phonological development.

She reiterates that second language acquisition research has found this continuing process of first language development to have a significant influence on the development of a second language.

Applying these well-documented findings about other bilingual children to Deaf children, expectations for achieving academic equality are likely to be further diminished for the many children who enter school without solid competence in any language. Even for those Deaf children who do have American Sign Language as a strong first language, there has traditionally been little schooling in that language, or recognition of ASL (L1) as an academic and cognitive resource that can contribute to the development of English skills *and* overall achievement. Collier's findings alone seem to explain many of the traditional problems in educating Deaf children. Based on this information, it may be very helpful to apply to Deaf children's education a greater understanding of second language learning processes, while continuing growth in all other areas through the first language.

Such findings call into question the practice of educating Deaf children without regard for the important ingredients discussed here, and provides a strong directive for change. Success does appear attainable in environments where the system:

- promotes early fluency in a first language for Deaf children,

- supports that first language as a tool for academic instruction and continued cognitive development, and

- includes a degree of realism about what is reasonable to expect regarding spoken, written, and academic proficiency in the majority language in the early years.

Educators in Sweden and Denmark are finding that receiving content through Sign Language is not only more comprehensible for Deaf children; in accordance with these research findings, they consider it the only way for the average Deaf student to keep up academically.

A Measure of the Need for Change

In taking a closer look at Deaf children's education and literacy development, one barometer of the need for change in a system[18] is the degree to which Deaf children are viewed simply as children:

- Are these children, their parents, and their teachers functioning the way other children, parents, and teachers typically function at various stages?

- Or is a large percentage of time and energy in the school and home spent in some kind of remedial activity (at first, trying to fix the children; later, trying to fix educational or literacy problems)?

If the latter is true, then it seems it is necessary to continue evaluating the configuration of service provision for children and training for parents and teachers.

The next three chapters focus on ways the system can support Deaf children, parents, and teachers in their normal roles—which appear to be among the most crucial ingredients in promoting the children's improved literacy, achievement, and participation in both Deaf and Hearing society.

---

18 "The system," as it is used frequently in this document, is meant to refer to various levels of service provision to Deaf children and their parents. This includes (but is not limited to) diagnosis and advice given by medical professionals, support/training for the parents, and education/socialization for the children. While the responsibilities of 'the system' referred to herein could conceivably be undertaken at the local or school district level, reference to the system here typically implies change at a much higher level (state and federal) in order to make changes at the local level possible.

CHAPTER TWO

Let Deaf Children
Be Children

*L*et *Deaf children be children* may have been the most important message that emerged from the interviews and observations during my second study in Sweden and Denmark. Parents, teachers, and researchers reported that they had begun to relax and rely on their intuitions, utilizing what they know about all children: the natural way very young children learn their first language without being taught, the way their curiosity leads them to want to know about *everything* as they become ready (including reading, writing, and the language spoken by their parents), the way they will set about meeting each new challenge when they are ready—and not a moment sooner.

In addition to supporting Deaf children in the many ways they are like hearing children, it is also very important for parents and educators to acknowledge the aspects of growing up that are *unique* to Deaf children as they are revealed both through research and through the rich experiences and insights of former Deaf children, who are now Deaf adults—within and outside the educational system. There seems to be a perceptible difference in environments where the presence and input of Deaf administrators, teachers, parents, and researchers—as well as of the children themselves—is considered a critical component in every decision-making process. In applying the theoretical principles described earlier, it is important to acknowledge not only how Deaf children are like other children, but the very important ways they *differ* from other children. How does perceiving one's world visually make a difference in approaching various tasks? What do the tasks we present and the language input we provide look like from the child's viewpoint?

There is growing recognition in Sweden and Denmark that Deaf children may have been limited most in the past by a general lack of understanding of children's learning processes and capacities for multilingualism. Both Deaf and hearing professionals feel there is much to be learned from today's Deaf children about how best to provide them what they need within the context of recent changes in attitude and practice. Even those who grew up in Deaf families seem to be raising their expectations about what Deaf children (and their parents) are capable of—when the children get the acceptance, language, and knowledge they need early and throughout their education. Hansen (1989) describes one group of 12-year-olds in Denmark who had been given the opportunity to become fluent in Danish Sign Language and to learn about their academic subjects through that language and through written Danish:

What is even more important is these children's development of cognitive, social, and academic skills as such. They can communicate about their world, they can control their own daily life through linguistic means, which include discussions of what is right and why. They have acquired the power of being able to influence what is going to happen to them. They can argue and understand an argument, often to an extent which is as subtle and irritating as it is with normally-hearing children, provoking their adult surroundings into new areas of explanation and thinking (p. 7).

A great deal becomes apparent now that we can observe an environment where more and more Deaf children of hearing parents are receiving encouragement to be who they are—not to mention crucial exposure to fluent users of a natural, visual language and role models who are Deaf. What is taking place does not seem as simple as imposing a different strategy on the same children; in some ways such a paradigm shift seems to have the effect of fostering a "new generation" of confident, attentive, better-prepared Deaf learners. Many of these Deaf children—whether their parents are Deaf or hearing—have enjoyed the benefits of language, acceptance, and trust in their abilities from the start. Some older teachers I spoke to felt they were truly challenged to come up with methods and materials to meet the needs of today's students. Their observation seems to be that education for Deaf children in some parts of these countries is beginning to move into uncharted territory. The *prerequisite* for a situation like this is hard to find elsewhere in the world: an environment where the parents are getting the kind of support, example, and language training they need to trust that their Deaf children will be OK—which in turn frees the parents to "Let the children be children."

For parents, a pivotal message can come from the simple experience of interacting with Deaf and hearing people who happily accept their baby as Deaf, are skilled at communicating in ways that capture the child's attention, and are committed to that child's growth as a *Deaf* child. Neither teaching, hypothesizing, nor counseling seem to have equal impact when it comes to impressing upon parents that their deaf child is still a child and can lead a normal, happy life. One parent in the U.S. who was fortunate to have such experience writes the following:

We lived near Philadelphia, and two Deaf women (Lillian Hoshouer and April Nelson) ran the Deaf Hearing Community Center to teach Sign and to help parents and hearing people and deaf people know and trust each other. DHCC nurtured us and changed our lives. Jesse would fly in the door on Tuesday nights and rush over to some lovely deaf grandmother and sign [something like], "If you take medicine out of the cabinet and eat it, you will DIE, my mother said!" And the grandmother would hug him and kiss him and tell him he was wonderful and bring him over to her friends, and Jesse would tell his story again, and they would hug him and smile and laugh and talk with him. I was convinced that Jesse was the most adorable wonderful child in America and so was he.

DHCC gave Jesse critical and essential pride in himself. DHCC was the family that hearing parents with deaf children don't have—that extended family of relatives and friends to admire and adore your child, to reassure you and make you feel both confident and capable and proud. Deaf people gave me back my child and empowered me.

How did this happen? At DHCC deafness was not a tragedy or an affliction. At DHCC, deafness was normal. Jesse was an ordinary darling little boy, and I was an ordinary doting mother. DHCC enabled me to see Jesse as a child and deafness as simply another way of being human (R. Thomas, 1989, p.8).

This quote is repeated often throughout the literature, but it is not because Ms. Thomas is the only one who has felt this way. On the contrary, the interviews in Sweden and Denmark revealed that many parents who have had such an opportunity see it as the gift of a lifetime. The scarcity of such reports (that hearing parents and their children not only survive, but thrive with such support) is due primarily to the fact that opportunities for such interaction are still rare in the United States. While such interactions, in general, are scarce for hearing parents of a recently-diagnosed deaf child in the U.S., opportunities for contact with Deaf families as role models are even harder to find for minority parents (L. Proctor, personal communication, July 12, 1994).

Genuine experience clearly contradicts popular fears that association with Deaf adults/caretakers will destroy the bond between hearing parents and their children. Parents who have had this opportunity early are adamant that it was this circumstance that *strengthened* their bond with their children; that helped them rebuild their ability to relate to their children as children—without guilt or sadness. Even occasional contact can go a long way toward this goal, if the parents are made to feel comfortable and welcome by members of the Deaf community.

Our lack of actual experience in the U.S. with this kind of "extended family" as a support for hearing parents seems to perpetuate a tendency to underestimate 1) the depth of the bond between hearing parent and Deaf child, 2) the willingness of the children's Deaf teachers/caretakers to support and facilitate that bond, and 3) the ease with which many hearing parents fully accept the indispensable role of Deaf adults in their children's lives.

No matter who their parents are, ensuring an adequate public education for Deaf children in Sweden and Denmark means providing them early with the linguistic, cognitive, and social environment they need to proceed with *being a child*. It means not asking the impossible or the unreasonable of Deaf children by engaging them in tedious tasks which lack meaning for them at ages when they simply need to be doing what other children are doing: communicating, discovering, playing.

As parents and teachers in these countries are finding, the better we get at meeting Deaf children "where they live," the more they will surprise us with what they can achieve. The tradition in countries around the world has been to panic about "language" (which has typically been considered to be synonymous with speech). The primary focus of deaf children's early years has often been on speech-learning tasks that bear little resemblance to other children's natural processes of language acquisition. I gleaned from the Swedish/Danish experience some dependable measures of the success of early service provision for deaf infants and toddlers. If we find that very young Deaf children are being asked to "practice" language (spoken or signed) and are spending much of their time doing things that other children of a similar developmental age aren't doing, it is time to reconsider our approach.

If these children are failing to reach developmental and linguistic milestones that other children their age are reaching, the system responsible for meeting their early needs deserves further scrutiny:

- What factors must be present so Deaf children can just be "kids?"

- How can we configure these children's environments to help them build their early resources with a minimum of undue pressure and a minimum of experience with failure?

Clearly, this places a big responsibility on the system. The previous chapter stated the need to trust the children's own learning processes in approaching language and literacy. The idea is not just to sit children in front of the T.V. or hand them a book and "trust their process"; the idea is to design early service provision for the parents and children that gives them what they need to lead very normal lives. Use of the label, "normal," as a standard is not always considered to be a sensitive term. Nevertheless, I use it because it reflects the remarks of preschool teachers, psychologists, speech therapists, Deaf consumers, parents, and educators (in both the U.S. and these countries) who are in a position to observe young Deaf children in environments that provide accessible language, peer interaction, and age-appropriate activities. Their overriding comment about the inquisitive, mischievous, noisy, bright, affectionate children they see every day has been, "They're just so normal!" Giving those children and their parents what they need—*early*—to be 'so normal' is considered one of the main responsibilities of the consumer organizations and the educational system for Deaf children in Sweden and Denmark.

Let the Parents
Be Parents

hat about the parents? This question, often raised in discussions among educators in the U.S., tends to function as an implicit argument against bilingual education. My own perception on both visits to Sweden and Denmark and some programs in the U.S. was that many parents not only accept, but embrace the idea of educating their Deaf child bilingually. Those parents who have had this kind of early advice and experience seem to be doing much better than the confused or angry parents I had previously encountered over the course of more than 20 years in this field. Common elements in well-designed bilingual environments seemed to be 1) trusting the parents' willingness and ability to make the needed adjustments, 2) acknowledging those parents—hearing and Deaf—for their important role, and 3) providing parents with a positive orientation, as well as the support, example, and training they need to make informed choices. This chapter focuses on some of the issues that directly involve parents: acceptance and support, decisions about first language input and early amplification for their child, placement considerations, and their own learning of Sign Language.

These very important people deserve both trust and help to function in their traditional role—as parents. In a moving statement during a recent panel of parents in the U.S., one parent of a grown Deaf child said she wished she had gotten the kind of support that would have helped her to relax more, to laugh more, to enjoy her Deaf child more—and to worry less (Hom, Laldee, Treesberg, Venturini, & Wilson, 1994). In many areas in Sweden and Denmark the focus of early support is on seeing that the parents of Deaf children are not alone and worried, that the children have an accessible first language, and that families have access to a circle of support and social interaction that includes their Deaf child. Such opportunities are provided in part through the educational/healthcare system, and in part through parent organizations and the Deaf community. This support relieves a great deal of the pressure on parents, who had functioned in the past as the primary speech and language trainer, playmate, teacher, best friend, and advocate for their Deaf child, often to the detriment of the family unit.

In short, every effort is made to let the parents "just be parents." In addition to a strong program of early orientation, home support, and preschools, some areas have camps, retreats, potlucks, and other social events sponsored by parents' organizations and organizations within the Deaf community to make sure families get the interaction and support they need. The following quote by a parent gives an example of one way the local parents' associations work with the preschools and the Deaf community to support very young Deaf children and their parents:

This is not really about government funding....The parents' organization in Denmark is strong. I am working in one of the local organizations that is very active. We have a lot of meetings with the preschools. The staff at those eight preschools in Copenhagen are meeting together once a month. Once every second week, they bring all their own children to another preschool. The staff is very concerned with seeing that the deaf children are meeting each other very often. So if you are sending your child to one preschool, they are not limited to only having social contact with those 5 or 10 or 12 children; you also make sure that they visit children in other groups.

Through the parents' organization, I am arranging to have different persons give speeches at one of the preschools and then the rest of the parents from the other preschools are invited. So that they have seen the other preschools....

Also, the parents organization has arranged monthly Saturday afternoons at the deaf school, when we bring together all the parents with their deaf children from 0 up to 6 years, and the hearing siblings. For the parents, they have a talk about something of interest to them. The hearing siblings have Sign Language classes. And the deaf children are supervised by adults, NEW deaf adults. Somebody who is different from what they see everyday, so that the children can learn that there are a lot of different deaf persons and that everyone speaks Sign Language a little differently. (S. Toft, personal communication, March 10, 1992.)

This quote also exemplifies the level of sensitivity to Deaf children's right to have a full, normal, social upbringing, with regular and frequent exposure to many other Deaf children and to a variety of Deaf adults.

Now that early development of language need no longer be a "wait and see" proposition, more energy can be given to the quality of the children's education and the breadth of their experiences and acquaintances as they grow. Parents seem more relaxed; much of the anxiety is reduced. They are not asked to make impossible decisions about their baby's fate at a time when there simply is not enough information available about that child's aptitude for hearing and speech. And, while their communication with the child is considered absolutely crucial, they are not asked to be the child's only model for Sign Language. It is simply seen as a fact that it takes time for parents, as adult language learners, to acquire real fluency. Early emphasis is on making sure that parents know how to communicate with the child, and that there is a natural language that is fully accessible to the child in his or her environment. This allows the child's natural predispositions toward spoken or signed language to guide the teachers and parents in facilitating that child's individual path to becoming a bilingual adult.

The Impact is on the Family

I was truly surprised at the lack of turmoil among most of the parents I met and interviewed. With support from the parents' group, the Deaf community, and the school, things do seem to fall into place.

Bonaventura, one national parents' organization in Denmark, has created a booklet of "advice," handed down from the "old" parents (who have already had some experience raising a Deaf child) to the "new" parents (see Appendix F). This brochure (Bonaventura, 1992, p. 1) states a very important fact:

The impact of having a deaf child is on the family.

When we realize that it is the family, not the child, that is in turmoil—that it is the family that needs to adjust to the situation—our outlook changes. In other words, in the early part of life, the deaf infant is—like all infants—happily going about exploring his or her world. As far as the child is concerned, all is well.[1] At the same time that the families' needs are in the process of being met, this awareness fosters a desire to do what is needed to make sure that child's spirit, inquisitiveness, confidence, and ability to acquire knowledge are maintained. It becomes a high priority to ensure that the environment, which was sufficient for the child's visual communicative needs in the first months, remains comprehensible as his or her cognitive skills and need for language begin to grow. Given this orientation, it makes sense that the child's natural development—as a child who is Deaf—is not interrupted by efforts to make him conform to the needs of the family, *who were expecting a hearing child.*

In the case of many Deaf families around the world, the kind of environment Deaf toddlers need to proceed on their own is present from the start. The idea that the baby might be deaf is not only acknowledged, but is sometimes celebrated (Erting, C., 1992b). The child is typically treated like any other child, and his or her natural capabilities and potential

---

1   The exception is when the discovery that the child is deaf occurs well beyond the age of one year. In this case, the child may not be "happily" going about discovering his world, but may be acting out anger and frustration at not being able to communicate.

to survive in both Deaf and hearing worlds are not questioned. This acceptance and confidence in the child and his/her abilities has been identified as one of the reasons Deaf children of Deaf parents (oral or signing) consistently scored higher on most measures of academic achievement (Corson, 1973), are often considered to be leaders by their teachers and peers, and have traditionally been interpreters of information for the other children in classrooms. In the setting of a Deaf family, there are typically no major interruptions or setbacks when the child is discovered to be deaf. Given a different orientation, it appears such an environment of acceptance and accessible language can become a reality for Deaf children with hearing parents, too.

While this can mean a *major* adjustment for hearing families, it seems to go more smoothly when it is acknowledged by other parents and professionals that it is really the family (not the child) that must be asked to adjust. Part of this child-centered mindset means recognizing that—for simple biological reasons—members of a hearing family have the choice of communicating orally or manually, whereas the deaf child, in most cases, does not (Erting, C., 1992b). Another part of the equation is acknowledging that the rest of the family has needs that deserve attention. Those needs, of course, are quite unlike the needs of the Deaf child—who is ready to learn language. Acknowledging these facts can free parents to make decisions, keeping in mind the differing needs of the child and the other family members. Finally, one of the main components in creating an environment of confidence, acceptance, and accessible language for the Deaf child is effectively moving parents beyond their grieving to the knowledge that all is well with their child.

Acceptance and Support

Grieving

Grieving can be a natural and healthy part of a family's process of re-adjusting. However, it appears that this process may go more quickly and smoothly when parents are provided a linguistic—rather than pathological—framework for viewing their child's interactions, education, and future. This includes opportunities to get to know other Deaf children and adults.

One parent at Kendall Demonstration Elementary School recently shared her perception about this issue at a meeting:

> *When we found out that our daughter was deaf, we were like a lot of parents. We didn't know anything about deaf people. I had lots of misconceptions about what it meant to be deaf, and no experience with happy, successful deaf people. In the beginning, I was very sad, because I thought my daughter would have a lonely, difficult life. Of course, everyone who meets her now—she's 5—sees a carefree and very social child.*

Parents shouldn't have to stay in that kind of pain for long. That's why it's so important to get information about how very normally deaf children can develop—given the right environment—into the hands of medical professionals, the audiologists, early-childhood educators, and social workers; the people who see parents first. Many parents in the U.S. struggle with their fears and grief for a very long time. Some never do figure out that it's OK to have a deaf child (Raimondo, 1994a).

While there is always a necessary adjustment in hearing parents' perception of the child they had expected, acceptance seems to come much more easily when the kind of early advice parents get helps them capitalize on the many attributes of their child that they can relate to immediately. Such advice does not contribute to a perception of the diagnosis as a tragedy, nor does it minimize parents' degree of shock, fear, loss, or anger. Professionals do not have any reason nowadays to cast a huge shadow on the child's possibilities to develop language as his or her skills and aptitudes dictate. The following quote, from a psychologist at the University of Stockholm, exemplifies the positive approach parents are met with—in the settings where everything is working according to plan—upon the diagnosis of their child's deafness:

When the professionals inform parents that they have a deaf child, they must let them know from the beginning that it is not a tragedy. They tell them, "What we know today is that communication, visual communication—the use of Sign Language—is comfortable for your child....Given this visual language through which to learn and communicate, we know your child will be much like any other child. Will learn like any other child—if you give your child opportunities to do it—and if we use what the child has. With that, this child is a whole person, and can lead a happy life. Right now, your baby can see, can touch, can get up and explore around his world, is bright, will learn language." This is good sense for parents....I want them to leave the room knowing this is NOT some kind of terrible event.

And because we don't know if these children will speak or not, I think it is terribly important not to say that your child will never be able to speak or to do this or that.... Because we really don't know yet. But what we DO know is that your child will easily be able to use Sign Language at an early age and will be able to communicate with you and you will be able to communicate with your child. And there are professionals who know about deaf children from infancy through high school age and there is a culture with other deaf people—and as you learn about it all, your family will lead a rich, full life. (G. Priesler, personal communication, March 16, 1992.)

Most parents I met in these countries really did feel that way about their lives. They did not seem distraught, nor were they raging about the problems in educating their child.

While they had had their share of difficulties, many commented that their families' lives had been greatly enriched by their experience with the Deaf community and this fascinating new language.[2] Parents in the U.S. who have been fortunate enough to get this kind of support and advice, whether early or late, make very similar remarks (personal communication: Sandy Harvey [California], August 18, 1994; Lauren Roberts [Michigan], October, 1992; Glenn Webster, [Colorado], March 30, 1994).

Opportunities throughout a Deaf child's life for support from other parents (Deaf and hearing) who have Deaf children seems to help parents relax and function simply as parents to their children during various stages of their growth. When I asked one teacher of a tenth grade bilingual class in Copenhagen what types of problems, complaints, and fears she hears from the parents, she had to stop and think. Finally, she said,

> *They don't really talk much about anything related to their child being deaf. They are most concerned with who their children are dating, whether to let them pierce their ears, whether or not they will survive driving a car, and other problems parents of teenagers grapple with (W. Lewis, personal communication, March 9, 1992).*

Support for hearing parents of young Deaf children has traditionally come from family and friends who have little information about the real possibilities. Often it comes in the form of sympathy, reinforcing the idea that the child's deafness is a tragedy. It is hard, under circumstances where the relatives and friends feel helpless to know how to interact with the deaf child, for parents to share or even recognize the wonderful milestones in that child's growth the way other parents do. Mather and Mitchell (1994) discuss this very basic loss many hearing parents experience:

> *These parents gradually give up their expectation of a "normal" hearing child, but are not offered a model of a normal deaf child. The family is, in a sense, deprived of the knowledge that deaf children are seen as normal by the Deaf community, a community that could be enlisted to provide the family with a sense of a positive future (p. 124).*

As Roberta Thomas noted earlier, it can be a turning point for both parents and children to be with Deaf adults and other hearing parents who are accepting of the child. It is important, at least some of the time, to be surrounded by people who appreciate their Deaf child's visual approach to the world, and are cognizant of the child's potential. This kind of support helps parents regain their ability to clearly see their Deaf child as a child,

---

2   Appendix F, the text of the Bonaventura Parents' Organization advice sheet, expresses these sentiments.

regain their faith in a bright future for the child and the family, and develop an awareness of that child's strengths.

Parents in Transition

Another kind of grieving, of which both parents and professionals may be unaware, is the grieving that takes place when parents have invested themselves in one method or approach for educating or communicating with their Deaf child, then have to make a change—either because the school is changing or because they, themselves, see the need for it. Either way, such change requires a very difficult "letting go" of the methods they had pinned their hopes on: this includes beliefs, activities, or structures which may have been the only thing that kept them going, as well as the important camaraderie of others who shared their philosophy. One parent in the U.S. didn't recognize until years later that she was in a very serious state of grieving when she let go of oral education for her 5-year-old son. She wrote:

> *"Language" methodology in deaf education becomes like a religious cult experience. Change involves a belief system change. This can be very powerful. When I accepted Sign Language for my son—even though it was one of the best things I've ever done—it was literally like having a bad case of the flu. Doesn't seem like it should have been that way, but for about 4 months, it was hell. It was not that it was hard to learn, or that I didn't see how good it was for Matt. It was just the change. I had to let go of a lot that I was holding on to (L. Proctor, personal correspondence, July 12, 1994).*

Parents in transition may also find it easy to blame their child's current problems on past choices they made. Sensitive professionals and other parents can help them through these stages, reminding them that they made the best choices they could, given the information and belief systems they had, and that our understanding of what Deaf children need has continued to evolve.

A Soft Start

While exposure to Deaf adults is very important, it seems it is also important, in some cases, not to overload parents of Deaf infants with too much outside contact, example, and training. The family also needs some time to get "re-acquainted" with their child as a *Deaf* child—within a supportive framework. I am not talking about prolonging their grieving period or keeping families away from Deaf role models. Rather, I am referring to a sensitivity I have seen among professionals supporting Deaf children in becoming bilingual: the idea that during the early stages of this process, the parents and family need to gain confidence in their own ability to communicate visually with the child and in the indispensable role they play in their child's development of language and self-esteem. One principal of a preschool for Deaf children related to me the gentle approach used by her Deaf and hearing staff with parents who are in the earliest stages of acceptance:

A soft start. So as not to overwhelm parents. Because the most important thing for the parents is to accept their children as they are. If they don't get through the crisis in a good way, you can never get them to accept the child, accept Sign Language, accept what we do here, accept the future—nothing. So that is why we are so careful in the beginning.

The home teachers do teach some signs, but very little at first. We think that when the parents first learn that the child is deaf, you have to be very aware in the beginning of their relationship to the child. It's not that the parents fear teaching the child Sign Language—it's something more. The home teacher will give the parents a few signs to get started, like for juice or teddy bear or something that they can use. That way the parents can start to communicate with their children on their own time, and in their own way. These early signs are really not for the purpose of teaching the parents Sign Language. That comes later. (Principal, Bøktrykarrvägen Preschool, March 15, 1992).

While it is considered crucial for the Deaf child to have frequent, sustained interaction with fluent models for Sign Language early in life, it is also recognized that hearing parents can do a lot in the beginning by building their awareness of what it means to communicate visually, and by starting to communicate with just a few signs that are part of their everyday interaction. Research has given us two important pieces of information that can support parents in their early efforts to communicate visually with their child: 1) many hearing parents have already developed—through reliance on eye contact and visual cues that accompany spoken communication with babies—remarkably successful communication with their Deaf child in the earliest stages (which they often are not aware of and therefore do not necessarily maintain after learning that the child is deaf) and 2) while Deaf parents use fluent and fast-paced Sign Language to communicate with one another in the presence of their baby, they also use a large percentage of single signs or short utterances, modified to be easily seen by the baby, when interacting directly with the baby (Erting, Prezioso, & Hynes, 1990; Maestas y Moores, 1980; Meadow, Greenberg, Erting, & Carmichael, 1981). When their Deaf child is attending to an object, they typically wait for eye-contact from the child and produce a single sign or short utterance about what the child was looking at, then let the child return eye-gaze to the object (Erting, C., 1994; Spencer, et al, 1992)—strategies hearing parents can use in the beginning with a little training.

The outcomes of studies on the importance of visual cues in human communication, as well as studies of mothers with their Deaf infants, suggest the following: hearing parent's *perception* of the importance of speech in establishing a connection with their child may be one of the main factors that causes a breakdown in the previous level of communication and rapport between parent and child. If this notion is further reinforced by professionals, parents may be able to focus only on that loss of vocal communication and may be completely unaware of the extra-verbal communication that had previously sustained parent and child. In the following quote, speech therapist and linguist Danielle Bouvet of France, describes what she calls "the shared handicap of communication:"

> In studying parental reactions to the diagnosis of their child's deafness, the psychologist Kathryn Meadow-Orlans (1966) found that hearing parents are more distraught over their child's inability to speak than over their child's inability to hear. Because mothers perceive their deaf child as being incapable of talking, they themselves become incapable of talking to their child. As seen earlier, maternal speech is a response and an adaptation to child speech. If the child doesn't speak, the mother feels at a loss, deprived of her ability to communicate....

> When deafness is diagnosed in a child, it is the mother who 'loses' her speech. The knowledge that her child is deaf squelches her anticipation of the infant's speech and makes her feel that she can no longer connect with her baby—her words won't get through. Consequently, she herself becomes communicationally handicapped, unable to speak naturally to her child.

> As long as a mother remains unaware of her child's deafness she can dialogue with her infant perfectly well. She understands what her baby is telling her in his or her own special way, and she knows that her baby understands her. Between them there exists true interaction based on multiple senses. But because she overestimates the importance of vocal speech to this exchange, the discovery of deafness leaves her completely undone (Bouvet, 1990, p. 108).

Based on what we know about language acquisition, it would seem a child-centered perspective would make choices about early visual language input fairly straightforward. But without adequate information and support for parents to re-establish communication with their deaf child, a perspective that appreciates the healthy development of this visually-oriented child can be hard to come by. As Dr. Bouvet goes on to explain:

> The diagnosis of deafness sweeps parents (especially mothers, who are generally more available) into a medical and paramedical world that focuses exclusively on hearing loss and the resulting absence of speech....

> The support parents receive...all centers on attempting to remedy their child's vocal deficiency. It would seem, then that mothers' expectations are met, for what distresses mothers is the fact that their deaf child doesn't speak. They believe that communication will 'get back to normal' once their child can speak and re-become for them a speaking being (Bouvet, 1990, p. 109).

American and British researchers Spencer, Bodner-Johnson, and Gutfreund explain their findings, which suggest that the relative non-responsiveness of hearing mothers with deaf infants (as compared to hearing mothers with hearing infants or deaf mothers with deaf infants) is due primarily to the mothers' attitudes and behaviors rather than any real differences in the children themselves. They assert, therefore, that:

Mothers' behaviors may be modified in a positive manner by assurance that their infants can communicate with them, regardless of hearing loss, and by mothers' learning more about communicative strategies which accommodate for their infants' special visual needs.

Thus, hearing mothers should be provided information about ways that infants with hearing loss, just like those without hearing loss, communicate about their interests through non-verbal behavior before they acquire language. For example, intervention programs should emphasize the information mothers can gain from observing infants' direction of eye gaze. It should be pointed out that these behaviors provide parents and other adults with opportunities to respond contingently, and that contingent responses provide excellent stimulation for language development.

It is also important to provide parents of infants with a hearing loss with information about specific strategies for visual communication used by deaf mothers in interacting with and providing visual language input for their infants who are deaf (1992, p. 75-76).

If professionals first focus on recognizing strategies that were already working, as well as providing a few new ones, this can work immediately to meet the crucial need for communication in the parents, as well as in the child. It is important that parents grow to feel comfortable, have fun, and maintain their union with their child while they get used to communicating and "listening" visually, and become acquainted with other Deaf children and Deaf adults (Erting, C., 1994).

Since most children who are deaf are discovered fairly early in Sweden and Denmark (see Introduction), there is some time available to lay this important groundwork toward acceptance. Consequently, a great deal of adjustment and practice with visual communication can take place early, before parents become involved in studying or producing grammatical Sign Language. This time factor may be one important component in parents' ability to move through their trauma. In many circumstances in the United States today, some children are not determined to be deaf until sometime after the age of two (Mace, et al, 1991). Because the first three years are such an important time for language acquisition, the parents' need for an adjustment period must be weighed against the child's urgent need for comprehensible linguistic and cognitive input from fluent users of a visual language.

Discussion of sensitivity to parent's needs does not imply that parents' early advisors must be hearing. Schools in the U.S. that have employed Deaf parent infant advisors (separately or teaming with a hearing partner) report these professionals can not only answer parents' questions from the point of view of someone who is Deaf, but are often recognized for their high level of sensitivity to the emotional and communication needs of hearing parents.

Differing Needs

Obviously, one component of good support is consciousness on the part of the professional that not all parents need the same kind of support. Some need emotional support, some need information, some need training, some want technical devices, some want to learn Sign Language. Chances are they will all—at some time—want all of the above, but at different times and from different sources. Some parents I spoke to felt professionals were *too* focused on their emotional needs, when they just wanted to learn Sign Language and "get on with it." Clearly, it's just as important to let parents *have* the Sign Language they need and meet Deaf people when they are ready, as it is not to push them if they're not. One parent, who lived just outside the area where she would have been eligible for services from Stockholm, shows that services are still not always what they are promised to be, and that over-focus on the emotional considerations can be just as detrimental as ignoring them. She relived her frustration as follows:

> *Well, I didn't quite understand why my daughter behaved the way she did and so then she was diagnosed as being deaf when she was almost two. After that a psychologist was sent around to determine her progress. But they never attempted to help us communicate with her or refer us to a sign language class, and by then we had started to go crazy.*

> *So we asked her for help and it was then that she said we could go to a psychological care center. What could they do?! I didn't need counseling, I just wanted to communicate with my child! Can you give me sign language? She just kept telling me, "Don't worry, Don't worry." Well, if you are worried, that is the last thing you want to hear, "take it easy, calm down, don't worry." (Anonymous, personal communication, May 30, 1990).*

It just so happens that these parents not only learned Swedish Sign Language, but later became quite involved in adult education within the Deaf community. Obviously, this level of involvement is not typical for all parents; however, I did not meet any parents who truly resisted involvement with the Deaf community, or who feared that the Deaf community would "steal" their child. Interaction and support from Deaf people was viewed by the parents I met as a very positive, not frightening, part of their Deaf child's upbringing. (See also "Yes...but" section on Deaf-hearing relationships). While the Deaf community and organizations in these countries are very strong, feelings of separation/alienation from hearing people have, many sources feel, decreased as a result of changes in the system and of Deaf people's growing role in political and educational decision-making processes.

Professionals need to be ready with resources, as many parents—given the opportunity— accept their child's needs for visual language very quickly. In many cases, it simply seems to make sense to them. A panel of parents at a recent workshop in the U.S. (Hom, et al, 1994) was asked the question, "How long did it take you to accept ASL as a language for your child?" One young couple said they had brought home videotapes about deafness when they learned their daughter was deaf, and noticed that she was riveted to the TV screen whenever there were people signing. At every opportunity to meet Deaf people, they felt their daughter was telling them she 'wanted' Sign Language. Acceptance of her need for other Deaf people and visual language was simply not a question for them.

Parents on the panel who didn't get opportunities to see their Deaf children interacting with other Deaf people until much later related how they struggled for years with their anger at the precious time their children had lost. One such parent answered the question about how long it took her to accept ASL by saying, "It took me about 5 minutes." She had been advised to keep her daughter away from Sign Language, and placed her in oral and mainstream programs, where she was considered successful. Yet, as soon as this mother first got a chance to see her child (at the age of 10) interacting with Deaf people who used Sign Language, she felt strongly that it was right for her.

Parents in the U.S. often share stories about support that failed to match their wish to do whatever it was their child needed. Sandy Harvey, president of the American Society for Deaf children, recently shared one such story:

> I spoke to a father of a 27 month-old yesterday. They were lucky enough to find out that their son was deaf at 7 months, but had spent the last year under the supervision of a parent training center, where they were inundated with information about grieving and advocacy and inclusion, but almost nothing about early language development—not even in speech. He finally walked up to some people signing in a grocery store and wrote, "My son is deaf, too," and that was the beginning of his finding the trail of information he needed. He was crying on the phone with me because he couldn't get over how much time they had lost. (Sandy Harvey, personal communication, August 18, 1994)

In addition to learning from Deaf parents and professionals, the support and sharing of other hearing parents has also proven to be a big factor in helping parents learn how to make their way under these new circumstances. One parent from Kendall Demonstration Elementary School, who is closely allied with Deaf parents, noted in a recent talk that she feels hearing parents need each other, too:

You hear so much about deaf children of Deaf parents and how much better they are doing than deaf children of hearing parents, it's easy to become discouraged. Hearing parents also need other hearing parents who have learned Sign Language and are managing successfully, as proof that it can be done, as role models, and to learn from (Raimondo, 1994a).

The experience of hearing parents in Sweden and Denmark is absolutely consistent with these remarks, revealing that—in addition to interaction and example from parents who are Deaf—they need another kind of empathy, sharing, and knowledge they can gain from other hearing parents (see "Yes, but...." section about dynamics between deaf people and hearing parents). The local parent organization in Stockholm has made up an extensive book of information to serve as a resource to other hearing parents. The book shares the kind of information that hearing parents don't seem to get from professionals or even the Deaf community. The booklet describes how to navigate the system, where to go for various services and peer support, and what articles/books have been helpful to other parents. It also has some first-hand accounts written by parents of their experiences following the discovery that their child was deaf—some positive and some exasperating. Parents in the Oakland Society for Deaf Children in Livonia, Michigan have done a great deal to provide similar kinds of support for "new" parents in their area. As part of this effort, they have compiled an annotated bibliography of articles they found to be helpful. Peer support for both deaf and hearing parents is a very important component in meeting the diverse, changing needs of parents. Interestingly, in the programs where Deaf children are thriving, it seems those children's parents are usually getting what they need, too.

Respect

One crucial component in providing successful support for parents is that they are respected for what they know about their child. Anyone who has talked much to parents of Deaf children has heard stories of how the actual discovery of the child's deafness was delayed because professionals did not take the parents' concern seriously. University of Stockholm psychologist Margareta Ahlström, who is conducting a longitudinal study of hard of hearing preschoolers, feels that this initial insult lays the groundwork for further minimization of parents' intuitions about their child. In her 1991 paper, *An (Un)ordinary Family*, she notes the importance of respecting parents' role and listening to their intuitions and observations throughout the course of the child's education. She explained in our interview:

If you are being listened to as a parent, if you are being treated like a "professional" when it comes to your child, then you will act like a professional and trust your intuitions. Sometimes parents are neglected or rejected in the whole process. I think this is very dangerous (Margareta Ahlström, personal communication, March 22, 1992).

Judith Treesberg (executive director of Louder than Words, editor of The Bicultural Center Newsletter,[3] and parent of a Gallaudet student who was an exchange student to Sweden during high school) has worked toward strengthening the parental support network here in the United States. The small-scale parent workshops she has conducted host a number of professionals speaking on a variety of issues. In addition to presentations by professionals to help parents build their base of knowledge, Treesberg reserves plenty of time for parents to have discussions strictly among themselves to compare what they learn in each presentation with their own observations and frame of reference. Based on her interactions with parents over the years, and as a parent herself, Treesberg has concluded that parents tend to hold their questions (for fear they should already know the answer) in the presence of professionals. They may fail to make valuable contributions to the discussion of what is best for their child because they haven't necessarily been encouraged to question what the professionals have recommended. Regardless of cultural background or socioeconomic status, parents are experts about their own children.

Professionals must actively invite parents' observations and questions, as they are an important part of parents' road to understanding and acceptance. As Philip (1994) points out, no matter how much professionals may think they know what is good for a deaf child, just telling parents "We know..." is not enough. Parents' investment in their children is such that they need to *understand* it for themselves. Professionals must accept that the other part of parents just being parents is having strong opinions and concerns about the welfare of their child, and needing to fully believe that what is happening is in the best interest of the child.

Parents, professionals, and Deaf consumers must work together to create for each child the model described here (Bergman & Wallin, 1989; Bergmann, 1994; Erting, C., 1994; Hansen, 1989). Given a safe, supportive environment and an orientation that helps them view their Deaf child in a positive light, parents can make decisions that take into account the whole child's development. Parents need clear, theoretically sound information about child development, communication, language, language acquisition, emerging literacy, and socio-cultural issues; as well as opportunities to assimilate this theoretical orientation with their own observations and with information from other parents, professionals, and the Deaf community.

3   See Appendix C for addresses.

A First Language: Whose Choice Is It?

A Win-Win Situation

For many Deaf children of hearing parents in Sweden and Denmark, childhood is a relaxed, play-oriented time that—by nature—includes spoken language, and—by design—includes signed language. The picture does not include hours and hours of intensive training any more than it does for a hearing child. In environments where the Deaf child encounters both spoken and signed language separately—as whole languages—during the course of natural interactions, it has become apparent to both parents and professionals that the child will be the guide regarding his or her predisposition toward a more oral or more visual language. In this win-win situation, the choice of a first language is clearly the child's.

In many countries, decisions about first language input for the deaf child weigh heavily on parents, who often have to make a choice between speech and Sign Language. Based on experience in Sweden and Denmark, it is clear that the pressure experienced by hearing parents can be substantially diminished. Much of the panic that parents experience seems to subside when there is a clear focus among those who give early advice to parents on 1) natural, timely acquisition of language and its subsequent influence on cognitive and social functioning, and 2) recognition of the crucial role of well-developed literacy in the majority language in Deaf peoples' successful participation in hearing society.

In these two countries, it is widely accepted to be the right of Deaf children to acquire a first language naturally and "on schedule." The objective for most Deaf children is that the language which is not acquired naturally will be learned as a second language as the child becomes cognitively/developmentally ready and interested. Rather than being presented with options that are mutually exclusive, parents are shown a model that is—ideally—infused with all the options at developmentally appropriate times.

Different Paths to Bilingualism

While the *ultimate* goal is that the children become bilingual adults, it is acknowledged that there is more than one path to that goal. As noted before, many Deaf children enter first grade with knowledge of Swedish Sign Language and written Swedish, gained through face-to-face interaction and frequent exposure to text through storybooks, fingerspelling, and environmental print. Others are reported to arrive with some grasp of the spoken language as well, even though little or no formal teaching of speech was reported in the preschools in Sweden. Some children who are hard of hearing[4] are in a position to learn the spoken language sufficiently for face-to-face interactions, as well as Sign Language.

For example, some of the children in a longitudinal study through Stockholm University Department of Psychology were described by the investigator as follows:

> *Some of the hard of hearing preschoolers used primarily Sign Language with their peers and deaf, hard of hearing, or hearing teachers in preschools, and had enough command of spoken Swedish to use with their parents, siblings, and with hearing peers in their neighborhood. They modified their way of communicating depending on the partner's prerequisites, i.e., they signed with signing peers and used spoken language with those who used speech (M. Ahlström, 1994).*

Although these children were diagnosed with fairly mild hearing losses, it is important to note that their parents, who agreed to be part of the study, began learning and using Sign Language very soon after the children's hearing loss was discovered.

Other paths to bilingualism include those children that have sufficient auditory perception to acquire spoken Swedish/Danish as a first language, who may be placed in a preschool with hearing children or other hard of hearing children. Some of these children also become bilingual because of their parents' efforts to see that they interact with Deaf playmates and adults who use Sign Language.

When I refer to the child's choice in determining these various paths to bilingualism, I don't mean to imply that adults should ask one- or two-year-olds, "Which language works best for you?" While it is very important for parents and teachers to talk in depth with the child as he or she grows up about what is and isn't working communicatively, societal variables may cause children at various ages to place a higher value on speech even if the auditory/aural world is not terribly comprehensible to them. (Children may also have been told that their speech is "good"—in a relative sense—which can be misleading to them in making decisions.) Reference here to the choice of a first language means that we closely observe and evaluate each child to see how he or she functions in both academic and social settings with each language. Or, as one preschool teacher at Kendall School put it:

> *When it comes to language, kids will eventually show you where their strengths and weaknesses lie. If you're really watching them, they're going to let you know what they need and what they can do and what they can't do (L. Erting, personal communication, July 22, 1994).*

---

4   Appendix A discusses use of the term "hard of hearing" in this book.

In those instances where the child's hearing loss is mild enough that both languages can be learned *through natural processes of interaction* (rather than training), the effects of this early bilingualism are not considered a threat to the child's development of spoken or signed language but rather a positive factor in the child's overall development (Preisler, 1983, 1990). Cummins and Swain (1986) cite numerous studies conducted since the early 60s reporting that bilingual children function at a significantly higher level then unilingual children on various measures of cognitive abilities. In a similar vein, Daniels (1993) found that hearing children whose first language was Sign Language had English skills superior to their monolingual peers.

Collier (1989, 1994) also summarizes the results of extensive research about bilingual children's potential. The studies she cites conclude that, if simultaneous and successive bilinguals continue cognitive development in both languages throughout the elementary-school years, they frequently outperform monolinguals on measures of cognitive flexibility, linguistic and metalinguistic abilities, concept formation, divergent thinking skills, creativity, and diversity.[5] In other words, exposing a hard of hearing child to Sign Language early is not considered to be risky or detrimental (Ahlström, in press; Preisler, 1983, 1990). Rather, for those hard of hearing children who do have enough access to the spoken signal to acquire speech naturally, the benefits of early bilingualism in Swedish and Swedish Sign Language are considered to be an asset for the child.

As we know from studies of bilingual homes in many different language settings, bilinguals are rarely equally fluent in both of their languages; and bilingual children gravitate toward a clearly dominant language, which may or may not be their first language. This is typically true in the case of hearing children in homes with one or both Deaf parents. These children often acquire Sign Language as their first language, but the spoken language of the majority eventually becomes their dominant language (E. Newport, personal communication, August 19, 1993). In many ways, the same is true of these hard of hearing children who have access to both languages. The choice is up to them.

I met one parent in Sweden who had determined that Sign Language would be the best language for his hard of hearing child's education. He was among a growing number of parents of hard of hearing children who were afraid their children would not develop solid enough competence in spoken Swedish to support academic work or comfortable classroom participation and peer interaction. These parents felt that their children would miss out on too much information and socialization if placed in their neighborhood school with hearing children. They wanted their child to go to the school for the Deaf. The man I met (and his wife) had gone to great lengths to learn the Sign Language of the Deaf

---

5   Collier cites, for example, De Avila & Duncan, 1980; Diaz, 1983; and Hakuta, 1986.

community and surround their children with it by attending activities at the Deaf club in Stockholm. (I learned from some Deaf people that the father had even become very active and was well-liked in the local Deaf club.)

While their son did learn some Sign Language during the preschool years (and may use it often later), the boy clearly preferred being addressed in and communicating via speech—sometimes to the dismay of his parents. Despite the parents' wishes, the school for the Deaf at that time rejected some of the children whose preference for auditory/aural communication was so clear. (Placement of hard of hearing children is discussed later in this chapter.) Conversely, it was reported that other hard of hearing children who could communicate through speech were accepted into first grade at the school for the Deaf, as they seemed to thrive in social and educational environments with Sign Language, and tended to choose playmates who were Deaf and communicated visually. In other words, *given the choice*, the determination of a primary language is still up to the individual.

The Whole Child

Balanced bilingualism is rare (Grosjean, 1992). Even in an environment such as these children had, it is unlikely that both spoken and signed language will be acquired in parallel or equivalent fashion, simply because of issues related to accessibility (see discussion on critical period). In the far more frequent instances where the child evidences *some* natural acquisition of speech skills, but is not likely to thrive in a speech-only educational environment, keeping the spotlight on the *whole* child is crucial in guiding decisions about the focus of language input. Preschool teachers and speech therapists (in bilingual preschools in both the U.S. and in Sweden) felt it was critical to foster development of these children's visual attention, as well as their receptive and expressive skills in Sign Language. It is recognized that these children's later academic and social functioning, as well as their ability to become fluent in the majority language through literacy, will rely heavily on solid language competence and ability to readily comprehend classroom instruction in Sign Language. Many teachers I interviewed felt that the importance of building visual attention and Sign Language competence cannot be over-emphasized in facilitating the normal development of the whole child. The comments of Sharon Graney, speech pathologist at the Sterck School in Delaware, are consistent with those of teachers of very young children in Sweden, Denmark, and at Kendall School:

> *Some of the hard of hearing children may be getting 60, 70, 80% here [points to her ears], but we know they can get 100% here [points to her eyes]; that's another reason we turn off our voices. It takes a while for them to become visual, but once they get it, then they learn that they can choose to give attention to different kinds of auditory and visual stimuli....*

Sharpening children's visual skills seems to help their attention to both spoken and signed language. The children have to be very tuned in to visual information in comprehending speech. [Texts about speechreading stress the need to develop visual attention.] Some of the hard of hearing kids are such "talkers" that they are moved to preschools with hearing children, but others seem to thrive in this visual environment and I don't see that their speech suffers. I know many older hard of hearing children who never had this opportunity. They are truly "non-visual," but they also ended up with minimal skills in spoken English. We need to help them learn early that vision is important to them. It takes a long time for some children to become visual learners. I see lots of children who need work with this, but I never find kids who need it the other way around.

She went on to talk about children in their parent-infant and preschool programs, and how she incorporates spoken English into their day:

Parents were at first concerned that their hard of hearing children would lose what speech they had when they entered a preschool where Sign Language is used primarily. But their speech seems to be coming along really well. I don't really understand why, but it is. Often I go in when they are playing at centers and spend time talking (no signs) with a child about what he or she is doing. With some children we talk a lot; with others, I play with the words and they like to imitate me (while we are pouring sand, for example, I'll make my voice go from high to low). Some children like what we're doing, but don't vocalize much. Others lose interest and go play in another part of the room and that's OK, too. Another teacher may precede or follow me, or join us in playing, talking about the same kinds of things, using signs without voice. We don't have teachers switching from one mode to another within an activity; we have certain people, certain times, or certain places when we use speech with individual children in natural, interactive ways (Graney, 1994).

Teachers in the preschool research classes at Kendall School noticed what appeared to be an initial cessation of vocalization in the more vocal children as they were starting to tune in to visual language, then a return to using speech in some contexts. Graney's observations were similar:

I have seen a number of hard of hearing 3-year-olds who stop using their voice at first for a while as they seem to be "getting it" about visual language. Then they come back to speaking as the situation calls for it. Like other toddlers who grow up bilingual, many of the hard of hearing children are amazing at code-switching and knowing with whom they should use spoken English and with whom they should use Sign Language. Once in a while a child will forget and will yell "Give me the ball," two or three times when standing behind a Deaf child, but in general they catch on very quickly about the two languages and the situations where each is of use. One hard of hearing three-year-old entered preschool relatively fluent at signing because she'd had a Deaf home teacher. While she understood her peers and staff when they signed to her without voice, she always used spoken English to the staff at first, because she knew we were all hearing. (S. Graney, 1994).

The Opportunity to See for Themselves

Nancy Topoloski, parent-infant teacher at Kendall Demonstration Elementary School, encourages parents to feel free to expose their infant or toddler to spoken English as well as American Sign Language (but not simultaneously) and to be observant of the child's interactions with Deaf children/adults and hearing children/adults in a wide variety of settings. If parents record early vocabulary and linguistic developments in both spoken and signed language, they often get a clearer idea what is working for the child. Deborah Nussbaum, audiologist at Kendall, explained during a presentation to parents and professionals:

> *Providing children opportunities to be exposed to spoken language and auditory stimulation during the early years when they are developing American Sign Language seems to help hearing parents move more quickly to a place of acceptance of American Sign Language. If both areas are addressed early, parents have the opportunity to see for themselves the role listening may have for their child in acquiring spoken language. For some students, this role will be very limited, for some this role will be greater. If parents see that ASL is providing their child a complete avenue for learning language, while listening is providing only minimal information and opportunities for skill development, they may be more willing to move quickly into promoting the development of a visual language for their child. If not allowed to see this for themselves, families may feel their child is missing out on something that could be beneficial. They may feel something is being kept away from their child (Nussbaum, 1994).*

This may sound implausible to people who have seen decades of over-focus on speech and hearing. However, when parents have early contact with Deaf professionals, as well as with speech and hearing professionals who are strong advocates for the child's right to a natural, visual language, the picture changes. Hearing parents who have truly had opportunities to learn Sign Language early and observe their deaf child's communication with Deaf peers and professionals are often extremely perceptive in their observation of what their child needs. In fact, the parents I have met who had such opportunities, whether in the U.S., Sweden, or Denmark, are sometimes the most adamant in advocating that their child's day include *less* emphasis on developing the spoken form and more emphasis on information and visual input in Sign Language.

Graney (1994) reinforced the concept of parents' willingness and ability to see for themselves, *given enough information.* She described three rough categories the Deaf children she encounters seem to fall into with regard to spoken English development during the preschool years: 1) those who are truly learning English auditorily, but seem to benefit from being in a visual environment, interacting with Deaf peers, and learning Sign Language, 2) those who show some aptitude for speech, but clearly do better communicating visually or would require a great deal of work with no guarantees of usable speech as an outcome, and 3) those who really have almost no potential for developing intelligible speech. In regard to the last group, she comments:

I recently dreaded going to an I.E.P. meeting. I felt it would be important to share with this child's parents that our time spent on speech didn't seem to be resulting in much progress. Much to my surprise, it was the parents who, themselves, had looked at their child and made that determination. When the meeting came around to the topic of speech, they said to us, "This is just not happening. This is not important for him right now. It's not fair to him or us to spend all that time working on speech...."

Before, there was no way we would consider telling parents, "Your child has very little potential for speech." No matter what, we encouraged them to use voice at all times and keep trying. We just kept telling parents to do this until finally around age 7-10, everyone would start to accept that it was going nowhere. I think if you ask most teachers and speech/language therapists who work with preschool kids, they seem to know farily soon who is more likely to have intelligible speech. I don't know how it is, but someone ought to do some research to see what it is they are picking up on. I've made a checklist that I use with parents to keep track of some of the factors that seem relevant and have been fairly reliable predictors for me.

There are some older kids at the school—I remember working with them as an aide in the parent-infant program many years ago—who now have absolutely no intelligible speech. These children had all the benefits; we gave them speech in the classroom, plenty of individual work, group work, and amplification. When I think back on how much time we spent with them on something we intuitively knew was not likely to happen, I still cringe (S. Graney, 1994).

One speech researcher at Gallaudet, after observing preschool speech "play" (in a primarily ASL preschool at Fremont, California, School for the Deaf), commented to me that when speech and Sign Language are kept separate, it becomes more clear which children have natural predispositions toward speaking. The children he observed all seemed to enjoy the auditory and speech play activities in which they were involved and were doing something meaningful to them, activities that also tended to be very visual. When adults in their environment do not talk and sign at the same time, it becomes much easier for the speech therapist (and the parents) to observe which children's speech is most intelligible, which children are more attentive to sound and spoken language input, and which benefit in interactive settings from wearing hearing aids. (J. Mahshie, personal communication, April 2, 1993). This observation helped explain to me the clarity I saw in Sweden and Denmark about children who were referred to quite young as "deaf" or "hard of hearing." When I asked how interviewees were able to make such distinctions (since early audiograms are not necessarily predictive of later aptitudes), teachers, psychologists, and social workers said they based them on observations of the children's behavior in different settings.

Speech professionals, teachers, and parents in everyday interactions with Deaf children use language in the way in which the children will find it in the 'real world:' either the Sign Language of the Deaf community, or the spoken language of the home or the majority—without supplementation of signs or cues. When this happens, parents and professionals seem able to get a better reading on whether or not individual time spent is resulting in speech the child can really utilize for interactions with hearing people.[6]

A variety of tools used in the U.S. for clarifying ambiguities in lipreading, such as visual phonics or cued speech, may prove to be helpful when the children are a little older in the actual teaching of speech within a bilingual setting. The ultimate goal, which is to communicate with individuals in the mainstream who do not know or use such aids to speechreading, must be clearly kept in mind so that the child's learning time is not used acquiring a skill that can only be used with a few individuals in a training context. It will be necessary, therefore, to re-assess the value of such teaching tools within the context of an educational environment which utilizes Sign Language *for primary, everyday interaction.*

Cognitive Academic Language Proficiency

A child's initial preference for attention to visual or auditory input can sometimes be observed relatively early by skilled personnel in parent-infant programs and in the child's home, incorporating information from their ongoing dialogue with the parents. This is important information for parents and teachers, but does not imply, for example, that

---

6   This is not a commentary on whether or not cues may be helpful for representing phonologic distinctions in the teaching of speech production or lipreading in an educational context where Sign Language is used primarily. Danish Sign Language, in fact, has traditionally incorporated such a system (based on spoken Danish phonology rather than spelling letters) as part of the Sign Language of the Deaf community; it is used in much the same way fingerspelling is used (although some children in Denmark are now learning a hand alphabet—the same one used in ASL—rather than this Mouth-Hand system). *The Mouth-Hand System: Exercise Material in English,* is a brief description of the Danish mouth-hand system, an element of Danish Sign Language which was designed as an aid to lipreading. Although it is more similar to cued speech than to fingerspelling, it is used in much the same way other Sign Languages used fingerspelling in conversation. Includes practice exercises. To obtain a copy, contact the Kastelsvej Center, address in Appendix C. (Author: Sv. Vognsen).

Sign Language should be dropped as soon as the child shows some predisposition for speaking. Lon Kuntze, Bilingual-Bicultural Coordinator at California School for the Deaf in Fremont, notes that many of the children that come to their school had sufficient hearing to pick up spoken English that could be used for basic communication as toddlers. Some may have been exposed to simultaneous communication, others to spoken English only. In either case, Kuntze asserts, such children often do not acquire spoken English competence on a deep and comprehensive level, as they do American Sign Language (personal correspondence, August 30, 1994). While spoken English may have been their *first* language, it does not necessarily remain the primary or dominant language for many hard of hearing children who are given the choice, in part because they may not be able to assimilate complex information or academic instruction through this language. When both languages are available, a Deaf child may initially attend more to one linguistic modality than the other. Nevertheless, understanding and evaluating these early preferences and their potential role in the child's education can be complex. As one audiologist in the U.S. recently observed:

> *And, we have to remember, even if the child can hear some sounds doesn't mean that child can* **learn** *auditorily. Many seem to do much better visually, even though they have quite a bit of hearing. The school's primary concern is educating the child. So, despite the fact that some hard of hearing children can get by with spoken English for basic communication, many of these same children do not have the ability to process and really utilize complex auditory information. This is a consideration we can't ignore (K. Caputo, personal communication, August 9, 1994).*

Cummins (1980) has identified a very important distinction in levels of language competence: *basic interpersonal communication skills* (BICS) and *cognitive academic language proficiency* (CALP). BICS is the level of language performance which is sufficient for face-to-face interaction, where the speaker can rely heavily on context, and the content is often somewhat predictable. CALP is the level of language competence needed for critical thinking, problem solving, and assimilating new information. Barnum (1984) refers to the distinction between BICS and CALP in discussing the common misconception that speech skills in deaf or hard of hearing children equal real language competence. She cites Thompson and Thompson, who observed the progress of one deaf girl starting at the age of one year. While this little girl had had all the benefits of oral training in preschool, a mainstream education, and intelligent, cooperative parents, they describe her at 13 as having "*normal intelligence and psychological adjustment, a severe hearing loss, adequate speech production, but extremely deficient language and educational skills....The striking feature being that she speaks well but has little to say*" (Thompson and Thompson, 1981, p. 399 & 395).

While it can be informative for parents and teachers to observe a child's performance or surface level of competence with regard to both languages, it is very important to be aware

---

of issues related to the deeper linguistic competence needed for high level thought processing, dialogue, and academic work. These issues are not always apparent during early childhood—a time when most communication is heavily reinforced by context and or is focused on activity and play—and therefore require focused observation and evaluation.

Keeping Expectations High

> *The hearing aid and 'early intervention' might succeed in teaching their deaf child to speechread a few words and even produce some, but that hardly makes for normal family communication. What seemed an appropriate response to the family's distress simply doesn't work. When the parents show consternation at their child's slow progress and the problems they are having communicating with him or her, they are advised to be patient and persevering—after all, it takes a lot of long, hard work to 'get' a deaf child to speak (Bouvet, 1990, p.110).*

Parents' ability to clearly observe their child's progress and trust their intuitions is facilitated when they become conscious that normal developmental and language milestones are well within the reach of Deaf children, and that they don't have to "settle for less" when it comes to their own Deaf child. Through preschools and parent group activities, many parents in Sweden and Denmark are in a position to regularly observe other Deaf children whose linguistic and cognitive development is proceeding "on schedule."

One preschool where expectations are particularly high is housed at the *Dövas Hus*, the Deaf club in Stockholm. Here at the *Skeppargatan* School, hearing parents and their children not only get to know Deaf adults, but these parents have frequent opportunities to see other Deaf children carrying on animated conversations with their parents—Deaf or hearing—when they come to pick them up from school. Through interactions with Deaf children of all ages at social events, hearing parents of Deaf toddlers can't easily forget about the intense, searching, interactive, playful dialogue that normally characterizes the communication of children between the ages of two and five. They are frequently reminded that children gain much of their knowledge and the answers to their constant questions through *language* well before they start school. Basic communication is not enough.

Efforts to bring Deaf children together where there are Deaf adults also result in important opportunities for hearing parents to see children who are growing up Deaf, communicative, and happy—with or without speech. Without such experience, this is often hard for hearing parents to imagine, even when they are told by professionals or Deaf adults. One parent from California (whose child is now grown) recently reminisced with me about her need to *see* other Deaf children. She was having trouble envisioning what she might hope for in her child at any given age, something most parents take for granted:

Unlike many parents in the U.S., I was lucky to meet deaf adults early. But I was sitting there with them, holding this baby in my arms, and I just couldn't make the connection between these adults and my tiny child. I really needed to see Deaf children. Even though I had another son, when I found out my second was deaf, there was this void in my ability to visualize what to expect. Once I began meeting whole families and saw Deaf children interacting with their parents and siblings, I started to feel better.

The parents in the Fremont area now are so lucky, because they regularly get to see other babies who are already signing "Mommy" and "milk" with their parents, and children a little older who can say and do the things hearing children that age say and do—only in Sign Language. They don't have that big breach in their knowledge of what deaf children are capable of. (S. Harvey, personal communication, August 18, 1994).

Given this kind of exposure, parents can no longer be satisfied that their child's communication at the age of three is limited to the few spoken words he or she can pronounce or lipread. It becomes crystal clear to parents that it really doesn't matter WHAT language it is—as long as their child can HAVE language, in all its richness. Parents in such settings are not encouraged to disregard normal developmental milestones or set lower sights for their children (K. Lindberg, Skeppargatan Preschool, personal communication, May 14, 1994).

Emphasis on Speech Skills

Parents I met in Sweden and Denmark did understand the potential benefits and conveniences of speech skills in their child's life. But they also understood some of the inherent limitations for deaf people to comfortable, unencumbered two-way spoken communication. Through their openness to learning from a variety of Deaf adults, hearing parents become aware that, for even the best of lipreaders, spoken interactions further deteriorate when talking with more than one person or in a slightly noisy environment. They want their children to have a language they can own; to have relaxed, pleasurable conversations with others on a deep and meaningful level; and to belong to a group of people within which they are not always seen as the one who is different, deficient, or needs an interpreter. They clearly did not judge the success or failure of their child based on speech and auditory skills.

The following quote from Bouvet shows that taking into account the whole child—and the experiences of a variety of Deaf adults—may be very important when parents consider choices about spoken language as the only form of communication for their child:

In other words, speech produced without the natural feedback of sound cannot be the privileged place of self-expression and identification for deaf people that it is for hearing people....The following testimony of a 22-year-old woman helps us to understand what the deaf person must deal with in such interactions. This young, congenitally deaf woman with a hearing loss of between 80 and 90 Db, learned at a very young age to articulate so correctly that it would take someone a while to realize that she was deaf. Yet here is what she has to say about growing up:

> "In play, deafness wasn't a problem. The trouble began when relationships started to revolve around discussions and spoken exchanges. I felt excluded then because no one talked to you 'just for the pleasure of it,' but only to transmit a practical message to you....I am uncomfortable in group discussions, even in friendly get-togethers. Even if someone agrees to be the go-between—and I have lots of friends who do—he will only be able to relate the 'skeleton' of the story, which by then has lost all of its flavor. I laugh to please him, but often it's no longer funny or I haven't understood. Everything I get is in past tense, so I have no chance of responding or contributing" *[Armengaud, 1979, p. 266]* *(Bouvet, 1990, p. 32).*

A Cost-Benefit Perspective

In Denmark and Sweden, speech is seen as a complement to—not a necessary component in—a Deaf child's normal development of language and literacy (Hansen, 1990; Wallin, 1988). The importance of perfecting a child's auditory discrimination or pronunciation is seen in the context of the whole child's development. Parents I met placed a very high value on grade-level academic achievement, and felt that time and energy put into intensive speech training must be weighed realistically against the potential benefits. Some children benefit greatly from time spent in training, in terms of usable skills. Others benefit only minimally in their prognosis for usable speech. Speech researcher James Mahshie (personal communication, June 11, 1993) characterizes this as a "cost-benefit" view of speech development and teaching: keeping the whole child's development and future functioning in mind as the critical consideration in determining how much effort is reasonable to expend (by both child and teacher) for developing speech skills.

As a bottom line, parents I interviewed in Sweden and Denmark seemed to accept the possibility that—with or without intense efforts and long hours of practice—oral/aural skills simply *may not* play a primary role in their children's life. They were not willing to put learning, socialization, and language on hold; or require that their children fail with spoken language before they are given opportunities for exposure to Deaf adults and fully-accessible visual language.

In an intense reaction to years of strict oralism in Sweden, the pendulum did swing far in the direction of support for Sign Language at first—sometimes with clear disregard for speech skills (see later discussion). This was not the case in Denmark. There, flexibility and individual rights have always been the hallmark of programs for Deaf children, and in most schools, signs were never completely banned; nor have hearing aids or speech development been disregarded. A number of avenues have opened up in both countries that did not previously exist when all education in Sweden was oral: new technology, the ability to communicate in depth in Sign Language about the speech being learned, a strong focus on literacy and competence in Swedish as a language (upon which speech teachers can capitalize for spoken language development), and involving Deaf adults in certain aspects of teaching about speech and its uses.

Nevertheless, when it comes to understanding and producing spoken language, it seems investment and outcomes continue to vary greatly from child to child, whether in these countries or in the U.S. Intelligibility scores of deaf children vary considerably depending on a wide range of factors and have shown little or no improvement over many years (McGarr, 1980). Daniel Ling, one of the foremost authorities in North America on teaching speech to deaf children—whose speech teaching methods are widely used by a large number of oral programs and by speech therapists in other educational settings—summarized studies that yielded the following conclusion:

> *Results of recent studies suggest that overall levels of speech intelligibility are utterly inadequate for oral communication and that typical speech errors of children attending special education for the deaf today are much the same as they were 40 years ago. Advances in acoustic phonetics, speech science, psychology, hearing aid technology, and other related fields appear to have made no significant impact on standards of speech production (Ling, 1976, p. 11).*

Six years later, speech researchers Osberger and McGarr (1982) assert that, "on average, the intelligibility[7] of profoundly hearing-impaired children's speech is very poor," citing a number of studies which show that "only about one in five words they say can be understood by a listener who is unfamiliar with the speech of this group" (p. 268).

While I have not found studies on more current overall intelligibility levels, it can be assumed that various factors may have caused intelligibility ratings of deaf children as a group to change in some way. Since 1990, for example, 2200 children in North America have received cochlear implants [Cochlear Corporation, 1994.] Therefore, some children (pre- and post-lingually deaf) who derive no use from hearing aids are now being fitted with cochlear implants (or tactile devices) and given intensive auditory and speech training. Previously, these children might have been candidates for early Sign Language from the start, in some cases with little or no emphasis on speech skills. While some of these children show degrees of improvement in production of isolated aspects

---

7   The term *speech intelligibility* is used by Osberger and McGarr to refer to "how much of what a child says can be understood by a listener."

speech intelligibility over what they would have otherwise been expected to produce, this does not imply that pre-lingually deaf children using these devices can come anywhere near an age-appropriate spoken dialogue with hearing peers or teachers (see section on cochlear implants for discussion and citations). In other words, since the time they were written, the phrases *very poor* and *utterly inadequate for oral communication* could still be considered accurate in describing the overall levels of speech intelligibility of deaf children as a group.

This does not imply that we stop trying to increase our understanding of how Deaf children can best learn to speak, or that we deny them opportunities for exposure to spoken language input. Rather, these conclusions suggest that our approaches to deaf infants and toddlers must take into account some long-standing facts about the real possibilities for the average deaf child to develop intelligible speech and use it as a primary mode of communication for academic, social, and later for career purposes.

There is a great deal to be learned about what makes some deaf children's speech more intelligible than others, and what factors would enable us to predict whether or not a child will become an intelligible speaker, with or without amplification and intensive training. After describing numerous studies looking at various kinds of production errors deaf children tend to make, Osberger and McGarr (1982) conclude:

> *In summary, we have relatively little information regarding the effect of errors, or combinations of errors, on the intelligibility of hearing-impaired children's speech, nor are we able to predict reliably if a child has the potential to develop intelligible speech (p. 273).*

Much more information will be needed about why and how some deaf speakers have successfully overcome the odds and developed intelligible speech before we can claim to adequately address these issues through teaching. Because of our relative inability to predict a child's potential for developing intelligible speech, choices about effort expended in the direction of structured teaching should be based on individual children's observed aptitudes, interests, and potential. Such choices must take into account the whole child. In other words, the child's timely development—linguistic, cognitive, and social—deserves center stage.

More and more professionals and Deaf consumers in Sweden are studying their current educational structure to make sure that those children who have an aptitude and talent for speech will get the training they need. At the time of my first study, the National Association of the Deaf had established as one of its political aims to study the question of how schools can realistically and effectively incorporate speech training into the Sign Language milieu they had struggled to create. At that time, a large meeting was held at which Deaf consumers and professionals were asked to complete a survey and came together to discuss what their speech skills really mean to them, how they use speech, and how they feel about their years of speech training. The fact that professor Arne Risberg, a prominent speech scientist in Sweden, sought the comments of Deaf adults to get at these issues shows an important attitude of respect for the experiences of Deaf people—many of whom grew up under oral systems—and what they know about the process of learning speech without full benefit of hearing. As this level of respect has become apparent and Deaf professionals have started to play a bigger role in the speech teaching process, concerns within Sweden's Deaf population about the potential for over-focus on hearing and speech appear to have subsided.

Residual Hearing

There is widespread acceptance among professionals in the United States of the premise that a child's aptitude for comprehending or producing speech cannot be predicted based on early audiograms. This is clearly explained by the classic text many speech therapists still rely on as a model for teaching speech. Ling (1976) equates the part of a young child's hearing that we DO know about with the shoreline of a body of water. He shows a figure in which we can see the edge of a lake or river, as well as the house and trees on the land, but we have no information about what is under the water. He states that the audiogram "merely indicates the dividing line between hearing and not hearing" in much the same way as the shoreline separates land from water:

> From this figure, it is impossible to deduce the water's depth, warmth, or its suitability for drinking or swimming. Similarly, from an audiogram having the same "shoreline" configuration, one cannot deduce a child's ability to distinguish one frequency from another, to track formant transitions, or to judge one sound as louder or quieter than another. Nor does an audiogram indicate a child's level of tolerance for amplified sound. For these (and yet other) reasons, it is possible for several children with identical pure-tone audiograms to differ greatly in ability to use residual hearing and to discriminate speech (Ling, 1976, p. 24-25).

Ling notes that not all pure tone audiograms are reliable; audiograms of children tend to vary from one audiometric test to another for a variety of reasons (Ling and Nash, 1975). Further, he explains:

> Sound has three aspects—intensity, frequency, and duration—whereas the audiogram is a two-dimensional plot of intensity and frequency. It provides no information on how well (or badly) a child may be able to process the time relationships which are so important to speech intelligibility. This has to be determined in the course of teaching. Also, the audiogram provides only a threshold measure, whereas hearing-impaired listeners generally require speech amplified to 20-30dB above threshold (Gengel and Foust, 1975). The audiogram provides no information on the quality of audition present at these levels (Ling, 1976, p. 23-24).

Osberger and McGarr (1982) note that, while the degree of a child's hearing loss is an important variable, this measure alone cannot reliably predict the intelligibility of a child's speech; in fact, it was identified as only a fair predictor. Rather, they explain that it is the ability of the child to make use of the acoustic cues available to him (i.e., to recognize phonemes) that is more closely correlated with speech intelligibility than is level of hearing. This ability is something that is determined not as the result of a single test performed on an infant, but based on the child's response to and development of spoken language over a period of time.

One audiologist from the Sterck School for Deaf children in Delaware explained that neither pure-tone measures nor brain-stem testing can provide information that gives a clear prediction about usable hearing and speech, until the child is well beyond the age when most children have already acquired language. Even then, tests of perception can be misleading:

> *While we can get information about reception (what the child can detect), we still don't know about **perception** (what the child can understand) until the child is about 4 years old.[8] In other words, we know something about what sound is getting through, but not what the child will be able to do with it. Even then, a child's ability to identify spoken words is in some cases obscured if that child has an impoverished vocabulary. Many of the tests depend on the child's vocabulary and concept development.*

> *For example, if the child doesn't know the word for "purse," then it doesn't matter if he can hear me, he may still choose the wrong picture. Many deaf children we see have not had first-hand experience with the object in the test (and its name), or haven't been sufficiently exposed to Sign Language so they can really discuss abstract concepts and learn about pictures in storybooks. This makes it very difficult to know if test failures relate to poor discrimination of speech or to lack of vocabulary and concept development (K. Caputo, personal communication, August 9, 1994).*

In other words, at the very early ages, when most children's language-learning is well underway, it is not technically possible to get an accurate picture of what sounds a deaf child can discriminate (either through behavioral or brain-stem testing), nor how the child's hearing will facilitate speech production and perception. While this fact is typically shared with parents, it is not necessarily incorporated into actual practice when decisions are made about the first language input to be provided to a deaf infant. Incorporating this information into practice would mean ensuring that each deaf child has access to

---

8   Erber (1982) discusses 4 levels of hearing: detection, discrimination, identification, perception (the last being the actual comprehension of speech).

visual language during the period while his or her facility for auditory language is being observed and/or facilitated. Instead, parents in the U.S. are often encouraged to focus on speech-based approaches first, or are asked to make a choice at a time when the child is still too young to predict later aptitude for hearing and speech. Parents can undergo extreme pressure attempting to make a decision that will affect their deaf child's entire future—based on information that many professionals in the fields of speech and hearing agree is insufficient. Current pressures on parents in the U.S. toward choosing—as a first option—efforts to teach speech (or to talk at all times when signing in English word order) are often fueled by the following popular notion:

> Almost all deaf children have residual hearing that
> could possibly be utilized toward development of speech.

For parents, this statement sends a powerful—and often misleading—message: There is a good possibility your child really can hear to some extent. If you do all the "right" things, that child may also speak.

Professionals I interviewed linked the move toward almost absolute oralism in Sweden and the hiring of only hearing teachers to a similar notion promoted by a Swedish doctor, Erik Wedenberg, who had a deaf son himself. Gunnell Blücher (personal communication, May 21, 1990) notes that some schools for the deaf were still using signs in the forties. Then Wedenberg, who also happened to be a highly-respected teacher trainer, conducted studies which indicated that almost all children had some residual hearing (Wedenberg, 1951). Therefore, he asserted, deaf children could learn to speak if properly trained and spoken to from an early age. Many educators and speech/hearing professionals I have spoken to over the years have accepted the belief that relatively few children with a hearing loss are totally deaf.

Hearing or Feeling?

In 1963, speech researchers began to question this concept, according to Arne Risberg, internationally-known speech researcher at Sweden's Royal Institute of Technology. In our interview, Risberg explained his findings, which indicated that the residual hearing philosophy that seems to shape much of our thinking about deaf children and speech was formed somewhat erroneously on the basis of many children's responses to *feeling* vibrations—rather than *hearing* sound (Risberg, Algefors, & Boberg, 1975). Their new technology was better able to sort out auditory response vs. tactile response. In other words, in regard to some of the profoundly deaf children, Risberg told me:

> *If you put the headphone on the ear or if you put it on the stomach that doesn't matter, you still get the same audiogram....If you don't call it hearing when it comes through tactile vibrations in the stomach, I'm not sure we should call it hearing when the same thing happens in the ear.*

So we started to make other kinds of measurements and more or less found out that about one third, at least, of the children in the school for the deaf at that time were totally deaf and had no residual hearing whatsoever; it was just tactile sensation in the ear. (A. Risberg, personal communication, March 9, 1990).

Many speech and hearing professionals in the United States are familiar with the concept of vibro-tactile "hearing;" for example, Ling (1976) points out that not all responses to sound necessarily indicate the presence of audition. He notes that some responses, particularly those to low-frequency tones, may result from tactile sensation, which may or may not be useful for certain aspects of speech discrimination (he cites Boothroyd and Cawkwell, 1970; Erber, 1972; Nober, 1964). Ling also explains that some children "may actually hear rather than feel sound, but nevertheless may be unable to differentiate sounds auditorily" (1976, p. 290). Even assuming a reliable audiogram can be obtained, Ling explains that these children cannot be diagnosed on the basis of an audiogram. He reiterates that the child's capacity for hearing cannot be evaluated at a single moment in time, but is unveiled gradually. He advises that speech training should be considered as *diagnostic* therapy, noting that our knowledge of what the child can hear is only reliably determined over time during opportunities to observe the child's ability to differentiate speech stimuli through audition.

Ramifications

This is not to say that a high percentage of profoundly deaf children have audiograms that are based on "feeling" alone, or that there are large numbers of children who may hear fairly well but not be able to differentiate sounds. Rather, the point is: The notion that all deaf children have some degree of residual hearing is often carried to the extreme in justifying early and intensive auditory and speech training or maintaining the practice of talking and signing at the same time. The problem is, because those involved may believe the deaf child is getting sufficient language input from these sources, minimal effort may be made to ensure that the child is frequently exposed to fluent models of Sign Language.

Despite limitations inherent in our ability to predict, many professionals continue to focus on giving parents hope by talking about what residual hearing *is* there. This well-meaning approach often has the unfortunate effect of stalling parents' efforts to provide deaf children with early access to a complete language they can acquire in a timely way.

As Ling has pointed out, it is not the audiogram that reveals to us what residual hearing will mean to a child, but rather careful observation of the child's behavior over time with regard to spoken language, through natural interactions and through attempts to teach that child to talk. Clearly, these things take time. I do not suggest we stop this process of discovering what each Deaf child will do with speech input, or even that we wait until the child can comprehend all aspects of speech practice before beginning it (as long as the child finds the process enjoyable). Rather, I suggest that whatever hopes parents attach to this notion of residual hearing be accompanied by a realistic perspective about the limits of the real outcomes for even the most successful of deaf speakers—and that hopeful advice also be tempered with appropriate alarm that, due to our inability to predict, many children are left with little or no access to language during what is often a long-term evaluation of their potential for using spoken language.

Many professionals who advise parents of deaf infants in Sweden and Denmark now seem to agree on one major premise: Whatever the infant's level of hearing or future aptitude for speech, the fact that it is even a topic for discussion implies the child's right to early exposure to Sign Language. In other words, if the child's hearing loss was severe enough to be discovered at a young age, the child is very likely to be lacking access to at least some of the spoken signal, rendering speech a deficient language model. If the child was responding to and developing clear speech "on schedule," the parents and professionals would not even be having this discussion. Rather than setting goals for the infant or toddler that rely on mastery of the thing he or she is failing to achieve through natural processes, the alternative is to give the child a "sure thing" upon which to build.

Studies have shown that access to Sign Language does not hamper Deaf children's ability to acquire speech. Israelite, Ewoldt, and Hoffmeister (1989) summarize numerous studies in which Deaf children of Deaf parents who use Sign Language from the start scored equally or higher when compared to Deaf children of hearing parents in measures related to spoken language—despite the intense early efforts to teach speech, denial of access to Sign Language, or use of simultaneous communication that have often characterized approaches used with Deaf children of hearing parents. (The Deaf children of Deaf parents also scored significantly higher on most measures of academic achievement.) As Stockholm University linguist, Inger Ahlgren states:

> Sign Language is no longer regarded as a threat to the normal development of deaf children, but rather the best possible guarantee for normal development (1989, p.1).

Deaf and hard of hearing children live in a world full of sounds and speech to which they may or may not have access. Since these auditory attributes are easy to find, efforts in Sweden and Denmark focus on making sure the visual part of this equation (including a language which is completely accessible regardless of hearing levels) is somehow made regularly available in the child's environment. These changes in early approach have gone a long way toward freeing parents to be parents by releasing them from impossible either-or decisions and configuring the environment to let the child's actual behavior guide considerations about language and educational placement.

Critical Period and Spoken Language

The need to capitalize on a "critical period" for language acquisition is often referred to in the U.S. as a rationale for placing the early focus on speech. The idea of a critical period is based on a hypothesis that there is a limited window in the brain's development when it is acutely predisposed to acquiring language. During this biologically-determined period, children's brains are highly responsive to any natural language in their environment (see section on early natural language input and the brain). When there are no limits to access, children acquire language naturally, through exposure and interaction. They do not need to be explicitly taught (Krashen, 1981). This early, natural acquisition of language is thought by some to be a necessary condition for children to achieve full fluency in language, which also influences their cognitive abilities and their capacity for learning other languages. If they acquire language after that period, their capacity for learning language is believed to have decreased, with adolescents and adults no longer able to call upon the innate mechanisms that work so well for young children.

Over time, this natural acquisition of language gradually becomes a more conscious and demanding process, with the information stored differently in the brain. Lenneberg (1967) has suggested that this "lateralization" (assigning of functions to two halves of the brain) is a slow process that begins around age two and is completed around puberty. Krashen's (1973) work indicates that the development of lateralization starts very early and is complete by age five. This is consistent with other first language acquisition research in which relative fluency in a language is often considered to be reached by age five (although development continues well beyond puberty). Brown (1980) discusses other factors that may influence the optimal period for language acquisition, including the effects of motor control (physical coordination) and cognitive development, both of which develop rapidly during the early years and much more slowly after puberty.

Acquisition vs. Learning

While there is still some debate about the parameters of this early critical period, we cannot ignore the question that is on the minds of many parents and educators of Deaf children:

> In approaches based primarily on early exposure to natural signed language, will the child miss the "critical period" for acquiring spoken language?

This is one of the questions I asked during my first visit to Sweden. One linguistic researcher from the Stockholm University Department of Scandinavian Languages expressed her concern over my assumption that critical period effects would apply to the learning of speech by deaf children. She explained their view (also held by linguists in the U.S.) that the distinction between *acquiring* and being formally *taught* a language is central to the discussion of critical period for both first and second languages (K.

Svartholm, personal correspondence, January, 1990). The term *acquisition* is used to refer to the subconscious process through which children acquire their first language, while *learning*, in this context, refers to the conscious process through which simple grammatical rules and other facts about the workings of the language are understood. Krashen (1981) asserts that these two kinds of knowledge are stored separately in the brain, and that only *acquired* knowledge is available for spontaneous and automatic language use. Learned knowledge can be accessed when there is time for reflection, as in writing, serving as kind of a conscious editorial device that Krashen refers to as the *monitor*.

Except in cases where the Deaf child has sufficient auditory processing to acquire the spoken language naturally through everyday processes of interaction, the learning of speech through teacher-directed repetition, feedback, correction, and explanation is not considered to be an "acquisition" process. If the child's hearing loss is severe enough that, with or without amplification, speech must be *consciously* learned through training and practice, the process is very different in character from other language acquisition processes in children (Risberg, 1968). This training of speech skills to children who have little or no auditory access to the speech signal is considered by researchers in Sweden to be more an intellectual or memorization task than a language learning task (Svartholm, 1993; I. Ahlgren, personal communication, April 2, 1990). It therefore is not regarded as falling under the purview of the critical period discussion as it applies to first language *acquisition*. In other words, *except for those Deaf children who can pick up speech through exposure alone, the "critical period" is not considered to be critical by linguists and many educators of Deaf children in Sweden.* What *is* considered critical for teaching speech is cognitive readiness—and motivation—for the learning task.

One American parent shared with me the reflections of her Deaf son (who has usable speech) about his perception of his own speech-learning process:

> *My son has told me that he didn't really "get it" about speech until after he learned to sign and read. Before that, the speech he was learning really didn't have meaning for him—he says he just didn't have a good grasp of the concepts for the words he was practicing to say, or the reason why he was doing it. Once he got that part, it became more of a challenge to him. He has shared with me some of the strategies he used to use to make sense of things and make connections as he started to learn signs. They were using the oral method in his preschool, which was part of Gallaudet College at that time. We decided when he was around five that it just wasn't working. He was always so frustrated, so we changed to sign communication before he left preschool and continued when he entered the primary department at Kendall School. After a few years, that's when his speech really started to take off. Now, as an adult, he uses his speech whenever he needs it, even though his main language is ASL and his friends are mostly Deaf. He had that speech training early, but speech didn't seem to develop until it made more*

sense to him. He just wasn't ready before (L. Proctor, personal communication, July 20, 1994).

Some readers might look at this testimony and ascribe this boy's eventual success with spoken English to those early years of oral training (even though he showed little progress or interest at the time). Even if we accept the assumption that this early training contributed to his later success in speaking, the whole child must still be considered. What was he deprived of during those years? Was it worth the price? We have no way of knowing if this child might have benefitted even more from his speech training in school if the focus of his early years had been on building a strong first language base and the kind of world knowledge most children attain well before starting school. What he did have was a very diligent mother who worked with him with books and toy animals and found ways to make sure he understood what was going on around him. Such parental attention can make a significant difference in a child's later functioning, no matter what approach is used.

In the model described here, however, a Deaf child is not asked to overcome the odds and to succeed *despite* impoverished early language input. Instead, the model is based on giving young children the optimum tools—whatever works for them—to build a strong base of language and knowledge. It is also important to note that, while this boy had every opportunity (including dedicated parents) to acquire spoken English early as a first language, he chose ASL as his primary language for education and for communication as an adult. Given the chance, each child will ultimately do the choosing. The operative phrase here is "given the chance."

I was told numerous times by teachers and speech professionals involved in educating Deaf children bilingually that many children are motivated to practice their speech and sometimes ask for more at certain stages: 1) in the early grades because they are curious about *everything*, as most small children are, 2) later because it can be related to the sentences they are learning to read, and 3) still later because they see the potential benefits of having skills in that area in their lives. Many also described a falling off of interest around fourth grade or fifth grade and a re-kindling of interest in the later grades (that is when children have access to Sign Language from the start).

The more experience professionals in these countries have with Deaf children who are exposed to Sign Language early, the more they trust that those who are going to acquire speech naturally through their hearing *will* acquire it even if they are addressed much of the time in Sign Language. Many Deaf parents around the world see that their hard of hearing children have some access to people who speak to them. Many hearing parents—whether or not they learn Sign Language—do tend to talk to their Deaf children, and do continue to talk to each other and to hearing children in the family. In other words, spoken language models are everywhere. When children do have sufficient hearing and tend to be responsive to speech, the hearing adults in their environment use it with them in many contexts. Studies in early mother-child interaction show that much of parents' early communication with their children is comprised of "automatic" responses that reinforce their child's efforts to communicate (see Bouvet, 1990 for extensive discussion). In other words, if the child begins to express him/herself verbally, the parents will follow suit, reinforcing the utterances verbally.

Unless a child is very isolated from hearing society, it is likely that no amount of exposure to Sign Language will keep that child from acquiring the spoken language that is prevalent in society or in his own home, if it is accessible to him through hearing (Axelsson, 1994). Conversely, there is much evidence that those children who do not have enough auditory access to the signal will not learn the spoken language *through a natural acquisition process* no matter how much they are exposed to it. These children will need to be *taught* much of what they will ultimately know about speech.

Access is the Key

If a language is being spoken around them and with them, and their auditory perception and intelligence are intact, most hearing children will, over a relatively short period of time, be able to understand and produce that language (Axelsson, 1994). For both deaf and hearing children, the same is true of signed languages, as long as the children's visual perception and intelligence are intact. If children have full access on a sustained basis to two languages at this early age, they will acquire both—whether signed or spoken (Petitto, 1994b). Conversely, a child who does not have access to the auditory or visual channels through which a language is transmitted, even if that child is addressed regularly in that language, will not acquire that language naturally (see section on early amplification).

The key word is *ACCESS*. We would consider it ludicrous to expect a blind infant to acquire Sign Language simply by being in an environment where it is used by the adults around him. This visual/gestural language—for an infant who does not have the sense of sight—simply does not exist. If that child has some sight, he might perceive movement, but not a language. With glasses, the child might perceive some of the signs and movements, but that may not be enough to constitute comprehensive linguistic input. Even if signs are taught, sign by sign, to the blind or deaf-blind child for the purpose of communicating with Deaf people through tactile channels, the child will not have full receptive access to the language as it is used among Deaf people in normally-paced conversation. Sign Language is, by nature, a visually-perceived language.

In much the same way, there are *very real* biological limits for most Deaf children to acquiring spoken language through natural interactive processes. These limits persist even if the child has some hearing or is taught the language through a step-by-step process that relies heavily on vision for reception. Such a teaching process, by nature, must often involve structured, repetitive practice. In most cases, such teaching cannot capitalize fully on the natural processes of daily interaction and conversation that are so important to linguistic and cognitive development (Vygotsky, 1962), nor does the *outcome* of that teaching give the Deaf child full access to normal-paced spoken conversation with a group of hearing people. Spoken language is, by nature, an auditorily perceived language.

Mahshie (J., in press) notes that speech learning by Deaf children appears to take place in one of two ways: 1) the developmental model, in which the momentum comes from within the child based on his own proclivity to use hearing and speech in daily spoken interactions (often made possible through amplification), and 2) the intervention model, in which the directives for learning are largely teacher-based or clinician-based. If we rely solely on the developmental approach (natural spoken interactions) with all deaf children, many will acquire little or no spoken language. In other words, Mahshie explains, if the goal for these children is to learn some spoken language, they must, primarily, be taught—a process that bears little resemblance to the more natural acquisition processes of hearing or hard of hearing children who do have real auditory access to speech (Risberg, 1968). Unfortunately, the intervention model (dependent on teaching) still does not produce intelligible speech in many of those deaf children with whom it is used.

Long (1990) describes a "sensitive period" during which hearing children can easily acquire second languages, claiming that, for the learner to acquire native-like *pronunciation* in a second language, exposure to that language needs to start sometime before the age of six. Long also claims that the acquisition of *morphology and syntax* (the way the language connects words and parts of words to create meaning) needs to take place between the ages of six and fifteen years for the child to acquire full, native-like proficiency in these areas.

In other words, learning before the age of six was found to be important for hearing children to speak with no trace of an accent, but is not critical to their attainment of a high level of knowledge and fluency in a second language. Danish children, for example, do not typically begin to learn their 3rd and 4th languages (English and German) until the ages of 9 to 11 years, yet can acquire very high levels of proficiency. This period coincides with Deaf children's learning the morphology and syntax of the majority language through reading, which Swedish and Danish educators feel provides strong support for those children who are learning the spoken form.

There are some critical considerations that cannot be ignored when generalizing such hypotheses to deaf children. Most notably, the children upon whom such hypotheses are based already possess solid age-appropriate competence in their *first* language. Speech researchers Osberger and McGarr (1982) note that, "Although some hearing-impaired children develop intelligible speech, many do not" (p. 222). It is therefore of major concern that some Deaf children, if exposed only to spoken language input during the first five years, may develop *little* in the way of a first language.

If first language development (signed or spoken) is not impeded, children have the linguistic and cognitive preparedness to acquire their second language without major setbacks in proficiency, even if teaching in that language is started later (Hyltenstam, 1992; Long, 1990; Svartholm, 1993, 1994). However, if first language development *is* impeded, neither the first nor the second language is likely to be learned fully (Cummins, 1984; Paulston, 1977; Schiff, et al, 1993; Newport & Supalla, 1987).

Access must be considered at the heart of every issue when generalizing to deaf children findings that are based on hearing children who have full auditory input from spoken conversation for natural, interactive acquisition in both their first and second languages.[9] If we recall the widely-researched premise that all language acquisition is based on comprehensible input, it follows that exposing deaf children to *more* spoken conversation or to *earlier* spoken conversation when they have limited auditory access to that conversation will result in very limited language development. Good pronunciation is of little use without knowledge of the language. In order for language to develop, the input simply must be comprehensible to the child. The development of the first language, which contributes to later success in acquiring the second language and other language forms, must not be sacrificed to insufficient input or intervention-type training processes in lieu of natural acquisition.

A Hard Reality

In addition to needing some knowledge of how a language builds meaning (morphology and syntax), Deaf children, to develop skills in the spoken form, must also master the phonology of that language—with little or no auditory feedback—and learn the motor and breath control needed to produce various sounds. This process includes memorizing productions or developing and practicing internal strategies for monitoring their own speech. Children who do not acquire the spoken form naturally must often rely heavily on feedback from the speech teacher or computers, since they can rely only minimally (if at all) on their hearing for information about their own productions.

While we are continuing to learn more through research about how best to teach the spoken language to Deaf children, one thing is clear: It is an extremely complex (and often unattainable) task. To quote Danielle Bouvet, a speech pathologist/linguist from France:

---

9   A parallel that *would* be relevant is Deaf children who acquire Danish or Swedish Sign Language as a strong first language, then proceed to learn American Sign Language. Like the hearing children in Long's studies, both the first and the second language, in this context, are completely accessible to the Deaf child and can be acquired through interactive processes.

Speech is a hard reality with its own laws and requirements. In disregarding or not respecting them because they are not simple, we certainly complicate the lives of the deaf children whom we want to teach to speak. We make them pay dearly for our lack of honesty, sometimes jeopardizing their entire equilibrium. The only way that we can better respond to deaf children and free them from our own false assumptions is to adopt an approach that 'recognizes the complexity of things.' (1990, p.34).

The more conscious learning process Deaf children must employ to master this extremely complex task requires a certain level of cognitive maturity, developmental readiness to attend to the tasks presented, motivation, and some way of gaining access to the form and structure of the language—typically through literacy—since that form and structure is not readily available through the spoken signal or through signs.

There are many speech-play activities for which some young Deaf children are highly motivated that may contribute to a child's growing awareness of speech and sound in the environment, and that could lay important groundwork for those who will later have varying degrees of success with speech or lipreading. Such activities as one part of the child's preschool experience, do not seem to capture the attention of some children, but are quite enjoyable for others. In either case, such activities do not constitute the interactive, productive, and meaningful processes that lead to the natural acquisition of a first language during the critical period. These processes depend on full access to the language. Wallin (1989) sums it up as follows:

The recurrent problem is that we, for natural reasons, cannot learn Swedish the way hearing people do. They acquire it "for free," so to speak, in their early childhood through hearing it spoken around them. This is not possible for many of us since it presupposes one important thing—perfect (or near perfect) hearing—which we do not have. We are dependent on instruction for learning the language. What is the best method of teaching us the language of the surrounding society, so that we can live and work on an equal basis with hearing people? (p. 2).

Deaf children who are learning speech skills, but do not have enough hearing to acquire the spoken language through natural processes, nevertheless need a way to develop competence in the *language* if they are to produce and comprehend spoken structures without auditory models or feedback. In other words, early, structured teaching of pronunciation will be of little use in actual communication if the child does not have a strong grasp of the morphology and syntax of the language (which Long claims can be acquired fluently between the ages of six and fifteen). Comprehending other people's connected speech is yet another set of skills that relies heavily on this knowledge of the language to overcome incomplete audition and ambiguities on the lips.

Because it provides a Deaf child *access* to the structures of the language, the written form of the majority language, acquired by Deaf children through sufficient exposure (R. Andersson, 1994; Svartholm, 1994) offers a basis upon which learned pronunciations of spoken words can be related to the language as a whole. Functional use of the spoken form of the majority language is then considered by some to be more "teachable" for children who do not otherwise acquire it naturally, because these children now bring to the task solid competence in their first language, world knowledge, and knowledge of the written form of the spoken language (Hansen, 1989; Kuntze, 1994).

The conclusion drawn by Wallin and others in Sweden and Denmark is that, for Deaf children, the one complete and fully comprehensible channel for acquisition and expression in the language of the majority is through reading and writing. Speech therapists in the most ideal settings in these countries (and now in more and more schools in the U.S.) not only support Deaf children's natural acquisition of Sign Language, but also work very closely with teachers to make sure the tasks they are teaching capitalize on concepts the child is able to talk about in Sign Language or can read. Since the children already know (or are in the process of learning) the Danish/Swedish language, training in pronunciation is not isolated from the structure of the language. Speech teachers regularly commented that the children have more to talk *about*.

Critical Period and Sign Language

The fear that deaf children may never talk unless they are exposed exclusively to speech during an early, critical period has had a pervasive effect on practices in raising deaf children. Yet, only recently have the concerns of Deaf people and a handful of Deaf and hearing professionals been recognized—serious concerns over the consequences of *not* exposing Deaf children to Sign Language during the critical period for language acquisition. The question asked earlier might be appropriately reworded, considering that many deaf children around the world still enter school with very little language of any kind:

> In approaches based exclusively on early efforts to teach spoken language, will the child miss the "critical period" for acquiring any first language?

This is the question posed in Sweden by linguists and psychologists who were concerned about the strict oralism that had persisted there for many years. If the critical period is missed because we are exposing the children only to speech, they pointed out, we run the risk that some children's limited or non-existent access to the spoken signal will result in almost no early language (other than the idiosyncratic systems they have pieced together to get by). The Sign Language competence they do acquire when they are later exposed to it will be increasingly less proficient depending on the age it was acquired (Hyltenstam, 1992; Newport and Supalla, 1987). This lack of early first language competence, which has been shown to hamper acquisition of any language, results in

---

the children progressing through their education only "semi-lingual" (Cummins, 1984; Paulston, 1977).

While it is hard to imagine a setting in our world that includes no exposure to spoken language, many deaf and hard of hearing children in the U.S. today still grow up in environments that provide no exposure to signed language (see figures in Prologue). Since we don't know and can't accurately predict some very important variables at the earliest stages, the possible consequences of even partial deprivation of accessible language at a critical time were important considerations in the decision to make Sign Language part of the early education of Deaf and hard of hearing children in Denmark and Sweden.

Early Amplification

Regarding some children, the discussion of teaching vs. early, natural acquisition of a spoken language is not black and white. They may evidence some real aptitude for speech but not enough that their speech would be intelligible without some work. Others *might* naturally acquire or have more success when taught speech if they could simply hear some frequencies better. Therefore, the question that logically follows the discussion of critical period is whether or not to assist a child's ability to hear more of the spoken language, and if so, at what age?

During times when the speech signal was the only linguistic input made available to deaf children, the answers to that question were more clear-cut. Since there was only one form of early language input offered to the deaf child, it seemed only natural for parents to do everything possible to make that input accessible. Many of today's parents understand the educational, social, and linguistic benefits of seeing that their children are exposed early to natural Sign Language. For them, these questions about early amplification are more complex.

I have encountered a range of philosophies related to this issue. I perceived a greater emphasis on and acceptance of hearing technologies for Deaf children in Denmark than in Sweden—and a greater reluctance to relinquish those technologies for any Deaf children in the United States. However, these are only my impressions. Policies, practices, and attitudes often vary from school to school; sometimes from class to class. Doctors, audiologists, social workers, home visitors, preschool teachers, speech therapists, classroom teachers, and administrators all advise parents on questions related to use of hearing aids—and are clearly not all of like minds. In addition, there are very different approaches to the use of hearing technologies in these countries for children who are considered hard of hearing and for children considered to be Deaf. I made no attempt to survey actual use or official policy of any country or school. However, in light of this discussion of natural acquisition of spoken language, it seems relevant to share a few related observations for parents and educators whose goal is to raise Deaf children to become bilingual.

If and When

Children who benefit from hearing aids typically accept wearing them. That is an observation mentioned by teachers in both the U.S. and Scandinavia who are conducting bilingual education. In the same way these professionals allow the children's behavior to inform them about early predispositions toward spoken or visual language, children's behavior can also guide the use of hearing aids. But many teachers and speech therapists immediately qualified this guideline as a bit of an oversimplification.

There are many factors surrounding children's willingness to use hearing aids. Some have little to do with whether or not the child is benefitting from sound when using them. For example, during some developmental stages, children say "No" to almost anything imposed on them by adults as a way of exercising their independence. At other times, they are very anxious to please their parents, teachers, or other important adults in their lives. And then there is peer pressure: "All the other kids are wearing them," or "None of the other kids are wearing them."

Parental attitudes in, general, were named as an important factor in children's willingness to wear hearing aids. For many parents, hearing aids carry a positive connotation because they were the one thing that seemed to give the parents some control over the situation after the child was discovered to be deaf. As one parent in the U.S. told me, "It was like my child was bleeding and I couldn't put on a tourniquet." Hearing aids can make parents feel better because it is *something they can do* immediately. If a high value is placed on hearing aids (i.e., "Mom likes me when I have them on...."or if wearing them is equated with "good behavior"), children may wear them whether they benefit auditorily or not. Conversely, if parents do not think aids are important and don't remember to put them on or support their use, children may simply become accustomed to not wearing them, or pick up negative attitudes about their use.

Some children will ask for their hearing aids daily during one stage of their lives, and reject them during others. Others reject them (or accept them) consistently. Some teachers and speech therapists make aids available and try using them for short periods of time, at periodic intervals, with children who don't seem interested. This practice is one way to acknowledge children's resistance while leaving open the possibility for changes in disposition. In some cases, aids of various kinds are used in schools primarily during the teaching of speech; in other cases they are not useful at all for speech reception but help some children to be more aware of environmental noises.

Developmental stages and peers' passing fads aside, children's resistance to hearing aids is often substantive and must not be discounted or ignored. The aids may be uncomfortable, or may amplify sound in a way that is painful or confusing. That is one reason some Deaf adults advocate not introducing hearing aids until the child has the language to tell us what he or she is experiencing. Yet some practitioners feel amplification must be in place *early* if the child is truly to benefit from it. Others question who this supposed benefit is for—the child or the parents? Nevertheless, while some children do not benefit at all, there *are* many children who truly function as hard of hearing (acquiring spoken language through natural processes) who would not have had sufficient auditory access to spoken language without amplification (J. Mahshie, personal communication, May 21, 1994).

Some of the resistance to bilingual education in the U.S. lies in the fear that attempts to facilitate hearing and speech will be neglected—and many children who might otherwise have benefitted from having sound amplified will miss that opportunity. Most advocates of bilingual education are not against speech for those children who can acquire it, it's just that there has been no need to advocate for it in the system since the focus of the system already includes spoken language. In Sweden, as soon as the fight for Sign Language in Deaf children's homes and schools was over, the National Association of the Deaf (SDR) designated as one of its main political goals to focus on the speech component within bilingual education.

Use of hearing aids, per se, has not been shown to preclude natural acquisition of Sign Language; nor has use of Sign Language been shown to preclude natural acquisition of speech in individuals who have sufficient auditory perception. Fears seem due *not* to hearing aids themselves, but to the extreme reactions that the battle over their use has come to represent:

- focus on speech skills to the exclusion of language development

- focus on use of Sign Language to the exclusion of speech training.

Some sensory deprivation studies of animals have been widely interpreted to indicate that if the auditory nerve is not stimulated early, it will atrophy. While this theory is still under debate by neurologists (L. Petitto, personal correspondence, October 10, 1994), it is nevertheless accepted in many educational environments that Deaf children must have early auditory stimulation in order to "learn" how to recognize and comprehend the sounds coming through their aids. This hypothesis has been used in supporting decisions to place hearing aids on infants immediately after discovering they are deaf. There has also, in some settings, been an overgeneralization of this atrophy hypothesis; in other words, an implicit assumption that any need for early auditory stimulation also applies to the need for early and intensive *speech* training (S. Graney, 1994). As noted in earlier discussions, there is more and more agreement among those working in bilingual settings that early spoken interactions should be natural, and meaningful or playful. Many feel that time spent on formal teaching or structured practice with spoken English might actually deter the child's natural wish to learn to talk, and that children might reap greater benefits in less time with structured practice when they have the cognitive readiness and motivation for the task, knowledge of English through emerging literacy, and a language with which to discuss the work.

Cochlear Implants

Many discoveries have been made over the past twenty years about child language in general, and about the normal development of Deaf infants exposed to visual languages. In light of these, we may not yet have enough information to know in which cases receiving amplified signals at an early age enhances or inhibits the brain's processing of natural language, especially with the use of cochlear implants. Nevertheless, new technologies such as cochlear implants are now being considered by some parents of very young deaf children.

Discussion of cochlear implants will not be addressed in depth within the scope of this book, except to re-state that the Deaf community is regularly consulted in Sweden and Denmark on issues related to Deaf children. This issue is no different. At the Second International Conference on Tactile Aids, Hearing Aids, and Cochlear Implants which was held in Stockholm in 1992 (Risberg, Felicetti, Plant, Spens [eds.], 1992), one of the invited presenters was from the Deaf community. The Karolinska Institute, now undertaking a new study of cochlear implants, has met with officials from the National Association of the Deaf to elicit their perspective before beginning this new research. It is clear that cochlear implant researchers in Sweden are interested in Deaf adults' and Sign Language linguists' perspectives on issues related to inserting cochlear implants before the child has acquired a first language. As a result of this more balanced look at the issue, there may have been some dispelling of some of the idea that this technology is a cure for deafness or that deaf children with cochlear implants will become just like hearing children.

The official positions of the National Associations of the Deaf of Denmark and Sweden on use of cochlear implants in children are as follows:

> *The Danish Deaf Association in its position paper [1993]... states the [cochlear implant] operation should not be performed on deaf children. They find a lack of research into the sociological and psychological consequences of the surgery, and a lack of information concerning Deaf culture on the part of parents.*[10]

> *The Swedish Association states, "Our organization, as well as the Association of Parents of Deaf, Hard of Hearing, and Speech-Impaired Children; and the Association of the Hard of Hearing do not approve of cochlear implants for children*

---

10   Dansk Döves Landsforbund, Postboks 704, Fensmarkgäde 1, DK 2200, Kobenhavn, Denmark.

under the age of 18, but accept the operation for deafened people over the age of 18."[11]

The perspectives of the NAD and organizations of Deaf people around the world on use of cochlear implants with children are, for the most part, similar to those above, pointing to the lack of scientific evidence to justify the highly experimental nature of this surgery for young children (see Lane, 1994, p. 23 for an overview of these positions). Some of the concerns shared by Deaf people in many countries were outlined by the World Federation of the Deaf in their recent address to the Conference on Bioethics of the Council of International Medical Organizations.

Much of the publicity on the cochlear implant controversy implies that Deaf people's opposition to the use of these devices with young children is based on a wish to preserve their culture. My perception is that this is a misinterpretation of their real concerns—which have to do with protecting the rights of each deaf child. For centuries, many deaf children have gone through early childhood with little access to comprehensible language. It is appalling to many Deaf adults and other advocates of deaf children to learn that—even though the importance of early access to Sign Language has been clearly established—still more deaf children are now being deprived of early access to a visual language during the process of implantation and the intensive auditory and speech training that follow. Many pre-lingually deaf children in countries all over the world are undergoing this surgical process based on little or no evidence that the implantation will result in their being able to comprehend normal spoken conversation or speak intelligibly as a result of this technology (Lane, 1994).

Results of research must be carefully scrutinized when making decisions about inserting cochlear implants in children who have not yet acquired a first language. Progress that is considered significant from a research perspective is often based on measures of children's ability to discriminate the difference between single phonemes, words, or short phrases, and cannot be assumed to generalize to ability to understand normal spoken conversation. Results tend to focus on ability to perceive such isolated distinctions, rather than on ability to comprehend a spoken conversation at a level comparable to other children their age, to produce spoken language that is intelligible, or to show evidence of solid acquisition of the structures of the language. Results that do show intelligible *production* and ability to understand *connected* speech tend to focus on children and adults who had already acquired spoken language before losing their hearing (see Risberg, Felicetti, Plant, Spens [eds.], 1992, for a variety of studies).

---

11   Available from Sveriges Döves Riksförbund, P.O. Box 300, 579327 Leksand, Sweden.

Furthermore, as Toby and Hasenstab (1991) note, "...it is difficult to separate contributions directly attributable to the multichannel cochlear implant from those associated with maturation or training" (p. 53S). This 1991 article describes a longitudinal study of the speech production of children participating in clinical trials for the cochlear implant approved for children by the U.S. Food and Drug Administration. The authors describe some increases in ability to imitate prosodic aspects associated with the melody of speech during the first year of use with an implant. They also note improved abilities to imitate segmental aspects associated with consonant and vowel production. However, they conclude the article by saying:

> *Some generalization of these skills are evident in increased accuracy of sounds produced under elicited, not imitative, conditions. However, only minimal changes in speech intelligibility or mean length of utterances is evident (Toby and Hasenstab, 1991, p. 54S).*

It is interesting to note that the researchers found this minimal change in intelligibility to be statistically significant. This points to the fact that a change can be statistically significant and still mean little regarding the ability of the child to function in a spoken conversation or display knowledge of the language. The abstract for this article, therefore, has the potential to convey a very positive impression to the lay reader. Rather than describing "*minimal changes in intelligibility,*" as did the concluding paragraph quoted above, the abstract said that "*Speech intelligibility was significantly higher postimplant than preimplant*" (p. 48S). The point is, those who are in a position to make decisions for deaf children must look further than abstracts or summaries of research. They must ask for detailed explanations of the actual tests given to the children and whether or not isolated areas of improvement generalize to intelligible speech.

Most importantly, children with cochlear implants must be looked at *not* in comparison to how they performed before receiving the implant, or even in comparison to other deaf children who are learning to speak. Rather, *their linguistic development must be compared to Deaf and hearing children who are reaching normal milestones in the development of language—whether it be signed or spoken.* If a deaf child is not able to communicate with parents and teachers on the same level as would a hearing child acquiring spoken language or a deaf child acquiring signed language, then the child is—by default—being deprived of important early language due to the process of implantation and exclusive focus on speech development (see section on the importance of natural language input). For these reasons, Sign Language—and familiarity with Deaf children who are reaching normal developmental milestones—is considered by many professionals in Sweden and Denmark to be an indispensable part of the picture for the families of children who do receive (or are being considered for) implants.

Medical professionals may be unaware of the timely development of language and cognition in Deaf children exposed early to Sign Language, and its important impact on literacy and academic achievement. Without such information, the need to ensure the child's early language development and facilitate fully accessible communication between parent and child can get lost in the process of medical evaluation and hope for a cure. Kerstin Heiling, a Swedish psychologist who is a member of the pediatric Cochlear Implant team at the University Hospital in Lund, Sweden, strongly recommends the following steps before application to a cochlear implant program or actual selection of candidates for implants:

A. Before application

    - If the child's deafness has recently been diagnosed, provide crisis intervention according to a regular program.

    - Provide sign language instruction. (Sign language will be needed for communication during the selection and training process and probably after implantation as well.)

    - Let parents and child meet deaf and hard of hearing adults and children

    - Give information about schools and services for the deaf and hard of hearing (Heiling, 1993b, p. 73).

At an international conference in Luxembourg entitled, "Education of Deaf Children with Cochlear Implants: A New Challenge for the Teacher," Heiling, who has conducted longitudinal studies of achievement in Deaf children, described the dramatic rise in the theoretical knowledge of Deaf children in Sweden today compared to orally-trained deaf agemates from the sixties. She first explains that instruction at schools for Deaf children is stabilizing after about 20 years of turmoil, but that education of children who are considered hard of hearing is "still subject to a heated discussion." (See discussion in this book under "Placement Decisions.") She goes on to state:

I have seen the beneficial effects of systematic use of Sign Language with deaf and severely hard of hearing children, both on reading achievement and on socio-emotional development. ...I have also seen the psychological and educational difficulties of many orally trained hearing impaired children. Based on this knowledge, I do not want [cochlear implants] to promote a new wave of restrictive aural/oral training (Heiling, 1993b, p. 75-76).

In the cases where parents do choose to go ahead with this surgery on their children, Heiling recommends:

If implanted children can be seen as belonging to the hard of hearing group with varying ability to perceive speech sounds and varying ability to speak intelligibly,

I think that would be a reasonable level of expectation. In most parts of Sweden today that would mean a bilingual educational approach where Swedish language would be the main mode of communication but with Sign Language as an alternative and complementary channel....but I want to stress that implantation should be undertaken only with great care and that psychological aspects must be considered (Heiling, 1993b, p. 77).

Insertion of a cochlear implant eliminates any existing residual hearing by destroying the fibers at the end of the auditory nerve (Lane, 1994). Comparable research results (Eilers, Vergara, Oller, & Balkany, 1992) indicate that tactile aids may be a less invasive, but perceptually-comparable alternative for children who do not benefit from normal amplification (but whose parents' are interested in finding a way for the child to get sound-based information).

Making Decisions

Clearly, the complex and emotionally charged issues surrounding early amplification (cochlear implants will not be discussed further here) require a great deal of knowledge, awareness, and sensitivity on the part of those making decisions for very young Deaf children. In the past, discussion of such issues was often limited to the input of a doctor or audiologist. Consulting Deaf adults at different stages, as well as keeping the lines of communication with the child open for discussion of such questions is very important. Learning from a variety of Deaf and hard of hearing adults about their personal experience with hearing aids can give parents a better idea of the range of responses: from total rejection (and often anger/resentment that they were forced to wear them), to seeing hearing aids as a useful tool for living, to seeing amplified sound as simply irrelevant and distracting in what is otherwise a visually-oriented approach to life.

Of course, the child's degree and type of hearing loss has some predictive value for judging which children are likely to really incorporate sound, music, and speech into their lives. But even with amplification, sound will not be experienced by children who are deaf in the same way it is by hearing children. It is sometimes very hard for parents to let go of the idea that their child has experienced a great loss in not being able to hear all the same things the parents can hear. But it is important to recognize that a large part of the loss is the parents'. They will not be able to share with the child music and the many other sounds in their lives that hold meaning for them or bring them joy. As people who are grounded in their hearing, it may be difficult for hearing parents to relate to the fact that many Deaf adults do not feel the label "hearing loss" applies to them; they never had hearing to start with so they do not consider it a loss.

Again, talking with members of the Deaf community can help parents see the range of individual choices that Deaf and hard of hearing people make about these issues when they become adults. Many Deaf people, even those who can hear sounds with hearing aids, have chosen not to use them as adults. Their lives are complete without them. Others wear hearing aids for awareness of environmental sounds, and can perceive music and many other sounds through the aids, but do not experience those sounds as pleasurable, interesting, or emotionally moving, as hearing people might. Some feel they never did benefit, and stopped wearing the aids as soon as they were allowed to make their own decision. Still others have had the world of sound and music opened to them through amplification and appreciate using their aids.

Hearing aids in and of themselves do not deprive Deaf children of early language or—as far as we know—preclude the learning of Sign Language. But the practice of placing hearing aids on infants has so often been accompanied by exclusive focus on hearing and speech that the two have become practically synonymous. Resistance by advocates of Sign Language is not so much to amplification but to what hearing aids often represent: the hope that the child will someday function like a hearing child, often resulting in over-focus on hearing and speech to the exclusion of the early development of language and the recognition of the child's many other important strengths. In bilingual environments where both languages are valued, there is an understanding that the ultimate motivation must come from within the child. Students' own ability as they get older to see the value of hearing aids in their lives (or lack thereof) ultimately becomes the most important determiner of hearing aid use.

One teacher who felt strongly that Deaf and hard of hearing children should be together in the same class, described the evolution of the children in their bilingual class with regard to hearing aids.

> I think we can see a line now going from kindergarten class where we used hearing aids up till about 4th or 5th grade. Around that time, the children said, "We are deaf. We do not need hearing aids." And they took them out and put them away. And they did not use them, up until 8th grade when they had a period of working practice out in the "real" world with hearing grown-ups and they were on their own. Nobody else was deaf around them. After that, some of them came back and said, "Well, we want some speech training again now. I think I know where my hearing aid is, so I can bring it, and maybe we can work with speech and hearing sometimes." And they got motivated. So we saw them go from speech and hearing training to saying "No, thank you," and then back to now where the work is different because they already know the Danish language from reading. This has been a great change, and I guess it's quite normal" (T. Ravn, personal communication, March 12, 1992).

In a fully evolved bilingual environment where competence in both languages is nurtured and the child's rights are primary, hearing aids can take on a different connotation. They no longer symbolize an either-or choice or a frightening denial of the child's rights to early language acquisition. Instead, they simply become, for some children, the facilitators of their unique path to bilingualism. For other children, they are not important—which is also perfectly acceptable.

In Sweden, the definition of a fully bilingual Deaf person is one who is fluent in Sign Language and the written language of the majority. Speech, as an added skill, is considered a plus in many settings, but not a part of this basic bilingualism. Those who evidence speech skills are not necessarily more competent in the language than those who do not; in some cases they are less (Barnum, 1984). Teachers in the United States who teach hard of hearing children share many anecdotes about children whose expressive and receptive speech is sufficient for face-to-face communication, but whose skills in written English are very poor and whose reading is not sufficient to support academic work. Competence with face-to-face language that is embedded in context requires a different level of competence than written language or language used for academics (Cummins, 1980; Cummins and Swain, 1986). Nevertheless, one of the facets of bilingualism for a hard of hearing person often includes use of spoken Swedish—facilitated by hearing aids—sometimes as a primary language.

There are now more and more audiologists and speech pathologists in schools for Deaf children in the U.S. who clearly understand the linguistic and cultural issues, who have learned Sign Language and are strong advocates for its use, and who embrace the goal of bilingualism for Deaf children. Such individuals are extremely valuable assets in any successful bilingual program for very young children. These audiologists and speech pathologists are in a good position to observe children's early hearing and speech behavior, and to contribute concrete information to the "cost vs. benefit" discussion of amplification or speech training for each child. They are often in a position to see most clearly that some children's gain from diligent hearing aid use or time spent in speech training is minimal. While the issue of hearing aid use is admittedly complex, a team, some of whom are Deaf, comprised of sensitive speech and hearing professionals, teachers, support personnel, and the child's parents can go a long way toward making decisions regarding hearing aid use that are respectful of each child's path to bilingualism.

The Importance of Natural Language

The Significance of a Community of Language Users

In Sweden and Denmark, many parents are advised today that the children's model for early exposure to visual communication should be the natural signed language of the Deaf community, and the model for aural communication should be the natural spoken language of the majority. Artificial or educationally-based attempts to represent the majority language manually are not considered to be comprehensible language input in either modality (see section on sign-based codes).

One of the main properties that defines a natural language is that it has evolved over time through use by a community. Natural languages, which include the Sign Languages used among Deaf people in various nations or cultural groups for daily communication, reflect the complexity of structure and function needed for in-depth communication (Petitto, 1994a). Exposure to such a language brings with it possibilities for interaction with a community of fluent users of that language.

The significance of a community of language users is far greater for the child than just having someone to talk with. Ongoing use of a language for everyday communication over generations is one of the main ingredients in making natural languages learnable for children—no matter what language community in the world they are born into. This use by a group of people has been identified as a mechanism through which natural languages regulate their level of complexity in a way that reflects the actual potentials of the human brain.

Linguists have overwhelming evidence that natural languages undergo constant change. In less than a century, many uses of English have become archaic, and many more have been added that would not be understood by someone living in 1894. Sign Languages are no different, changing fairly rapidly over the course of generations (Frishberg, 1975, 1976). Since natural languages are developed through use by humans, they are suited from their inception to the constraints and capabilities of humans' mechanisms for communication. Then they are continually regulated—through ongoing use—so that new elements or constructions appearing in the language are modified toward what linguists refer to as greater "naturalness." Natural Sign Languages, like spoken languages, undergo phonological and morphological processes that keep the structures of the language within a range that can be produced easily and efficiently (Battison, 1974, 1978).

Studies in many languages, including Sign Language, have looked at children in language-deprivation settings, that is, when their adult model for language was somehow deficient, impoverished, or not matching the parameters of natural language. The laws of naturalness that underlie languages are so strong that something in these children seems to resist reproducing what was presented to them. Instead, they improve on it, creating their own version of the language or gesture system that is more consistent with the properties of natural languages than was the input they received. Likewise, when Deaf children are presented with artificial sign systems or incomplete models for ASL, their production gravitates away from many of the artificially imposed, sequential features of these speech-based systems and toward inclusion of spatially-based features that are part of natural signed languages (Gee and Mounty, 1986; Goodhart, 1984; Livingston, 1983; Mounty, 1986; Singleton and Newport, 1987; Supalla, 1986). *This occurs even when the children have had no exposure to role models for natural signed language*—strong evidence that natural languages are self-regulated to fit children's mechanisms for perception and production of language.

In addition to these very real biological considerations about the importance of a community of language users, the idea that children need people of all ages and all walks of life with whom to comfortably converse throughout their lifetime is an extremely important consideration. This consideration is often overlooked in widespread decisions in many countries to base the education and upbringing of Deaf children on artificial sign-based codes, cued speech, and other efforts to manually represent the majority language.[12]

The rationale that continues to be given in the U.S. for using manual representations of English is that children who are deaf will otherwise be isolated from the hearing world. But the fact is that few people in that hearing world know or use these manual codes or cues. Methods that accompany speech with manual symbols are generally used only by a child's family or teachers; the rest of the hearing world *just talks*. Furthermore, while there has been ongoing use of sign-based codes and cues in schools for twenty years, there is, to my knowledge, no documentation of a community or large group of deaf or hearing young adults in the U.S. who use manual codes for English, or cued speech, as a primary mode of communication among themselves.

Based on information about the importance of natural language in acquisition processes, the early visual language input for Deaf children of hearing parents in Sweden and Denmark is considered to be one that includes two important components:

- Parents, siblings, and others who are in the process of learning Sign Language

- Deaf children and adults who are already part of the community of people who use Sign Language as their primary mode of face-to-face communication.

The concept seems to make sense to parents. Efforts to ensure the child's early linguistic, cognitive, and social development by providing natural signed language input (whether or not speech will eventually be found to be an accessible modality) take some of the pressure off parents to be sole language models for the child.

---

12   The U.S. Commission on Education of the Deaf report states, "...too seldom recognized is the need for a deaf child to have other deaf children as part of this or her peer group, and to be exposed to deaf adults (1989, p. 9).

Early Natural Language Input and the Brain

There is now further evidence from neurological research supporting the premise that input of natural Sign Languages is equivalent to spoken input in the development of language and human thought. Laura Petitto, working at Harvard University, the Salk Institute, and currently McGill University in Montreal, has engaged in 20 years of intensive studies about the acquisition of language in two different modalities—spoken and signed. During the past 10 years, she has looked at a variety of infant populations in different home language settings: 1) hearing infants exposed primarily to spoken language, 2) hearing infants exposed primarily to signed language, 3) hearing infants exposed to both spoken and signed language, and 4) Deaf infants exposed to signed language. These infants were in homes where one or more of the following natural languages was used: spoken English, spoken French, American Sign Language, and Langue de Signes Québéquoises or LSQ (the language of the French Canadian Deaf community).

Petitto & Bellugi (1988) remind us that, while both signed and spoken languages convey identical kinds of linguistic information and are used to perform the same communicative functions, they differ in some very fundamental ways. They involve different types of signals and are perceived through different sensory mechanisms (visual-gestural vs. auditory-aural), they handle information differently, they are remembered using different memory structures, and are supported by different neural structures. Despite these many variables, Dr. Petitto observed striking parallels in all the children's ability to achieve all linguistic and cognitive milestones. In other words, her data revealed no significant differences in the children's onset, timing, rate, sequence, and content of early linguistic/cognitive milestones across these two radically different language modalities (Petitto, 1993a, 1994b; Petitto and Bellugi, 1988; Petitto and Marentette, 1991).

Part of what is so important about Petitto's studies is that they have provided new information to scientists about how the human brain learns language. In fact, her findings fail to confirm existing scientific theories about the earliest determinants of language development. Until recently, speech was thought to be synonymous with language, and was considered the only natural language for the human species. Many scientists have also assumed that the onset of expressive language in humans is determined by the maturation of speech production/perception mechanisms.

In looking at this assumption, it is important to note that the neural framework (substrate) for the motor control of the speech mechanisms and the neural substrate for the motor control of the hands are represented differently in the brain. Maturation of these two areas of motor control happens at different rates. Similarly, the mechanisms for perceiving spoken and signed language are also distinctly represented in the brain, and do not mature at the same rate. Furthermore, the structural properties of signed and spoken language are in many ways constrained by the perceptual, cognitive, and motor capacities that underlie *hearing and speaking* vs. *seeing and signing* (Bellugi & Studdert-Kennedy, 1980).

Based on this information, one would predict that there should be fundamental differences in the time course, sequence, and content of spoken versus signed language acquisition. Instead, Petitto discovered that *regardless* of which of the four languages (two signed, two spoken) the infants in her study were exposed to, they all achieved the same linguistic milestones at approximately the same times (vocal and manual babbling, first word and first sign, first two-word and two-sign utterances, and so forth).

It is even more significant that the hearing children who were in homes where both signed and spoken languages were used actually achieved all linguistic milestones in the signed and spoken language within the same time frame. *In some instances, they were achieved in the same day!* This occurred despite radical differences in the modalities of the languages.[13]

Petitto's careful study is regarded by scientists as very powerful evidence. It overturns our most basic assumptions about the *biological primacy* of spoken language, indicating that the human brain does not seem to show a preference for one modality over the other.

Beyond Modality

In light of prevailing views, Petitto's next question, then was: "Why *didn't* we find a difference between signed and spoken language acquisition? How could the child's brain possibly be structured such that the behavioral consequences of having 'switched' the child's modality at birth results in no developmental delays, loss, or modification to the language acquisition process?" (L. Petitto, personal correspondence, March 11, 1994).

In her recent writings, Petitto provides a theory about the neurological foundations of language that best explains both her own findings and some of the more fundamental findings in the field. In a nutshell, she has proposed that the only way the brain could tolerate such radical differences in the modality of language input was if modality, per se, was not the key component of the input. Rather, it seems the structure or pattern encoded *within* both the signed and spoken modalities is the key. She further hypothe-

---

13   In addition to the obvious fact that spoken and signed languages have significant differences in
      production and perception, there are also important differences among languages of the same
      modality. For example, Petitto noted, the sign for "cup," is different in ASL than in LSQ. One sign
      is very iconic—looks like someone holding a cup—while the other is more abstract. Nevertheless,
      children all acquired this concept in the same time frame, and were not found to delay acquisition
      of linguistic concepts based on degree of production difficulty or iconicity.

sized that infants are born with a sensitivity to some distributional patterns found in natural language.

Her findings suggest that children's brains are predisposed to be attentive to certain rhythmic patterns related to natural language *prosody* (timing, stress, and contours) as well as to contrasting units common to the *syllable* in both spoken and signed languages. Petitto's data show that these patterns occur consistently in the modifications of adult language (commonly known as "motherese") that users of natural spoken *and* signed languages employ when they engage in communication with infants. Thus, rather than being born with a peaked sensitivity to sound, per se, it would appear that infants are born with a peaked sensitivity to particular types of structures common to natural languages (be they auditory or visual).

When infants perceive these patterns (signed or spoken), it appears that corresponding patterns of neurons are activated. According to Petitto, this would be similar to the way groups of special-purpose neurons are activated when infants see familiar faces. Such activation patterns are thought to be laid down in memory and serve as the most basic input to the production and processing mechanisms involved in the achievement of later language mastery.

In addition to dispelling any myths about the supremacy of speech as the mode of communication favored by the human brain, Petitto's conclusions further reinforce the idea of placing fluent users of natural Sign Language in the child's environment at an early age to ensure that normal development is not interrupted. Her findings also call into question the following practices: 1) relying *solely* on children's incomplete auditory reception of spoken language; in other words, the brain is sensitive to patterning that may be absent when parts of syllables are distorted or not heard; 2) simultaneously using manual signs to represent spoken sentences; this practice produces linear strings of signs that violate the structural properties of natural signed languages and differ greatly in timing from natural languages in general (Bellugi and Fisher, 1972; Bellugi, Fischer, and Newkirk, 1979; Marmor and Petitto, 1979); and 3) adding inflections (suffixes/prefixes) to manual signs in a linear direction, rather than simultaneously incorporating such inflections into the sign as do natural Sign Languages, which further disrupts the timing (Supalla, 1986). Supalla discusses this distortion in timing and the effect it has on the listeners' ability to take in the information:

> *Temporally, a sign, due to its larger physical articulation, requires twice the length of time to produce as a word (Bellugi & Fischer, 1972; Grosjean, 1977); however, the proposition rate (the time involved in producing a sentence) is found to be equivalent in both ASL and spoken English (Bellugi & Fischer, 1972). MCE [manually-coded English], on the other hand, is found to exceed the proposition rate of both ASL and spoken English by a factor of two (Bellugi, Fischer, & Newkirk, 1979). This result may derive from the nature of MCE's sequential structure, in*

which the number of signs in a sentence is found to be higher than in ASL. Bellugi (1980) suggests that MCE fails to meet the proposition rate requirement imposed by the brain's central processing mechanisms. This may very well overload memory, and cognitive processes coupled with the perceptual distortion of MCE's morphological organization, may result in preventing natural language acquisition of English through MCE (1986, p. 5).

Such alterations to natural language input, as well as the halting grammar of adult language learners—as the child's *only* input—may significantly alter the timing and rhythm of the linguistic patterns to which children's brains appear to be sensitized.

Petitto's work serves to further reinforce the Swedish/Danish conclusion: While parents can become excellent communicators with their children very early, it is also important to have fluent models from a community of natural Sign Language users present in the child's environment. When such an environment is provided, their child's timely acquisition of a first language need no longer be a "wait and see" proposition for parents of children who are found to be deaf or hard of hearing.

Use of Simultaneous Communication and Sign-based Codes for the Majority Language

No one I interviewed in Sweden claimed that it would be advantageous to use Signed Swedish with infants and young children as a strategy for promoting mastery of the majority language. I asked many questions to try to understand why each of these countries experienced a comparatively short "signed Swedish/Danish period" before they identified the Sign Language of the Deaf community as the most accessible and complete source of early language input for the largest number of children who are deaf. No single answer was given, but it appears that the rejection of such signed-based codes in both countries was closely tied to the dissemination of linguistic findings.

The Rise and Fall of Sign-based Codes

In Sweden

Older teachers in Sweden told me that, near the end of Sweden's long period of strict oralism, many teachers began to use signs occasionally (often behind closed doors) to support their spoken Swedish. In 1968, a study by Blücher had revealed that many deaf children entering school after 3-4 years in an oral-only preschool had appallingly low skills in understanding spoken Swedish (receptive vocabularies averaging 30-40 words) (Gunnell Blücher, personal communication, May 21, 1990). Concerned teachers responded by starting to use what they referred to as "sign-supported Swedish" in an effort to make their oral-only lessons more comprehensible to the students. Then for five to ten years, schools began accepting manual communication, and teachers were encouraged to learn and use "Signed Swedish."[14] This more formal representation of Swedish, which included manual devices for representing Swedish inflections (suffixes and prefixes), was increasingly used in schools for the Deaf. It was also taught to parents and other adults who took classes to learn "sign language."

During the same period in which this use of manual symbols to represent Swedish was becoming increasingly popular, research was emerging that described the linguistic features of Swedish Sign Language (Bergman, 1975, 1979b). Brita Bergman (now an internationally-known Sign Language linguist), was hired by the Swedish Board of Education to describe Signed Swedish in 1972—a time when she knew nothing of Sign Language. She proceeded to analyze Signed Swedish using principles linguists rely on to analyze any language. It became clear to her rather quickly that there was not enough syntactic and morphologic information (the tools for building meaning) in the visual output of Signed Swedish to make it like other languages (Bergman, 1977, 1979a [English version]). Although she was hired to investigate this promising new approach to teaching Deaf children, a number of problems were revealed during the course of her study that did *not* appear promising.

Furthermore, as she proceeded, she became aware that Deaf people were using a different form of manual communication among themselves than what she had been taught by Deaf people in classes. At first, she had thought she just wasn't proficient enough in Signed Swedish. Later, when she *knew* she was among the most proficient, she still could not understand Deaf adults in conversation with each other. During our interview, she recalled the moment when she had a significant realization:

> *I asked a simple question of a deaf woman, whom I did not know well, about whether or not I should get my car. She did not seem to understand me at all, even when I repeated myself. By then, I knew neither of us was incompetent. It was as if we were not even speaking the same language! (B. Bergman, personal communication, March 9, 1990).*

In order to comprehend what was happening, Bergman ultimately analyzed the structure of both the form of communication that was taught to hearing people in classes and the form that Deaf people used among themselves. This work resulted in not only the intended description of Signed Swedish, but also the beginnings of an in-depth (and still ongoing) description of Swedish Sign Language (Bergman, 1975, 1978, 19979b, 1981, 1982, 1994, and many others). Her analysis revealed that, unlike Signed Swedish, the

---

14   Signed Swedish is capitalized in this context because it refers to a formal, published version called "Signed Swedish."

communication Deaf people used among themselves had all the identifiable properties of a language. In many ways, Bergman's research paralleled and reinforced William Stokoe's seminal analysis of American Sign Language (Stokoe, 1960; Stokoe, Casterline, Cronberg, 1965), the primary difference being that Stokoe's discoveries were initially ignored or repudiated by most American educators of Deaf students.

Over the next few years, Bergman's discoveries about Swedish Sign Language were widely communicated to Sign Language teachers, Deaf adults, and parents, as were findings from another important experiment that set out to look at language development in small Deaf children exposed to Signed Swedish (Ahlgren, 1978, 1980, 1994; also see Davies, 1991b). Much of the information was shared through workshops and classes or through guest lectures, by linguists and Deaf scholars at parent organization and Deaf club meetings.

What followed was a realization among those groups that the "language" typically taught to hearing people who went to classes to learn Sign Language was actually a form of signed Swedish, and not the Sign Language Deaf people really used among themselves. Deaf Sign Language teachers and consumers began to learn more about the grammatical structure of their language, and how it differed from the structure of the Swedish language. Efficient dissemination of ongoing linguistic findings to parents, educators, and policy-makers led both to the eventual recognition of Swedish Sign Language in schools—and to recognition of the problems inherent in trying to represent spoken Swedish manually.

In Denmark

Britta Hansen (1989) summarizes the adoption and later rejection of the simultaneous use of signs and speech in many schools in Denmark. She describes an initial sense of success when teachers in the late 1960s began to use "total communication" or sign-supported Danish and speech, followed by a gradual recognition of some very basic problems with this form of communication:

> *What happened was that, although the communication between deaf children and their hearing surroundings improved drastically [over the days when most classroom instruction was in speech], their Danish skills did not improve to the same extent—and they continued to communicate amongst themselves and with deaf adults in a sign system completely different from the one the hearing parents and teachers used with them—a system the teachers and parent could not understand.*
>
> *In the early 1970s the Center for Total Communication started doing research in deaf children's mutual signed communication as well as in the Sign Language used by deaf adults. Our results showed that this visual system of gestures was*

actually a language in its own right with phonological, morphological, and syntactic rules. We published dictionaries, teaching tapes, books—and set up intensive week and weekend courses for teachers and parents introducing DSL to them. Also, we were asked by teachers of the deaf to evaluate what they actually did while communicating through simultaneous use of spoken language and signs. Our findings questioned the whole concept of teaching deaf children through a monolingual approach, even if this approach now included some visual clues.

She goes on to describe how teachers themselves began to look at the actual communicative potential of what they had been signing:

We taped the teachers' signed/spoken communication, and later on presented the tapes to them without sound—just like it must have been for the deaf children. And more often than not, the teachers could not fully understand their own simultaneous communication when the sound was turned off. Also they realized that, although they believed that they were conveying Danish language to the children using a sign for every word and some of the grammatical signals to convey the actual grammatical patterns (e.g. inflection, time, and plurality), they never did this consistently. Producing a sign takes longer than producing a spoken word, so to keep up the normal speed of speech, they omitted signs as well as salient grammatical visual clues. The children did not get a visual version of Danish—instead, they got a very inconsistent linguistic input, where they often understood neither the signs nor the spoken words. They tended to become "half-lingual," mixing parts of the two languages to survive communicatively, but they had no idea where one language ended and the other began (Hansen, 1989, p. 2).

Sign-based Codes as Input for the Acquisition of a First Language

The Signed Portion of the Input

Bergman's initial analysis uncovered some very basic inconsistencies in the linguistic structure of Signed Swedish, even in it's "textbook" form. She then analyzed the visual output of Signed Swedish in practice and discovered that it was regularly lacking in the inflections and other structures needed to create a manual representation of Swedish. Realizing that her own perception of her subjects' manual signals was influenced by the spoken signal, Bergman always studied her videotapes of Signed Swedish with the volume turned down—in an effort to describe the actual visual information perceived by Deaf people. She found that the visual information the signers produced depicted neither Swedish nor Swedish Sign Language. It became clear to her that, in order to get any information about Swedish while watching the message, one must rely heavily on the spoken part of the signal. For this reason, Signed Swedish seemed to work much better for those who, like late-deafened or hearing individuals, already knew spoken Swedish, and could therefore fill in the blanks. For this reason, it also "feels" easy to learn for people who already know the language, because they are simply being asked to plug in a sign for each spoken word. However, producing all the morphemes represented in their speech actually turned out to be far from easy; it was a cumbersome task that was not performed satisfactorily even by well-trained signers making a conscious effort.

In addition to describing Signed Swedish, part of Bergman's study addressed the question: *Do deaf children exposed to Signed Swedish learn Swedish grammar or pronunciation as a result?* Bergman was not sure how such learning of Swedish could be possible, as her analysis of competent signers had shown that there was little in the output of the manual signal—or what could be *visually* perceived of the spoken signal—that would give the child information about the language of Swedish or the spelling or pronunciation of individual Swedish words. Like signed forms of English, the signs themselves had no connection to Swedish phonology (the system of speech sounds in a language) or orthography (the system for writing in a language) and therefore could not be expected to provide support for learning either. Bergman found that, while basic communication can take place, there is so little information on the lips that a deaf child still does not seem to really learn the makeup of spoken or written Swedish words (or even be aware of their existence) until he learns their form though print. In a 1978 paper to the British Deaf Association, she cautions:

> Signed Swedish, from the child's point of view (and remember that the child has not heard and does not know Swedish), consists of visually perceived lip movements and signs. The child can learn the signs, i.e., the form of the sign and the meaning (concept) conventionally attached to it. The child may even produce lip movements that look similar to those grown-ups use with that sign. But this does not mean that the child really gets hold of the form of the word, spoken or written. (Bergman, 1978, p. 1)

Bergman began this part of her inquiry through informal observation of children whose parents and teachers were diligent about using signed Swedish, and who believed that the children's utterances were also produced "in Swedish." Bergman first asked some parents who had been using Signed Swedish to try to raise their awareness of what their child was actually producing. After observing more closely, most of the parents realized that they had previously thought they were seeing Swedish word order and grammatical inflections signed by their children, but were actually filling in the gaps by relying on their own knowledge of Swedish. Some even called Bergman and explained that, while they were satisfied that they could communicate with their children, they could also see that the children's expression did not show much grasp of the Swedish language.

One couple, however, maintained that their child did sign in Swedish word order, and also mouthed Swedish words simultaneously. This first grader's teachers also felt that the boy signed in Swedish word order. The parents were recognized as being among the most competent at using Signed Swedish, which was confirmed by Bergman's evaluation of their skills. Bergman videotaped the boy talking first with his mother, then with his father. Analysis of the conversation in which the boy talked the most (reminiscing with his father about his stay in the mountains), revealed little evidence of competence in the Swedish language.

Bergman found only one instance during the twenty-minute videotaped segment in which the boy's signs represented a relatively grammatical Swedish sentence, despite the fact that the hearing observers *perceived* that the boy was signing/mouthing Swedish. That sentence was,

"*Jag äter bara god mat*" (I eat only good food).

Bergman analyzed this sentence more closely, but could not find evidence that the boy had a grasp of the spoken words behind the signs. While hearing adults had felt they were seeing the words on his lips, her analysis of the tape showed only lip movements corresponding to the following spoken sounds:

a ä ba o ba

It appeared the boy was neither aware of nor attempting to mouth the Swedish words to correspond with his signs. Rather, throughout the tape, he seemed to be producing lip movements as a non-manual part of each sign. These more open vowels and the bilabial closures (which might represent the consonants M, B, or P) are indeed those movements that could be detected on the lips if one watched this sentence in signed Swedish with the volume turned off. It seems he had learned lip movements to accompany each sign, as these movements were part of the visual input he received when perceiving the communication. However, these lip movements do not necessarily represent the under-lying spoken or written form as they would for someone who knows the language through speaking or literacy. This hypothesis, Bergman asserts, was supported by the fact that, during the rest of the videotape, no speech sounds were represented in the boy's lip movements or utterances *except* those that can be easily lip-read. In other words, she notes:

It is reasonable to suppose that anyone who grows up with Signed Swedish learns to associate certain lip movements with signs....

Even if a deaf child spontaneously produces sentences in which the rules of Swedish sentence formation apply (as in the example above), one must not draw the conclusion that the child knows the spoken or written form behind the *words....For every sign, he must still learn how the corresponding word can be written, pronounced, or manually spelt.*

It may be objected that there are children who grow up with signed Swedish who can read and write. If so, it is the result of teaching—teaching in the sense that the Swedish language has been brought into the child's consciousness at nursery school already, or even in the home. The child's attention has been drawn to its existence, and later the form of the words has been demonstrated in writing and manual spelling. But knowledge of the forms of the words cannot grow automatically, merely through communication in Signed Swedish (Bergman, 1979a, p. 159).

This study became the catalyst for closer scrutiny of children's acquisition of Swedish through exposure to only signed Swedish. Educators and parents began to look more closely at pre-reading deaf children and recognize that, although ideas may be communicated through signed Swedish, young children were still largely unable to respond with sentences (signed, spoken, or written) that demonstrated a knowledge of Swedish, until they begin to learn about the language through text, fingerspelling, and speech training. In dramatic contrast were the levels of grammatical competence in the spoken language of pre-reading hearing children, and the levels of grammatical competence in the signed language of young deaf children in environments where a natural Sign Language is used (Newport & Meier, 1986).

Further Research Support

Since the early '70s other studies in many countries have, like Bergman's, called into question various communication methods intended to manually represent spoken languages for purposes of first language acquisition or classroom instruction. Linguists argue that these manual coding systems do not evidence the salient characteristics common to natural languages. Petitto (1993b), summarizes some of the primary inconsistencies below:

Indeed, there is general scientific agreement about the status of these invented sign-based codes: Invented sign-based codes that are used as a pedagogic tool with deaf pupils are not "real" or natural languages. Instead, (i) they are artificially-invented teaching devices that are not used spontaneously by any native deaf community anywhere in the world, (they do not delineate cultural communities), (ii) they are not passed down from generation to generation of deaf people, (iii) they do not demonstrate the formal linguistic changes that natural languages exhibit over time, and (iv) there is substantial evidence that they are processed in the brain differently from natural language, be it spoken or signed [e.g., Bellugi, 1980; Klima & Bellugi, 1979; Marmor and Pettito, 1979]. (Petitto, 1993b, p. 1).

Furthermore, it is claimed that manual codes for spoken languages (which are widely used in the education of Deaf children in the United States) do not successfully serve as a model for children to learn the language of the Deaf community or the language of the majority (Bergman, 1978; Charrow, 1975; Hansen, 1980b; Hoffmeister, 1992; Hoffmeister & Bahan, 1991; Klima and Bellugi, 1979; Livingston, 1983; Marmor and Pettito 1979; Maxwell, 1987; Quigley and Paul, 1984; Stevens, 1976; Supalla 1986; Svartholm, 1993).

Most studies that *have* attempted to correlate the English skills of Deaf children with various forms of manual English have tested children ages 7 and older (typically much older). It is important to remember that, even by the age of 7, most of these children have had many years of exposure to text for the learning of English. In other words, it cannot be reasonably claimed that the knowledge these Deaf children possess of English was acquired through signed codes, unless that knowledge is measured well before they have learned to read—during the same time period when very young Deaf children exposed to ASL and hearing children exposed to English are already becoming quite fluent in grammatical use of their own language.

Researchers continue to find that the constraints of simultaneously communicating in two different modes result in problems for both the communicator and the receiver. Due to inherent differences in spoken and signed languages, it is not considered possible for individuals to produce both an accurate string of manual symbols for units of meaning in the spoken language and many of the features that are syntactically important in the visual mode (Hansen, 1975, 1989; Marmor and Petitto, 1979). While there is a higher rate of success among signers already fluent in a natural Sign Language, it has been repeatedly demonstrated that these artificial sign systems are not effectively produced by hearing signers who are talking at the same time. In an effort to speak at a fairly normal rate while signing, even the most proficient signers are likely to modify and delete a significant number of the manual symbols needed to represent the words they are speaking (Baker, 1978; Bergman, 1977, 1979a; Crandall, 1978; Hoffmeister, 1992; Johnson and Erting, 1989; Kluwin, 1981; Luetke-Stahlman, 1988; Mahshie, S., 1994; Marmor and Pettito 1979; Nover, 1994; Swisher, 1984).

As a result, it has been asserted, comprehension of the various forms of manual English used in simultaneous communication (talking and signing at the same time) relies heavily on reception of the speech signal and prior knowledge of the grammar of the spoken language needed to fill in linguistic information that is missing in the manual signal (Bergman, 1978, 1979a; Erting, C., 1986; Johnson, et al, 1989). The next section expands on problems with this reliance on the spoken signal for comprehension of sign-based codes.

The Spoken Portion of the Input: A Child-Centered View

Without first-hand experience trying to learn a spoken language through hand signals and lip movements, it is understandable how hearing parents and teachers have felt that signed English (Swedish/Danish/French) is a reasonable way to impart the spoken language visually. As Bergman explains:

Hearing people often find it difficult to understand what it is like for a deaf person only to perceive the spoken language by looking at the movements of the mouth. One way for a hearing person to put himself in a situation similar to the deaf person's is, of course, to turn down the sound during a news bulletin on the television, when the speaker as a rule is shown in close-up....

To a person who lacks hearing, Signed Swedish is a visually perceived combination of speech and signs.... The (adult) deaf person who knows Swedish, who himself reads, writes, and speaks, has of course some chance, if only a limited one, of lipreading connected speech. Anyone who already knows the language can himself supply what cannot be seen, and also has a certain chance of reconstructing what was not understood at an earlier stage, but was clarified in the continuation of the utterance. The more Swedish one knows, the greater one's capacity for lip-reading spoken Swedish. For anyone who knows Swedish, the signs accompanying the speech may function as a help to lip-reading.

For anyone who does not know Swedish, a deaf child for example, the situation is different. All that child perceives of Signed Swedish is lip movements and signs. The child has no knowledge of the forms of the words, does not know how they are pronounced or written or manually spelt, and cannot therefore perceive the lip movements as visual symbols or a visual representation of the (unknown) words. Many of the sounds of the spoken language are simply not visible on the lips. Furthermore, speech is a continuous flow in the sense that there are no gaps between words, which means that only people who know the language can decide where the word boundaries are. Another important point to be mentioned is that the prosodic features (intonation, stress, and quantity [duration]), so important for the understanding of spoken language, are entirely lost in speech perceived visually, not auditively (Bergman, 1979a, P. 159).

Bergman found a way to roughly simulate for hearing people a first-hand experience with trying to learn an unfamiliar spoken language through simultaneous communication. Over the years, she has given a demonstration many times in which she involves the audience—deaf or hearing—in trying to learn a nonsensical sequence of mouthed words paired with Signed Swedish the audience already knows. Even though many in the audience may be able to lipread fairly well, the support of signs (which lends meaning) is of no help at all in learning the form of these new spoken words. Even when slowed and presented one-word-at-a-time, most have great difficulty and do not succeed in figuring out the mouthed words. They catch the vowels and a few visible consonants, similar to those produced by the boy in Bergman's study.

The parts of the words that the audience (and the boy) do see on the lips are somewhat predictable based on our knowledge of the ambiguities inherent in perceiving spoken language without sound. It is common knowledge among those who lipread that there are a few consonants that are visible on the lips, and others that are formed further back in the mouth and therefore cannot be as clearly seen. Even those consonants that can be seen on the lips cannot be easily differentiated from their other "homophones," sounds that 'look' alike (see chart). Without the benefit of hearing whether they are voiced or not, and without knowledge of the language, it would be very difficult to guess possible combinations that result in a word in that language, or to get clues from the rest of the word or sentence (also being lipread) to create some context in an attempt to decrease the ambiguity (see discussion of lipreading under literacy development).

Visually Perceived Consonants
(Homophones)

On the Lips			Further Back		
P	F	WH	CH	T	K
B	V	W	DZ	D	G
M		R	SH	N	H
			ZH	L	
			Y	S	
				Z	

After the demonstration, Bergman points out to the audience that the vowels (which often involve visible opening or rounding of the lips) are the part of the words they could perceive most consistently. But, she contends, these lend little information when differentiating words. She gives an example of a childhood word game she and her friends played, the "E" language. In this "language," all the vowels are substituted by the speaker with a long "e." If the listener knows the code, they can still understand most utterances with no other vowel than "e", which makes possible a kind of secret communication. The same is true if one replaces all the vowels in a sentence with "o" or "a." In other words, the specific vowels are, in the context of full spoken sentences, somewhat expendable. But were one to replace all the consonants in a sentence with "B," no meaning would get through. It is ironic that, although vowels are the parts of the sentence that can be perceived in lipreading without a great deal of ambiguity, they are not the part that gives the listener much critical information, at least not in English, Danish, or Swedish.

Those who take part in this demonstration find that the task changes when the written forms of the words are finally revealed to them. Once they have "learned" the nonsense words in their written form, the mouthed words can be more clearly perceived when the sentence is repeated, as the lip movements have come to represent an underlying word in its complete form.

It is very important to understand that a sign does not "mean" an English word. It represents a concept. For example, the American Sign Language sign "horse," (the same sign used in sentences intended to represent English) does not represent the English word for horse, it represents the concept: *a large four-legged animal....* This concept can also be represented in Spanish or Swedish or Morse Code or English or Venezuelan Sign Language. But the sign "horse" has absolutely no connection to the written or spoken word for "horse" in English, any more than it does to the written or spoken word for "horse" in German. They are simply representations of a concept in different languages. We can no more expect a child to learn the English word for horse by presenting it in American Sign Language (or 'signed English,' which uses primarily ASL signs) than we would expect a child to learn the English word by saying or writing the Japanese word. If we wish to *teach* the correlation, then the child eventually comes to connect the ASL sign with both the concept, "horse," and with the English word. But, in order to do this, the child still has to *learn* the form of the English word (spoken or written), as would Dutch or Spanish-speaking students have to *learn* the English word for the concept "horse" before they could mentally connect it to the word for "horse" in their own language. If we fingerspell "h-o-r-s-e," then we at least have a one-to-one correspondence with the English letters used to spell the word. But the letters still have to be learned through reading or speaking, as there is nothing in the sign that gives information about the *form* of each written or spoken letter (Mahshie, S., 1994).

Bergman's demonstration had great impact. It helped impress upon Deaf adults the difficulty of the task they had been expected to master. And it convinced many parents and teachers that signed codes—though they feel easy to use for people who already know the spoken language—impart insufficient information for the purpose of *teaching* the Swedish language through interaction.

Use of sign-based codes while simultaneously speaking may be sufficient to meet the child's and the parents' early need for basic communication, but most of the meaning seems to be communicated through the sign. However, the signs themselves bear *no* phonological connection to spoken or written words. Therefore Deaf children, like the audience for the demonstration, are forced to rely on what comes through on the lips (complete with the ambiguities described above) as their source of information about the spoken language—until they learn the words through print. The people who participated in the demonstrations could also see that, even if one understands the signs, one does not necessarily have any grasp of the word connected with that sign—until one sees it in print or studies its pronunciation. Unlike the audience, small children are not even looking for or aware of the presence of an underlying spoken word.

Input in Two Modes

When I have conducted this demonstration myself, two interesting things happen. First, some of the Deaf people in the audience initially don't seem to think the demonstration is such a unique thing, because they are *used* to seeing voiceless signed English accompanied by some lip movements—that is what they get during simultaneous communication. (In fact, one time none of the Deaf people watching realized I was signing the sentence without voice, because I had, at first, forgotten to mention it. Clearly, they were not accustomed to relying heavily on the auditory part of the signal.) Second, both Deaf and hearing members of the audience focus on the signs the first few times through, since that's where the meaning is comprehensible to them. (Typically, they are so thrown by seeing unfamiliar lip movements with signs they know that no one has been able to tell me the meaning of my signs the first time through). Once they get the meaning, I remind them that they are being asked to "learn" the spoken words on my lips; then no one looks at my signs at all. Although they understand the meaning communicated through the signs, they quickly realize that the signs are of zero value in helping them to lipread an unfamiliar word. From then on, they focus all their attention on my mouth as I slow down and repeat each word/sign pair separately. It becomes clear to them that they have to pick one form of input or the other, but cannot not concentrate on both at once and still get information about the spoken signal through the lip movements.

Even for some hard of hearing children who have acquired speech naturally and can hear more of the signal, it appears that this bi-modal input may create some kind of linguistic or cognitive overload. Psychological researchers at Stockholm University made an interesting observation during a study of the language development of a group of hard of hearing children attending three different preschools with Deaf children. Analysis of videotaped interactions with their teachers and Deaf and hard of hearing peers revealed that these children could understand utterances in Sign Language, and many utterances in spoken Swedish. However, they often lacked comprehension, or asked for repetition, on those occasions when the teacher happened to sign and speak simultaneously (Ahlström, in press[15]). Consistent with observations noted in earlier sections, use of simultaneous communication in homes and classrooms of very young Deaf children

15   Some of Dr. Ahlström's reports on this study are available as of the spring of 1995. Requests may be forwarded to her at Stockholm University Department of Psychology, S-106 91, Stockholm, Sweden.

seemed to disguise from parents and teachers the children's true level of aptitude (or lack thereof) for hearing and speech (M. Ahlström, personal communication, March 22. 1993).

The rationale for the use of simultaneous communication in many countries has been twofold: to communicate with the child and to impart knowledge about the majority language. Since the second goal has not proven to be successful with pre-reading Deaf children, professionals in Sweden and Denmark recommend that—for communication—the children and their parents be given the opportunity to learn a full-fledged language that is fully accessible to the children, is already in use by a community of individuals, and will ultimately support the learning of the majority language (Israelite, Ewoldt, & Hoffmeister, 1989).   I

Use of Signed Codes by Older Students Whose First Language is Sign Language

The teachers of some bilingual classes in Denmark have found that, as the students became confident in their skills in reading Danish, they also became increasingly skilled at using "signed Danish," even though this was not how they were addressed growing up (W. Lewis, personal communication, March 12, 1992; T. Ravn, personal communication, March 14, 1992).

In much the same way that hearing adults and Deaf adults skilled in English have the capability to produce signed English (because they KNOW English grammar), these students' knowledge of Danish grammar through literacy was sufficient that many students in the older grades found it easy to produce signs in Danish word order. (Unlike invented codes for signing in Swedish or English word order, signed Danish does not attempt to represent all suffixes, prefixes, and some other aspects of Danish grammar.) The students' growing skill in signing in Danish word order is consistent with earlier findings by Hansen (1975) which showed that Deaf people were typically much better at producing signed Danish than hearing people. (See Valli & Lucas [1992] for discussion of the influence of language contact on hearing and Deaf signers.) Successful production is based on fluency in both languages and knowledge of how to use space efficiently to clearly communicate the message. This phenomenon must be kept in mind when looking at correlations between Deaf adolescents' ability to produce signed English and their reading skills. Teachers and researchers in Denmark have noted that students' increasing ability to produce signs in Danish word order is based on knowledge of the language through high levels of literacy, rather than high levels of literacy being brought about by using signed Danish. In other words, there *was* no structured attempt made by the teachers in these bilingual classes (who stayed with the students throughout their compulsory education) to use signed Danish to represent Danish grammar until after the children were good readers and writers. As one teacher explained:

We were always very keen on separating the two languages at first—Sign Language without speech and Danish without sign. We would never mix them. But now when the children have chosen to mix the codes, we do it more, too, and we are mostly still communicating fluently. That is because they know the difference between the two languages, so we all just find the code that fits in that room, depending on who is present and what we are talking about.

Visitors who did not know what we did in the early years might see us going in and out of the codes and using both speech and signs in different ways like this and say our sort of bilingualism is the total communication of the old days, but I don't agree. We have approached Danish and Danish Sign Language very differently than back then, which is what got us to this place with both languages (T. Ravn, personal communication, March 2, 1992).

A number of teachers in Sweden and Denmark observed that when children start out with a whole language approach to reading in the second language (and ongoing linguistic development in their own language), they seem quite ready to focus on breaking down and studying the grammar of the written or spoken language by the time they reach high school age. The students in this class were confident that they could read and write Danish. They also understood fully that Danish was not only their second language, but a language they could not know through hearing. It had become clear to them that they would need to pay close attention to both the grammar and the usage of the language. As they got older and more aware that they would be going out into the work world, they became especially motivated to find ways to practice—in the safe environment of their classroom—their knowledge of Danish coupled with whatever speech and lipreading skills they had acquired. This practice took two forms: interacting with the spoken form only, when the context was very clear, or using spoken and signed Danish simultaneously some of the time during their Danish lessons.

The teacher of this experimental bilingual class described to me how they could have a short spoken Danish conversation in her small reading group, relying heavily on context from reading:

If we are having dialogues about a topic we are learning about, then we would, of course, use Sign Language. But as long as it is a relaxed group—I mean there is open, honest communication between students and teachers—and all the children have strong Sign Language, we can also use more time on speech and pronunciation when they are working through certain Danish texts. If they know what it is about and it is a relatively simple text for them, then you have the opportunity of presenting Danish speech in a natural, interactive way. For instance, my small reading group has already talked about the text in Sign Language. We have written about the text on paper. And then we can try to make a little Danish conversation over this text: In the text, what is going on? Who is there? What did he do?

As long as we stick firmly to the text, and the words in the text, and the persons in the text, I guess we can have a fine little conversation in Danish. But suddenly somebody might, oh, want to say something about his dog at home, if the text was about a dog. But that was not in the text. It did not include the words, the vocabulary, and all the things that we knew were there. And another would say, "What did he say?" and then we would switch to Sign Language and continue from there, "What was it with your dog?" and so on. That is a natural way of using some spoken Danish and of switching codes (T. Ravn, personal communication, March 12, 1992).

A high degree of switching between codes and borrowing phrases or colloquialisms to best express their meaning is common among bilinguals talking to other bilinguals. The situation has been no different between hearing or Deaf bilingual speakers of Sign Language and the majority language (Grosjean, 1992).

The students in this bilingual project class had been with these teachers for many years (as is often the custom in these countries). It seems they not only felt comfortable with them, but were used to being open about communication dynamics and honest about communication breakdowns. The complex interplay between the two languages in their world was clearly a topic for ongoing discussion in this group. While their teachers were diligent about keeping the languages separate at first, the students were not bound by strict parameters that limited them to use of one language or the other. They knew they could always fall back on Sign Language for more in-depth discussion if interactions in spoken or signed Danish with their hearing teachers did not seem capable of carrying the message.

As face-to-face communication has different properties from written communication, and is rich in context, these students who had mastered written Danish found it instructive to utilize their skills for face-to-face interaction with their teachers. This use by older students of signs to represent Danish is consistent with the notion that successful production and reception of sign systems is based on knowledge of the structure of the language. That knowledge, which these students seem to have acquired through literacy (and speech instruction that was tied in with their emerging knowledge of Danish), could now be put to use for interaction using approximate Danish syntax represented orally or manually.

Sheltered Subject Matter Teaching

This face-to-face use of students' second language during their Danish lessons seems to have some parallels with what is known in the bilingual literature as "sheltered subject matter teaching" (Krashen, 1991). In other words, when students have had some years of exposure and are fluent in their second language, they can begin to receive limited instruction through that language—but *only* in areas that are context-embedded (surrounded by activity and context clues) and are *not* cognitively demanding (Skutnabb-Kangas, 1994). This is in some ways like the "spoken conversation" to which Lewis refers, where the students knew the Danish text inside-out before trying to talk about it in the spoken form of their second language. One factor in successful sheltered subject matter teaching is that the teachers are fluent in both languages and can readily switch to the students' first language if there are misunderstandings, or if a complex explanation of a concept is required.

This practice, however, cannot be borrowed directly from other bilingual or ESL (teaching English as a second language) methods. First of all, these methods assume that children enter this second language instruction with a solid base in the first language as a prerequisite, and their cognitive and linguistic development in their first language is, ideally, supported throughout their education. Similarly, the teachers in Denmark expressed to me that they did not use these methods with the children they felt were not yet fully competent in Sign Language, were struggling with written Danish, or had some confusion about the differences between Danish and Danish Sign Language. Furthermore, the Danish teachers conducted these activities only as reinforcement during lessons where the focus was learning Danish, and not as a way to teach other subject matter where the content—not the form—is the main focus. Another critical difference from the ESL literature is that the children and adults in those bilingual or ESL classrooms generally have access to *both* the spoken and written form in acquiring their second language and in receiving sheltered subject matter instruction. Finally, as discussed earlier, using a code to represent a language in a different modality is not the same as using that language. Despite these qualifications, it was reported that the students and teachers in this setting perceived that there were some benefits from practicing with these face-to-face representations of Danish.

The situation described here should not be over-generalized. It was given only as an example that the progression of Deaf students' language learning—and their capabilities and flexibility with both languages (or in the case of these students, four languages)[16]—is being further revealed as such language-rich, visual educational environments are being put into place. What was described has not been formally tested in other environments, and seems to rely to a large extent on these highly aware teachers and students who know they can offer feedback about the process at any time.

---

16   These students were learning English and German (and, in some cases, American Sign Language) in addition to their own Danish Sign Language and Danish.

Furthermore, the notion that older, more literate Deaf children are capable of producing and comprehending sign-based codes should not be taken to mean that students at older ages can be expected to understand teachers or interpreters who have no skills in the Sign Language of the Deaf community, but who learned only a one-word-one-sign correspondence. As discussed earlier, unless the listener has the benefits of substantial auditory perception, the communication of such signers lacks the syntactic "glue" needed to be comprehensible—providing a comprehensive representation of neither spoken nor signed language for the receiver. The teacher with this training does not possess the skill needed to clarify misunderstandings through clear explanations in Sign Language or to understand the students' conversations—important attributes of any teacher.

There is still much to be learned about optimal methods of teaching the majority language at various stages of a Deaf child's development in an environment where Sign Language is considered the student's primary language. For example, if the goal is *truly* to represent English structure for purposes of reinforcing knowledge of the language through face-to-face interaction, then other more phonetically-based ways of making the spoken language visual (cued speech, visual phonics) might prove to be more useful in these limited contexts than simultaneous communication.

When I shared news of this strategy with teachers in Sweden, they could not imagine putting aside the clear, concise, rich communication they felt they had with their students through Swedish Sign Language for even a short time in lieu of what they considered to be the incomplete, inferior, limited level of communication they could achieve through spoken or signed Swedish. Admittedly, the signed Danish used was not a whole language in itself, and therefore would not be comprehensive input for learning a first language or for communication of highly technical material. Since the Danish students' first language and ease in communicating with their parents and teachers was well-established by this age, the students' increasing facility with signed Danish and their use of it in some educational contexts was seen as just another manifestation of bilingualism in their everyday world.

The Learning of Sign Language by Parents

As noted earlier, the rationale for the use of simultaneous communication in many countries has been twofold: to communicate with the child and to impart knowledge about the majority language. Since the second goal has not proven to be successful with pre-reading Deaf children, professionals in Sweden and Denmark recommend that—for communication—the children and their parents be given the opportunity to learn a full-fledged language that is fully accessible to deaf children, is already in use by a community of individuals, and will ultimately support the learning of the majority language (Israelite, et al). In the U.S., even though linguistic research results have ruled out sign-based codes as a comprehensive form of first language input, it is commonly argued that they should still be used in hearing homes. When I traveled throughout Sweden and Denmark, I asked questions during interviews and observations about parents learning the Sign Language of the Deaf community: *Can they really learn Sign Language? Do they have the time? Have Sign Language teachers found effective ways to teach them?*

Given a child-centered approach to evaluating the quality of language input to the child, as well as opportunities to get to know Deaf adults, parents seem quite motivated and able to learn Sign Language—rather than threatened or confused by it. For the most part, parents in Sweden and Denmark are given excellent opportunities to learn, since teaching parents the language is seen as part of ensuring an adequate education for the child. The target language being taught to parents is Swedish/Danish Sign Language, the language of the Deaf community, or "Deaf Sign Language," as it was referred to by parents and teachers in both countries to differentiate it from signed Swedish/Danish.

Choices

The fact that parents are taught Sign Language does not mean they will use it at all times to the exclusion of their own language; nor does it mean they will be the sole language models for the children. But those who learn Sign Language come to respect it as a result of that study. They support it as the fully-valid language of their child and therefore are not trying to correct the child's Sign Language grammar in the direction of the majority language; they recognize that it is a completely different language. Their use of Sign Language is about interaction and communication, not about the teaching of Danish or Swedish grammar.

According to social workers, linguists, teachers, and the parents themselves, parents who learned Sign Language have a different kind of communication with their child than parents who learned a signed version of the majority language, even when they choose to use simultaneous communication. The signed part of their communication is then based on the spatial principles and inflections (incorporated into the sign) that are characteristic of natural signed languages (rather than adding them linearly, as do spoken languages). Even when parents do talk and sign at the same time, it is reportedly because that is the mode of communication that seems to work best under certain circumstances where both Deaf and hearing children are present—not because their goal is to teach or represent Danish. Britta Hansen, founder and director of Cogenhagen's Kastelsvej Center, explained to me that parents' signing while talking not only was more comprehensible because it came from a knowledge of Deaf Sign Language. This knowledge also carried with it opportunities for interaction which then increased parents' awareness about what this language is for Deaf people:

> *There is a huge difference in the signed output and the quality of the communication when the thing parents learned to understand and produce is Danish Sign*

Language. It is as different as night and day from the days when parents learned only "signed Danish" vocabulary, and the communication was based on single signs paired with spoken Danish words. First of all, they can understand their children, and their children's friends, and can carry on meaningful conversations with deaf adults (Hansen, Personal Communication, December 14, 1990).

Hansen has a no-nonsense attitude about the fact that the language of the home of most Deaf children is spoken Danish. No matter how fluent family members of today's Deaf child become in Danish Sign Language (DSL), the language used by parents and other family members in communicating at home will sometimes be spoken Danish. Professionals accept that talking and signing at the same time is probably the mode used for practical reasons at least part of the time in the hearing families of Deaf children. Nevertheless, Hansen notes that, with training in Deaf Sign Language, the parents have the skills to communicate the visual part of the message in a way that their Deaf child is more likely to understand. These parents also have the consciousness about what is getting through to the Deaf child. They can then choose, at the first sign of misunderstanding, to stop the sign-supported Danish and communicate clearly and directly—without voice—to include the Deaf child. Depending on the setting, family members sometimes have to make a choice to speak Danish, speak Danish and sign, or use Sign Language.

There is much talk about choice in the education of Deaf children in the United States, but if parents are never taught American Sign Language, which is a very different language from English, they cannot make the choice described above. Parents in the United States, many of whom are only taught signs in English word order, are not given the chance to move into the arena of Deaf Sign Language, which brings with it the skills to understand their children conversing with friends as they grow more fluent, and the tools to have conversations with Deaf adults in their own language. Hansen describes the parents of children in the first bilingual class in Copenhagen in 1982, their progression in learning Sign Language, and their resulting motivation to create opportunities for their children and themselves to spend time with Deaf people:

The parents were not a homogeneous group—although they had agreed to the same ideology. Several parents continued using simultaneous communication at home—also because they felt it was the easiest and most functional means of communication within a hearing family, but others slowly changed their style of communication into still more DSL-like signing. They applied for courses in DSL made especially for them as a group, and engaged our Centre for Total Communication to set up the courses. We found that, because their signing skills were very different, it was helpful to use videotapes of their own children's signing during the courses, which provided a very beneficial approach. To study the spontaneous signing of one's own child proved to be very motivating to further one's own understanding of DSL.

Also, the parents started to organize special events for themselves and their children where they, for example, went camping together with many other parents of deaf children and engaged deaf adults as assistants—and they arranged activities where their deaf children could meet other age-groups of deaf children and deaf adults (Hansen, 1989, p. 3).

In many areas of the U.S., parents are not taught Sign Language, but rather have learned single signs to correspond with English words. Without sufficient opportunity to learn the Sign Language of the Deaf community, parents will likely have a very hard time understanding Deaf adults, or their own children in conversation with their friends.

From an early age, Deaf children whose parents do learn some signing generally modify their signing to match their parents' skill level (Philip, 1994; Valli & Lucas, 1992), so one-on-one communication between parents and their own child can proceed. However, without sufficient opportunity to learn Sign Language, parents cannot be expected to understand their children's conversations with other users of American Sign Language. For this reason, Sign Language lessons in Sweden and Denmark often focus on building receptive skills in Swedish or Danish Sign Language, to ensure that parents and teachers *understand* the children, and can make choices about how they—as parents—will communicate in various settings.

While Sign Language lessons in both countries often focus on building receptive skills in Swedish or Danish Sign Language (including studying tapes of children signing to ensure that parents and teachers understand the children), it was rather adamantly explained by Britta Hansen, that the teaching goes much further than talking about receptive skills and language models. The emphasis at every stage in the child's development is on letting parents know that they CAN communicate with their children, and on encouraging them to feel comfortable and make the most of whatever level of Sign Language they have mastered. It is important that parents see their own competence, and the crucial role they play as active participants in an ongoing conversation with their children. While parents may not be the primary language models for their Deaf children's first language— it is made clear to them that they *are* the primary communicators in their children's lives. Messages about life and love and family and safety and security and values come through them, so their expressive skills are very important.

As explained by Gallimore (1994) at a workshop in the U.S., parents must do whatever it takes to communicate their meaning—and their love—to their Deaf child, even if it means using lots of pointing, gesturing, and pantomiming at first. It is important that parents be themselves, and are animated and involved, and get their message across. Being concerned about whether or not they can adequately model manual English or American Sign Language grammar is not the primary role of hearing parents of very young Deaf children, but rather to find ways to make sure the child understands what is going on around him or her, to spend happy times with their Deaf child, and to see that both Deaf and hearing children are full participants in family interactions.

The Parents' Own Language

A common motivation for teaching parents manual codes for English in the U.S. relates to the question raised often by professionals, "What are the consequences of teaching the children a language that is different from the language of the home?" When considering this question, it is important to be very clear about the fact that, whether it is English or Spanish or Japanese, the language of the home of most parents of deaf children is a *spoken* language, which is not fully accessible to the child no matter how much the parents want the child to acquire their own language. Giving the Deaf child very early access to natural Sign Language is seen, in Sweden and Denmark, not as a barrier between parent and child, but as the *best* way for the Deaf child to acquire ultimate fluency in the parents' language. Given a linguistic orientation to the two approaches, parents seem to rather easily grasp the concept that signed codes do not accurately represent the spoken language of their home, nor do they provide a tool for the child to communicate with extended family and mainstream society.

Learning the language of the child's home and society will clearly be a priority in the Deaf child's education and upbringing. But parents can accept that the language of the home may not be the *first* language their Deaf child will learn or the primary language that child will use for face-to-face communication throughout life. One parent I interviewed in Sweden described an attitude of mutual respect and sharing of knowledge that tends to grow over time between Deaf children and their parents: As the children get older, they are motivated to learn more from the parents about the written or spoken form of the parents' language—Swedish. And they come to realize that the parents, likewise, are life-long students of the children's language—Swedish Sign Language. For parents who are willing learners of Sign Language—their own Deaf children and their children's friends can be parents' greatest resource for continued learning.

Something In-Between

There has been a popular movement among parents and educators in the U.S. which acknowledges that invented sign-based codes with all their sequential suffixes and prefixes are, indeed, impossible to produce during conversation in a way that accurately represents the English language (see earlier section on sign-based codes). It is also claimed that the English skills of children whose parents and teachers produce a less rigorous representation of the spoken form are as good as or better than those whose linguistic input was based on an attempt to represent all the inflectional morphemes of English. Furthermore, it has become clear that, while Deaf children may use some of the markers of English structure their parents and teachers *do* produce (for example, overgeneralizing the sign for "-ing" in inappropriate contexts [Maxwell, 1987]), the children have not been found to produce them with consistency, nor do they produce the many other morphemes needed to reflect English structure. Therefore, it is being advocated that parents do not need to sign every word, suffix, and prefix, but can use what they refer to as a more "natural, relaxed" version of manual English which is colloquially referred to as PSE or pidgin sign English.[17] Ideally, users of this form of signing also attempt to make their signing more "conceptually" consistent with ASL (i.e., vocabulary is chosen on the basis of a word's meaning, not its English spelling), even though they may have had little or no actual contact with individuals who are fluent in ASL.

On one hand, advocates of this approach are making an important acknowledgement that the closer parents and teachers move to the biologically-evolved production found in natural signed languages, the more successful their visual communication with the Deaf child will be. On the other hand, the same people are still resisting ASL in the classroom and asserting that "PSE" must be used because "the children must have a chance to see English." I recently heard a parent adamantly opposing ASL and arguing for use of simultaneous communication (in this case, employing PSE while talking at the same time), so that her child "would be exposed to a visual representation of English." During this conversation, someone asked her about the efficacy of representing each English morpheme (and pointed out that she was not even coming close to representing them in her current conversation). She explained that one did not need to represent every part of English, but just needed to use signs in English word order comfortably while speaking as a way to give the child 'visual English.' It is certainly true that what works for the parents is crucial for communication in the home, and that communication may be the most important thing in the home. Clearly, parents must be comfortable and the communication must flow easily. But this parent and others are advised to be careful not to fool themselves into thinking that this *communication* is presenting the child with comprehensive input in the English language.

Unfortunately, this parent's argument is a very circular one. If one claims that it is important to represent English for language input purposes, then one must *really* represent English. Yet, English is an auditory-aural language, and much of its organization and meaning are represented through vocal prosody (timing, stress, intonation). We may decide to disregard these important auditory cues and attempt to represent every part of the English language manually. However, we then encounter problems with human beings' ability to physically produce all of this sequential grammatical information through manual movements in a time frame that matches the receiver's short-term memory and other perceptual constraints (see earlier explanation about timing under

17   See Valli & Lucas, 1992 for more accurate descriptors, as well as theoretical discussion of the outcomes of language contact between ASL and English for both Deaf and hearing signers.

section on natural language.) Furthermore, there is no phonological connection between the signs and the spoken or written forms of English (see earlier discussion). Because of these inherent problems, the participants' need for fluent real-time communication results in the speaker taking short cuts and leaving out what cannot be conveniently produced while speaking. This short-cut form, then, no longer represents English visually, resulting in children needing to rely heavily on ambiguous lip movements (and finally reading) for the learning of English. If children must learn English through these other forms, then they may as well be allowed to learn a natural, visual language for the acquisition of internal linguistic competence that will later contribute to proficiency in English.

One educator at a school in the Midwest that has been rigorous about using Signing Exact English for many years recently shared her observations about their success with *not* trying to represent every part of English. Based on evaluations of students who had received different forms of input, they had decided it would be best to encourage parents to use ' PSE.' She asked me if I had information from Sweden and Denmark about how best to teach PSE to hearing parents. My answer was consistent with practice in Sweden and Denmark: *Teach parents the language of the Deaf community and the influences from their own English grammar will naturally result in PSE.* In the process—their signing, which is likely to roughly approximate English word order—will become more spatially based, they will become familiar with the linguistic sophistication and efficiency of ASL, and they will gain knowledge of the structure of the language, as well as the culture of those who use it, to build upon in understanding their children and other Deaf people.

Sign Language Teaching

Sign Language researchers and teachers in Sweden and Denmark have learned a great deal about the benefits of teaching Sign Language to hearing parents and teachers in large, intensive blocks of time (periodic 3-day weekends and one- or two-week courses) with one or more of their teachers being Deaf. This large block of time allows parents to focus all their attention on learning, lets them have more interactive opportunities for practice with their Deaf teachers and with other learners, and provides an opportunity to share experiences with the other parents they meet in the classes.

Although parents seem to learn well under these circumstances, I also noticed among both parents and professionals a degree of realism—a recognition that these parents are adult learners of a second language who have jobs, lives, and often have other children in addition to their Deaf child. Nevertheless, according to the preschool and first grade teachers I interviewed, a high percentage of parents in these countries DO learn enough of the language of the Deaf community to communicate high-level concepts to their children well before those children enter first grade.

The parents do not communicate like native signers, but many become quite fluent. Most importantly, they can *understand* their children and form lasting relationships with Deaf adults. It is often the parents who advocate the hardest for their children to have consistent access to fluent models of Sign Language, as they have become aware that their sophistication with that language will take time. Brita Bergman described in 1978 some of the hearing parents who were among the earlier groups to start learning Deaf Sign Language:

> The Sign Language production, of course, is likely to be more or less influenced by Swedish. If hearing people are taught Swedish Sign Language rather than Signed Swedish, they will acquire greater sign language skill with more possibilities of variation. They will then be able to choose to use either a more genuine Sign Language or to sign and speak simultaneously (with or without voice). This is perhaps the most natural and simplest for hearing people, and with a base in deaf Sign Language, they can sign more in a manner adapted to how deaf people sign.
>
> The greatest benefit, however, of giving hearing people instruction in Swedish Sign Language rather than signed Swedish, is that they will be able to understand what deaf people sign. (Bergman, 1978, p.2).

Minority Parents

Parents who are recent immigrants and whose home language is not Swedish/Danish are not always in a position to learn Sign Language, as their livelihood depends more on first learning the language of the majority. The content of Sign Language courses *is* fairly accessible to speakers of other languages, as instruction relies on face-to-face interaction with a Deaf teacher rather than on ability to read or speak Danish/Swedish. Nevertheless, parents in this situation do not always get the information they need or have the time/language skills to petition for support, childcare, and release time from work to attend the classes. More attention and support is being given to these parents, but the situation is still far from satisfactory. Formal instruction in the home language for their Deaf and hearing children is supported in the schools. And there are attempts to get language support for home visitors to families of Deaf children. However, a better system still needs to be developed for getting instruction to parents of other cultures and improved early services for their children.

In addition to practical obstacles to learning Sign Language, Leslie Proctor, an African American parent who is Coordinator of Family Education at Kendall School, describes an important attitudinal obstacle:

> Since language carries power, minority language users inherently view ASL as a language without power in the majority community. For example, Black English, although powerful "in the streets," does not bring jobs or inclusion in upwardly

mobile society. And parents who grew up in another country struggle daily in the U.S. because of their accent or their insufficient command of English. Their minority deaf child is viewed by parents as having a double language burden. This may not be openly expressed, but rather felt in the "gut." English, then, is the option for overcoming the barrier, and ASL is viewed as "backward" English. There is resistance. (L. Proctor, personal correspondence, July 12, 1994).

Because minority parents tend to value the spoken language of the majority over Sign Language, and because a higher percentage of minority children were deafened after learning to talk (due to injury or illness), it is also more difficult for minority parents to find Deaf adults who use Sign Language *and* who adequately know and appreciate the language of the family.

Whatever it Takes

Adding that parents who were recent immigrants were too often the exception, one parent (who had been coordinating a 3-day weekend Sign Language retreat for parents in her area every fall for years), asserted during our interview, "Almost all parents of deaf children today in Sweden sign" (Berret Mayor, personal communication, August, 1990). After dealing with hundreds of parents who have attended the workshops, she has concluded that such broad-based learning of Swedish Sign Language by parents is due to their real acceptance of Sign Language *as a language their children will be using for life.*

In the U.S., we rarely have a chance to observe such outcomes, because our system is not set up to provide parents with intensive Sign Language instruction and with timely opportunities for interaction with Deaf adults. Hence, we come to underestimate hearing parents. When parents do have such opportunities, both their Sign Language skill and their attitude toward their child's language become more like these Swedish parents. This was true of the parents I met in Livonia, Michigan who got a positive early orientation to their children's being Deaf, excellent Sign Language instruction from Madonna College, and considerable support and encouragement from Deaf adults; also in those parents affiliated with the schools named in the introduction who have had a high degree of interaction with Deaf adults and were given a linguistic and cultural orientation with which to view their infant.

The hearing parents who have had such opportunities, whether in Sweden, Denmark, France, or the U.S., have often become the strongest advocates of other parents' right to similar opportunities for themselves and their child (Bonaventura Statement (Appendix F); Thomas, 1989; Treesberg, 1988, 1991). Mas's description of the parents involved in the experimental bilingual classes in France is typical of parents I have met in the U.S. whose children have had the opportunity to become part of an educational environment that truly understood and supported their full potential:

The parents, with deep emotion, discovered what their deaf children could become, regained hope, learned sign language, and became a totally committed part of this unknown world (Mas, 1994, p. 74).

Given the opportunity, it seems parents do want to learn Deaf Sign Language and become facilitators in their children's building of strong ties with other Deaf people. The Maryland School for the Deaf, which recently instituted a policy of bilingual education, offered ASL classes to parents for the first time in the fall of 1993. The administration was hoping that about 50 people would show up the first night. More than 180 arrived! One family brought 10 in all, including siblings, aunts and uncles, and grandparents. The school was happy to ensure that there was room for everyone in the classes (Tucker, 1994).

Despite the popular belief that some form of manual English is easier to learn for hearing parents, my sources observed that hearing parents become MORE, not less, likely to stick with their efforts to learn when they are taught the language of the Deaf community. Parents reportedly feel that Sign Language offers a dynamic, efficient way to communicate with some very interesting, alive people whose experience is relevant to them in the raising of their Deaf child. This feeling differs radically from the one associated with learning a one-word-one-sign code from a book or without opportunities for interaction. Because they are learning the Sign Language used by Deaf people, parents can interact more easily with Deaf children and adults, which gives them ongoing opportunities for reinforcement and continued learning. A few instructors in Sweden commented that fathers seemed to get more involved than in the days when parents learned Signed Swedish primarily from a book or sitting in a class. Now many parents have opportunities for real interaction with Deaf adults and children, and the communication takes place in the context of an activity, a ballgame, or a job to be done.

Hearing parents on a panel at a recent workshop in the U.S. (Hom, et al, 1994) agreed that, while they might not sign as proficiently as they would like, their real satisfaction is in seeing their child use language so freely and fluently in all the ways that really develop their identity, their "humanness." One parent explained that, after years of what was considered a successful oral education, she felt that acquiring ASL finally gave her child the means to express her 'essence.' This was much more important to the mother than her own ability to communicate in her own language. Another parent noted that, while her own communication is sufficient for making herself understood by her child and other Deaf people, she would not be considered fluent. However, she feels the main thing is that her son, now grown, knows she can always understand him. She said he can go 'a mile-a-minute' and she will understand, because he talked to her so much over the years about anything and everything.

It seems clear that parents will go to great lengths to do what they think their child needs. Many parents in the United States today spend countless hours conducting auditory and speech training activities with their children. Professionals who have worked with parents in bilingual settings observe that the type of parents who "bent over backwards" to pursue oralism, or cued speech, or to learn Signing Exact English—when that was what they were told their child needed—are the same type of parents who will expend the energy needed to learn ASL and to build ties with the Deaf community—if *that* is what they are convinced their child needs.

One Swedish parent I interviewed discussed this willingness. She learned Sign Language when her hard of hearing son (who now has intelligible spoken Swedish *and* English) was six. She saw the other world that was opening up for him as he began to interact with peers who were Deaf. She also learned Sign Language, she said, because he couldn't understand her when he had a cold, or when they were in noisy environments. She speaks for many parents, who will do whatever it takes:

> *If they told me that you have to learn Chinese, or you have to stand on your head when you are talking to your child, I would have done it because I think it is one of the children's rights that their surroundings should be understandable. And this was a way to get it completely understandable for him — to use Sign Language (M. Ahlström, personal communication, March 16, 1992).*

Placement Decisions

Integration of Deaf Children into Classes with Hearing Children

"No one in Sweden today advocates regular mainstreaming of prelingually deaf children." (Heiling, 1989, p. 13). Although this may sound like an overstatement, it sums up the general attitude I encountered in Denmark and Sweden. The topic simply did not come up unless I raised it as a question in the interviews, apparently because it is not currently an issue in the education of children who are profoundly deaf. While educational settings with hearing children are known to be excellent in their efforts to include children with various types of disabilities, providing a free and appropriate education for Deaf children is seen in these countries as a very different undertaking. Policies regarding Deaf children reflect the premise that linguistic, cognitive, and social competence are best achieved in environments that provide full communicative access to curricular content and socialization. The priority is to ensure Deaf students full participation in Swedish society through bilingualism, and an excellent education through two fully accessible languages, Sign Language and literacy in the majority language. While Deaf children also work to develop their skills in spoken Swedish/Danish, their success or failure as students and their ability to fully integrate into society as productive, well-educated citizens is not based on this variable.

When I asked about the mainstreaming of Deaf children in Sweden, one fairly high-level government official claimed, "For the most part, they have always been educated in separate schools. In the 1970's, there was a move to integrate Deaf children into public schools, but it was unsuccessful." Interviews with such individuals "on the periphery" tended to minimize the extent and impact of the mainstreaming experiment that took place during that time. But Deaf consumers saw it as a serious threat. The following quote represents the viewpoint of many Deaf adults that efforts at mainstreaming posed a very serious threat to Deaf children and to the system of state schools.

> *The early 50's saw the beginning of the notion that deaf children should be placed in schools for hearing children. Audiological equipment had been greatly improved and deaf children were now being diagnosed as having "residual hearing." It was considered possible to communicate with them via speech with the use of technical aids. The best environment for doing this was thought to be schools for hearing children. These new ideas were carried through. During the 50's and 60's and a good deal of the 70's more and more deaf children were placed there in groups, but later on it became more common that one deaf child was placed in a group of hearing children.*

> *At first this process was called "normalization."...Then, normalization was renamed "mainstreaming." Deaf people should not isolate themselves and form a group of their own it was now said. They had to become part of society. It was believed that this aim would be achieved more easily by starting in schools for hearing children.*

> *It was a sign of the times that handicapped people should not be treated as different and put away in special institutions. They were now to be treated as "normal" people, attend ordinary schools and lead an ordinary life in the community, just like everybody else. Special schools for the handicapped were a segregated school form and should be abolished. All groups concerned, except deaf people, supported this ambition, which was seen as something noble. Since deaf people did not support the new idea it was said that we did not know what was best for us. Nobody could understand why we wanted to keep segregated schools for the deaf. Mainstreaming became prestigious and segregation was something ugly. Many special schools were closed and the schools for the deaf only just made it" (Bergman & Wallin, 1989, P.13).*

The political discussion described by this scholar closely parallels one that is currently under way in the United States. Many advocates of children with various disabilities are fighting hard for "full inclusion," the idea that all children should be educated in their local school district. They claim that the least restrictive environment for all children is the public school classroom.

Wallin's views, presented at the international DEAF WAY conference in 1989, represent a Deaf individual's account of the struggle and embody arguments that do not appear to be openly opposed in Sweden today. His comments continue as follows:

But we thought about the well-being of deaf children. We realized the disastrous consequences of mainstreaming at an early stage in the process. We differ from other groups of handicapped people when it comes to one thing, something that is crucial to the success of mainstreaming—we cannot communicate by way of hearing. They all can. ...If mainstreaming is to succeed, all communication has to take place in sign. There are no shortcuts, which is something the supporters of mainstreaming had not acknowledged.

Our view was that if deaf children are to develop as other children, only using another language—Sign Language, they must be allowed to attend a school for the deaf. A school for the deaf, with a signing environment will be just like any other school. There will be no difference in instruction and relations, apart from the fact that everything will be based on sight instead of hearing. In a signing environment deaf children can develop together. There will be deaf children of all ages, as well as deaf adults who work there. The presence of deaf adults is important if the child is to find role models in an otherwise hearing society. In a group of other deaf people they can feel that they are just like everybody else, with their advantages and their shortcomings. Not being able to hear becomes something peripheral and of minor importance....(Bergman & Wallin, 1989, p.13).

Wallin credits cooperation between parents and Deaf consumers in referring to the changes that have taken place since the days of integrating children who were profoundly deaf. He states,

If this cooperation with the parents of deaf children had not started, there would probably be no schools for the deaf in Sweden today.

But he also traces the history as a difficult one in which hearing parents and Deaf adults did not always see eye-to-eye.:

Of course parents did not oppose the idea of mainstreaming.... Since deaf children will grow up to live in a hearing society it was considered best if they could start getting used to it as early as possible. Promises were made that the children would get all the assistance they needed and thereby not miss out on too much of the instruction. No wonder parents were very happy, and pleased with this generous offer from society. Nobody really considered how the children would feel, until it was too late....

It was not a simple task to convince parents that deaf children need a school of their own with a signing environment. Faced with the choice of sending their child away to such a school or keeping their child at home they naturally chose to keep the child at home. When we tried to argue for schools for the deaf, they said we tried to separate deaf children from their parents....By not living among hearing people from an early age, they would be denied the right to learn to speak and write Swedish. We were regarded as conservative and it was said that we wanted to keep the schools for the deaf for nostalgic reasons. In short: we were denying deaf children their right to live in a hearing society.

But it was the other way around. The schools for the deaf with their signing environment would give deaf children a place where they could build their mental and spiritual resources in peace and quiet, just like any other child. This would give them the strength to live satisfactory lives as deaf adults in a hearing society with the inherent security of having found their identity and their role in society.

After a while, influenced by their positive contact with the deaf community, more and more parents began to see that the schools for the deaf were important and worth fighting for. Today, most parents send their children to schools for the deaf, and many parents move with their children to a city which has one....Today we cooperate on a number of issues which concern deaf children and we complement each other in a good way. We are a strong force which it is very hard for society to neglect.

Although the history of such political struggles in Denmark will not be discussed here, the situation with regard to mainstreaming in Denmark appears to be similar, with a few schools remaining that are centers for integrating students or conducting self-contained classes in schools for hearing students—and integration into all-hearing classes is reported only for children with mild to moderate hearing losses. Mogens Rasmussen, principle of the Kastelsvej School, explained that there had been a political effort to mainstream deaf children, but they were no longer considered candidates for integration. To quote Rasmussen:

So blind children, children with physical disabilities, children with learning disabilities—most of them are integrated. But some of the centers for [mainstreaming] deaf children or hearing disabled children closed because it didn't work and now there are only two left in this area or three, and one of them is almost closing because the parents want the children to come to deaf schools to have Sign Language and to develop their personalities through Sign Language (personal communication, April 19, 1990).

When children in Sweden and Denmark today reach school age, placement in classrooms with hearing children is an option; however, parents in these countries tend to choose it

---

only in situations where the child's hearing loss is such that he or she can function in a classroom of hearing students without an interpreter.

'Segregated' Placements

Today, integration is perceived as a symbol of American democracy by many members of the dominant society, and inherent in that process of integration is the masking of differences. The argument that the dominant society is "color blind" and does not attend to differences among groups lends credibility to the American motto "One nation under God"....

Integration, introduced [in the 1800s] as a symbol of Democracy for Deaf people, became a strategy of normalization. By declaring integration as a normal endeavor of American society, the dominant culture presented integration as a legitimate goal for everyone. And if integration was normal, then segregation was abnormal (Jankowski, 1994, p. 5).

Segregated placements is the terminology used in the U.S. today by education officials to refer to separate schools for educating Deaf children.[18] Implementation of an education that supports both American Sign Language and English, by nature, involves such placements—bringing a critical mass of Deaf children of all ages together in a school where there are Deaf adults and other fluent users of Sign Language. Interestingly, many parents who have had opportunities to see their Deaf child growing up around other Deaf children and Deaf adults would consider placing their child in a school with mostly hearing children to be the segregated setting.

Most of the parents interviewed in Sweden and Denmark simply would not tolerate the segregation of their children from Deaf peers, adult role models, and an environment where they are full, unrestricted participants in every aspect of their education. While this was not always the case, as explained above, parents in Sweden and Denmark now seem very comfortable with the concept of bringing Deaf children together to best educate them. The views of today's parents in these countries are much like the views espoused by Deaf people during their fight against mainstreaming.

These views about the vital role of separate educational placements and the complications of mainstreaming are also shared by many parents and professionals in the United States (CCE, in press; Johnson & Cohen, 1994). However, at the time this book is being written, there is a very strong popular movement to change current law to favor "full inclusion"

---

18   As per officials addressing the founding meeting of the ACTION Coalition, December 12, 1993 (See Appendix C for ACTION address and full name).

---

for all children. Were the demands of the full-inclusion lobby to be met, every disabled child's neighborhood school classroom would be regarded as preferable to other placement options. Furthermore, the continuum of options that currently provides the political mandate to maintain state schools for the Deaf would be virtually eliminated.

Deaf children are currently considered identical under the law to disabled children who have full access to English through their hearing (children who therefore have very different educational and communicative possibilities in a public school classroom.) As Lane notes in his report to the U.S. Commission on Education of the Deaf, Deaf children seem to have somehow fallen between the cracks in current legislation:

> *Thus, there exists legislation to protect language minorities; there is also legislation to protect the handicapped; but those children who become members of a language minority because of their handicap are not protected (Lane, 1992b, p. 175).*

The American Society for Deaf Children (ASDC), a national organization representing 20,000 parents, friends, and professionals, has expressed strong opposition to any implicit or stated assumption that a classroom with hearing children is the best possible placement for a Deaf child. This organization testified on April 28, 1994 before the U.S. House of Representatives Subcommittee on Select Education and Civil Rights, in support of maintaining separate placement options under the law in the reauthorization of the IDEA (Individuals with Disabilities Education Act). The act, they state, "has a profound impact on the education of deaf and hard of hearing children, and therefore on their life achievement."

They are also fighting against any predetermined formulas for placement that run the risk of disregarding individual Deaf children's educational needs. Like the Deaf consumer's perspective shared above, parents' strong feelings about this issue are best communicated by parents. Therefore, I will quote at length directly from the Congressional testimony of the American Society for Deaf Children:

> *Some parents, national organizations, and LEAs [Local Education Agencies] believe that the neighborhood classroom is preferable to other placement options. For some deaf children, that assumption is correct. Often, however, this kind of inclusion is of a purely physical nature. When it comes to real interaction with people, and access to all information in the environment—sadly, this arrangement often amounts to nothing more than exclusion [see also Nover, 1994; and Ramsey, 1994]. This placement, thought to be the least restrictive environment, may turn out to be the most restrictive.*

> *It is also imperative that each option be considered equally valid as a first choice. Our children must not fall victim to a "fail first" mentality, whereby they must fail in the neighborhood school before they are permitted to see a part-time resource*

teacher, then they must fail in that situation before they are permitted to spend all day in a separate classroom, and so on. Such a cycle of failure jeopardizes a child's chance for future success, damages self esteem, and wastes precious limited educational resources.

We at the American Society for Deaf Children firmly support separate schools and programs for our deaf children. Often parents of deaf children who attend schools for the deaf are asked,

"Why doesn't your child attend a regular school?"

Our children do attend regular schools. They attend regular schools for deaf children. There they experience the kind of environment that hearing children take for granted. They have free, direct, communication with everyone at the school: friends and peers as well as teachers, principals, guidance counselors, the school nurse, the bus driver, the cafeteria workers, and even the maintenance staff. There are deaf role and language models. Classrooms are set up in a way to take advantage of visual space. Seats are arranged so that all the students can see each other and the teacher clearly. Filmstrips and videotapes are captioned. Fire alarms have flashing lights. Students have full access to the world around them, just as hearing children attending hearing schools do. Rather than being isolated, "segregated" institutions, schools for the deaf nurture and challenge deaf children. These schools do so the same way the best hearing schools do: They meet the children's needs and stimulate them to advance. This option must be maintained for our children....

In addition, often separate schools and programs are better able to meet the needs of the families of deaf children than neighborhood schools. While a neighborhood school has to "reinvent the wheel" every time a deaf child comes through the system, separate schools and programs are used to providing information to families.... Family support is essential to the educational success of any deaf or hard of hearing child.

They go on to discuss problems that have become apparent over the past twenty years with the concept of providing adequate services to deaf children in their local school district (LEA). They assert there are a number of individual needs that are often disregarded due to lack of information or resources in a public school classroom:

Linguistic needs of the child should be considered [in making decisions about educational placement]. Teachers and educational staff must be fluent in the language of instruction in order to be effective and to serve as appropriate language models. LEAs should be required to provide such educators. Unfortunately, at this time, many LEAs claim to be providing teachers who are competent in Sign

Language when in fact teachers' skills are seriously lacking. A placement that is, for example, supposedly a self-contained classroom with a teacher who signs is not that at all if the teacher has minimal signing skills. Similarly, Sign Language interpreters in educational settings should be qualified. In too many cases, individuals who "know some sign" are given the important role of interpreter. The child is dependent for all his or her communication on an individual who can neither properly convey information to the child nor properly convey information from the child to the teacher and peers.[19] LEAs must provide not only the appearance of a placement, but a quality placement that has meaning for the child in that placement (Raimondo, 1994b, p. 3-4.).

The configuration of the system in Sweden and Denmark has facilitated Deaf children having the same benefits in school as other children do, building their knowledge, skills, and confidence through successful social interactions and academic experiences. It also tends to facilitate parents of Deaf children in functioning much the same way all parents do. In other words, parents' degree of confusion about placement options does not seem to greatly exceed what parents of most hearing children go through—that of advocating for a high quality education (see also description of the Denver Magnet School in Chapter 5). While many settings are still very much in a process of transition, the system in principle considers it a priority to place each child in an environment like the one described in the quote above—one where lack of hearing is not seen as his or her primary attribute and where the focus is on building each child's strengths as the best way to meet the challenges of functioning in mainstream society. This philosophy helps to release parents from some of the familiar struggles parents in the U.S. go through—often as a matter of course—to secure for their children the kind of educational environment that lets them have the same kinds of social, linguistic, and learning experiences other children do.

Educational systems may eventually be able to find a way to place Deaf children in schools with hearing children without sacrificing these attributes. But this is likely to happen only when such attributes become an unquestioned part of a Deaf child's education, and the early access to language and teachers' attributes discussed in this book are a matter of course. One very wise teacher in Denmark recently described to me her vision of a two-way bilingual school with both Deaf and hearing children who started out together in preschool, and Deaf and hearing teachers. In such a school, all children would use Sign Language and attend classes together, play together, and become truly bilingual. Teachers in such a program would need to have the expertise to sustain the children's achievement in subject areas, while addressing the Deaf and hearing children's differing needs in attaining cognitive and academic proficiency in both the majority language and

19   Sometimes, parents are even brought into this interpreting role when there are no other individuals in the community who can sign.

Sign Language. While such an environment seems far off, more and more bilingual preschools for Deaf children are including hearing children of Deaf parents (Evans, et al, 1994; also see p. 203).

Placement of Hard of Hearing Children

Hard of Hearing Children Integrated into
Classrooms with Hearing Children

There was consensus among interviewees that—except in isolated cases—the only children mainstreamed in both countries are hard of hearing children who can function successfully in an auditory environment *without* Sign Language interpreters. Although many individuals initially referred to this integration with hearing children as a satisfactory situation, further inquiry revealed that there are many complex issues surrounding placement of children with less severe hearing losses. These issues are among the biggest challenges current educational systems for Deaf children in any country face.

Discussed earlier was the practice of exposing all children to natural Sign Language as well as the language of the majority and observing the direction of their development of a primary communication mode, and that many hard of hearing children may benefit from Sign Language even if their primary mode of receptive communication is auditory, not visual. Under these circumstances, parents whose preschoolers are clearly regarded as hard of hearing by the time they reach school-age have to make a decision. Some children are moved into preschools with hearing children fairly early. Even so, the choice of where the child should pursue compulsory education is far from straightforward. Either decision—placing the child in a public school or in a school for the Deaf—can present distinct problems, creating a quandary for some parents.

While the practice of mainstreaming children whose obvious choice in communicating is through auditory/aural channels sounds satisfactory, reports of negative social-emotional consequences have created cause for alarm. And for those children who fall somewhere on the edge of that functioning level, there are a different set of concerns. Some teachers expressed conflicting fears that these children would stand to miss a great deal of content and interaction in public schools, but might suffer for lack of spoken communication if placed in the primarily Sign Language environment of the state schools.

Many of the sources I interviewed commented that the national organization of hard of hearing adults in Sweden has become quite insistent about hard of hearing children's right to early exposure to Sign Language and interaction with other children who have a hearing loss. This organization has joined the National Association of the Deaf and the National Parents Organization in the political fight to achieve many of the changes this book describes. Some of these hard of hearing adults claim they were denied (through lack of knowledge of Sign Language and lack of opportunities for interaction) the right to the support and socialization of the Deaf community. They assert that Sign Language would facilitate communication among their hard of hearing peers, and among family members in noisy environments. To this end, many hard of hearing adults are reportedly taking Sign Language classes, hoping—in addition to gaining increased opportunities for interaction—to gain better access to lectures and other events where Sign Language interpreters are now provided. Psychologist Kerstin Heiling explains:

Young hard of hearing people in Sweden, most of whom have had oral education, are now marching for their rights to have sign language as a second language or as an alternative mode of communication in situations where spoken language does not work. Many of the hard of hearing leaders who have been quite successful at school and have a university degree, still feel deprived of an easily accessible mode of communication for social use. She says, "They deign themselves as 'socially deaf' and are striving towards a group identity as not hearing, not deaf, but hard of hearing" (Heiling, 1993, p. 77).

Even for children who seem to get sufficient speech input through their hearing, public school placement is no longer a foregone conclusion in Sweden or Denmark. In two studies (Tvingstedt, 1985; Tvingstedt & Hartman, 1989), the Swedish National Board of Education investigated the quality of support services and the social-emotional status of children who were fully integrated into hearing classrooms. Researchers found that such environments may be less than optimal. In short, Tvingstedt found in her sociometric study that 47% of the 215 hard of hearing subjects in public schools (grades 7-11) were not chosen by any classmates when all students were asked to list the names of their friends. The researchers characterized hard of hearing teenagers in hearing classrooms as generally lonely and isolated, with immigrant youths having even fewer friends and daily social contacts than the other hard of hearing students.

Regarding support for the students, the researchers found that teachers were not always trained in use of the available technology or methods of optimizing the environment for their hard of hearing students. Nevertheless, fairly impressive attempts were being made by many teachers to use technology and accommodate hard of hearing students in their classes. Despite these efforts, only 55% of the students said that they could readily follow what the teacher said. More important, just 6% could hear their classmates' comments, questions, and discussion.

While only 25% of these hearing aid users were disturbed by the noise level in the classroom, 81% complained of the noise level in common areas of the school, areas where students would be most likely to build social relationships. Figures such as these contribute to the concern parents of hard of hearing children experience regarding the most appropriate placement and mode of instruction for their child.

Placement of Hard of Hearing Children in Schools for the Deaf

As a result of this recent development, many parents of hard of hearing children are demanding that their child be placed in a school for the Deaf. Enrollment figures reflect this change (Gunilla Turesson-Morais, personal communication, March 14, 1990), and the phenomenon was referred to by many interviewees as a growing problem for these schools. Although many of the parents are convinced of the importance of Sign Language for their children, staff at the school for the Deaf have found that the children with less severe hearing losses, who are accustomed to talking in their preschool environment, tend to continue talking to each other—and to hearing teachers—during classes at the school for the Deaf.

At first, many teachers were confused by this, feeling they couldn't meet the needs of all the children. School personnel have worked hard during these past years to create a Sign Language milieu in the schools. In other words, spoken Swedish is not intended to be the language of instruction in the classroom. The idea of re-introducing spoken Swedish as the language of the classroom to meet the needs of a few was seen as a major setback.

I interviewed the Manilla School psychologist that administers readiness tests to pre-schoolers. She also coordinates a program where preschoolers scheduled to enter first grade the next year spend one day a week at the school for the Deaf to ensure a smooth transition. She commented about her efforts to deal with the new enrollment demands for the upcoming first grade, which had 24 potential students as opposed to the usual average of 10. She stated:

We hope the school for the hard of hearing will take on more Sign Language. Parents want it NOW. But that's just not possible. I've been visiting families, saying "It's not good for the kids to be here and be talking to each other. Their deaf friends won't trust them—won't know what they're saying."

In the trial program for the 6-year-olds before they start, we have told the parents that we will inform the kids, "If you come here, you have to turn off your voice, the way we all do it. This school is for the deaf, so if you 're hard of hearing and you want to come here, you have to "turn deaf" during this time.

We could very clearly see that some of the children could not do it. It was so important for them to talk. So, we sent them to Alvick [the school for hard of hearing children in Stockholm]. After our trial period, parents were willing to say, "OK, they've made their choice." (Gunilla Turesson-Morais is, personal communication, March 13, 990.)

Traditionally, critics of approaches that rely on speech or simultaneous communication have claimed that instruction catered to the children in the class who had the most speech and discriminated against those who had poor speech reception and relied only on Sign Language. When bilingual education started to take hold in these countries, there was some concern at first that those students who rely primarily on speech would not get the oral/aural input they need if placed in schools for the Deaf.

But teachers in the environments with the most experience assured me that attending classes where Swedish Sign Language is the language of instruction is not detrimental for these children. They assert that the children who have adequate hearing will get plenty of spoken input in the majority language from their daily environment. And those who do not should be receiving instruction in Sign Language anyway to gain complete access to curricular material. Nevertheless, there was—at first—concern about the social consequences and classroom repercussions observed when children who have a natural predisposition to speak in Swedish as their first language are placed in this environment. Britta Hansen relates some of the potentially complicated dynamics observed in such a classroom in her description of the children who entered the first experimental bilingual class in Copenhagen:

> Clearly the children who quickly developed or already knew DSL became the most popular "storytellers," whereas the Danish speaking children had problems in being "listened to" by the other children. On the other hand, the hearing teachers at first found it difficult not to react faster and more spontaneously to the Danish speaking children, simply because at the beginning of the process they understood them better, and as they say themselves in the reports they have published: Sound is very powerful for hearing people! (Hansen, 1987, p. 84) .

Teachers who have had more experience with the Sign Language milieu (including those who made this comment) claim that hearing teachers can establish a mode of communication that includes all participants in a group (i.e. signing without voice whenever there are Deaf children in the group so everyone gets equal input). These teachers have disciplined themselves not to attend to spoken utterances when the current mode is Sign Language. In the early stages, they remind the children that their peers won't hear what they have to say, or simply explain that, "We are using Sign Language right now." Hard of hearing first graders (those described earlier who are acquiring both spoken and signed language) do not seem to have the same problems knowing when to talk and when to sign if they attended pre-schools with Deaf children.

Other teachers related their strategies for trying to give the children what they need, including talking rather than signing to the hard of hearing children in some one-to-one situations. Some classrooms with team teachers divide the group for parts of the day and provide primarily spoken lessons in Swedish/Danish/English or an occasional context-embedded lesson in another subject (see the description of such groupings in the next chapter).

In some schools where class size is large enough (in some classes at Fredereccia School in Denmark, for example), children with greater auditory perception are placed in separate groups on the same campus with their Deaf peers. This approach was not considered satisfactory by many of the teachers at that school, as these children are generally labeled "hard of hearing" by their peers and teachers, reportedly causing segregation and some identity conflicts for those who perceive being "Deaf" as preferable (or vice versa). Groups where children with more and less hearing were placed together were reported to be having the most success. But it was also noted that the teachers in the more successful classes were very perceptive about the complex interactions between the signed, written, and spoken languages in the children's worlds.

Deaf, Hard of Hearing, and Hearing Children Together

Commitment to supporting both languages seems to be the key in questions about hard of hearing children. SignTalk Children's Centre, Inc., in Winnipeg, Canada (a daycare center for Deaf and hearing children belonging to Deaf parents and to hearing parents who have some connection to the Deaf community) is one example of a system where Deaf and hearing staff work successfully with Deaf and hearing children—including hard of hearing children—respecting all children's rights to access to both languages. Re-searchers recently published a concise, helpful booklet as part of a federal grant to track the children's development in both languages (Evans, et al, 1994). The communication dynamics of this mix of hearing, hard of hearing, and Deaf children, staff, and parents has presented some complex issues to the staff at the Centre, but they have worked through each challenging communication setting on a case-by-case basis in their goal of creating an environment that meets the needs of Deaf and hearing children, parents, and staff. Their commitment to keeping both languages whole and keeping both languages separate has forced them to find ways to employ the same kinds of strategies used in other settings where two languages co-exist.

Since ASL and English (like Japanese and English) are two distinct languages, the staff is committed to addressing various situations without talking and signing at the same time. English and ASL—much like English and Japanese—cannot successfully be mixed or performed at the same time. Therefore, for example, in a setting where a hearing teacher is having a conversation alone with a hearing child and the Deaf parent arrives to pick her up, one solution is to continue the conversation in English with the child briefly until they reach a good stopping point, then summarize the conversation for the parent in ASL, rather than using simultaneous communication. (Again, if the same situation happened with Japanese and English, there would be no way of mixing the two.) The rest of the conversation can then proceed in ASL, which is accessible to all three. Their book describes solutions that do not compromise the integrity of either language by using the two simultaneously.

Because of the attitude of respect for both languages, staff from this school noted that a level of trust has built up, making it perfectly acceptable to summarize a brief conversation that took place in another language, just as it might be in other situations where speakers of two languages interact; for example if my husband summarizes for me what the French shopkeeper said to him. The staff support the idea that both languages have a place in the environment and that this kind of translation is one way to handle situations where it is perfectly natural for hearing teachers to speak English to hearing children when there are no Deaf children around. I share this information here because this program and others that place Deaf and hearing preschoolers together (see "Yes, but..." section in Chapter Five) may be a helpful model when exploring ways to meet the spoken language needs of some hard of hearing children whose first language may be the spoken language, but who thrive educationally in a primarily ASL environment.

Placement in Classrooms with other Hard of Hearing Children

In addition to the options discussed above (mainstreaming and schools for the Deaf), there are some self-contained classrooms for hard of hearing students on the campuses of hearing schools. In these classes, the students are addressed in spoken Swedish, and have specially-trained teachers who take full advantage of available technologies. When I interviewed a group of high school students who had grown up in such classes, 6 out of 7 said that they were content with their education, except that they had such a small group of friends (only their 3-4 classmates). And while they said they were enjoying meeting Deaf students and learning Sign Language in "gymnaseum" (the level of upper-secondary education we would consider somewhere between high school and college), they did not feel part of the group of Deaf *or* hearing students.

In Stockholm, there is a separate school for hard of hearing children which is currently undergoing some changes. At the strong urging of the parents, staff at this school is now meeting regularly with staff from the Manilla School for the Deaf to find ways to see that the students get plenty of exposure to Sign Language and their Deaf peers, so they will experience less of the alienation from either world that the students above described to me.

While placement of hard of hearing children is clearly one of the harder issues parents in Sweden and Denmark face, things are changing. Now that Sign Language is completely accepted in the schools for the Deaf, more energy is going toward figuring out how to support children who can utilize speech and enjoy music and vocal stories. Most importantly, it seems we must give the children real opportunities to interact with both worlds, and talk with them often to understand what they are experiencing, where they feel most comfortable, and where they are able to learn the most.

CHAPTER FOUR

Let the Teachers
Be Teachers

Starting to see Deaf children as children seems to foster the attitude this teacher demonstrates; one that is mindful of variables beyond deafness in looking at her students:

> I think you have to be aware of the fact that different individuals have different abilities in language, in learning languages. I can see that it is this kind of spectrum in any class—in a hearing class—there are good readers and not-so-good readers and so on. It is the same thing with our kids. Some of them need 3 years to become readers. (S. Dahlen, personal communication, March 15, 1992).

When both languages are truly accepted, teachers can observe each child more clearly. Teachers who are skilled in watching for and responding to cues about the child's aptitudes and pace in various areas, and who trust the children's natural interest in their world and desire to learn, observe ongoing growth in both languages. When there is agreement among parents, teachers, administrators, students, and the Deaf community that both languages have equal status as languages, but differ in function and value in the students' lives, the dynamics change. A great deal of energy is redirected to the business of how best to *teach* each child. It is apparent that there is more to teaching Deaf children—like all children—than deciding what language to use in addressing them.

Trust

Trust—not only in the children and their learning processes, but also in teachers' ability to discover how to proceed—seems to have emerged in the programs where educating Deaf children bilingually has become a matter of course. In order to let the teachers be teachers, the system must give current and incoming teachers the theoretical orientation and training that prepares them to be vigilant about each child's rights to normal linguistic, cognitive, and social development. Their training must prepare them to have the skills to impart knowledge about history and science and math and other subjects through Sign Language during the early years, as well as using text through many different avenues as the children's developing literacy skills become a primary avenue for learning. Being well-trained in their subject matter and having the theoretical footing needed to explore new teaching methodologies becomes of primary importance. In addition, the teachers I have observed in the U.S. and Scandinavia who seem most focused on issues related to teaching in this bilingual context tend to have some qualities in common—attributes that are especially critical for teachers of younger grades if bilingual education is to succeed. Before discussing these attributes that are important for every teacher, I will first focus on the teachers who are an indispensable part of a bilingual education for Deaf children: teachers who are, themselves, Deaf.

Deaf Teachers

Deaf teachers are absolutely crucial to the success of any bilingual program. The importance of their understanding of and rapport with Deaf children, their skill at communicating visually, and their role as adult models of Deaf children's culture and heritage cannot be overstated. Woodward (1978) quotes Vorih and Rosier in their discussion of the successful Rock Point Navaho-English bilingual program: "It was felt it would be far easier to prepare Navajo aides to teach than it would be to teach certified Anglo teachers to speak Navajo, so Navajo aides were trained [to be teachers] on site." (p. 268).

Referring to successful approaches to bilingual education, Paulston (1974) has stated:

> *Mother tongue instruction in minority languages usually implies that the teacher comes from the same reference group, from the same minority culture, and that by willingly speaking the native tongue, he demonstrates an acceptance of that culture (Paulston, 1974, p. 24)*

In her article, "Linguistic Human Rights: A Prerequisite for Bilingualism," Skutnabb-Kangas (1994) describes principles in educational models which succeed in making children high level multilinguals. The most successful models she refers to are those that support (use as the main medium of education) minority children's first language up to a high level, teach L1 (the first language) as a subject throughout schooling, and teach all languages in a way that reflects what they are for each child (i.e., first languages are approached differently than second languages or foreign languages). Because of the importance of the native language throughout school, she stresses the need for teachers to be bi- or multi-lingual, with high levels of fluency in the language children are least likely to be exposed to through the majority culture:

All teachers have to be bi- or multi-lingual. Thus they can be good models for the children, and support them (through comparing and contrasting and being metalinguistically aware) in language learning. Every child in a school has to be able to talk to an adult with the same native language.

This demand is often experienced as extremely threatening by majority group teachers, many of whom are not bilingual. Of course, all minority group teachers are not high level bilinguals either. But it is often less important that the teacher's competence in a majority language is at top level, for instance... because all children have ample opportunities to hear and read native models of a majority language outside the school, whereas many of them do not have the same opportunities with native minority language models. High levels of competence in a minority language is thus more important for a teacher than high levels of competence in a majority language (p. 155).

Unlike most children for whom the majority language is a second language, over 90% of Deaf children (those born to hearing parents) are not likely to encounter native models of their primary language in their own home. Therefore, the presence of teachers who are native models becomes an even *more* important ingredient in linguistic and academic success.

Through the course of interviews with parents, educators, students, and government officials in both Denmark and Sweden, it became clear that Deaf people employed in the system were almost unanimously regarded as great assets. A desire to have more Deaf staff members was mentioned very frequently when people were questioned about their "wish list." Teachers who had worked in teams with Deaf staff were particularly aware of the enhanced communication and rapport between Deaf teachers and their students.

Although there exists a high degree of respect for the knowledge Deaf people possess regarding their own language and culture, the ratio of Deaf to hearing staff in education remains low. Deaf people were completely banned from teaching in Sweden during the many years of strict oral-only education; however, most of the state schools for the Deaf in both countries have employed Deaf dorm counselors, coaches, or kitchen staff over the years. Changes are evident, though. Not only are there more Deaf teachers, but also more Deaf members on the school boards. Deaf people are involved in writing the Special School Curriculum, as well as in teacher training.

According to Wallin, there were, in 1988, about forty qualified Deaf teachers of the Deaf working in education from the preschool to the university level. He also states that the majority of these were teaching Swedish Sign Language and Swedish in the schools for the Deaf and the upper secondary school. The Manilla School in Stockholm, considered best-situated in terms of attracting Deaf teachers, had 10 Deaf teachers out of 55, with the first credentialed Deaf teacher having started in the late '70s. Clearly, building a pool of Deaf teachers takes time. In preschools, where Deaf staff are considered particularly crucial, the situation is better, but a shortage persists. Of the eight preschools in the Stockholm area that accept Deaf children, 7 had at least one Deaf staff member in 1990. (The ratio is higher now). The highest ratio I was able to find during that first study was at the well-regarded Skeppargatan School, which is housed in the annex of the Stockholm Deaf Club. Here, there were 2/3 Deaf staff—12 out of 18. (This figure includes aids and support personnel as well as credentialed teachers.) I do not have any figures about Denmark.

All the state schools and most preschools have what is known as *Fritidshem* (roughly translated, "free-time home"), supervised after-school activities on the school premise. The ratio of Deaf staff is generally high in the Fritidshems, lending a feeling in school hallways and lunchrooms that there are a number of Deaf adults, even though they are not all teachers. Children quickly become aware of who holds positions of power. While having Deaf adults in all kinds of support positions is important, it is more critical yet for students to set their sights high by seeing that Deaf administrators and fully-credentialed teachers play a significant role in their education. Even in schools for the Deaf in the United States, where there are Deaf teachers and dorm staff, students have been very curious and excited about Deaf speakers who have come to give presentations to the staff on ASL, bilingual education, and Deaf empowerment. The Sterck School in Delaware is now opening up some of these presentations for teachers to their older Deaf *students*, who seem hungry to observe a variety of self-confident, articulate Deaf adults.

Although no research was cited, collective reasons given for the shortage of Deaf teachers are similar to those given in the United States: traditional barriers to college and especially graduate-level education for many Deaf people (barriers which seem to be lifting in Sweden as a result of higher achievement and literacy levels, and rising awareness of the validity of Sign Language as a language). There is also the simple demographic fact that the ratio of Deaf to hearing people is very small. In Sweden, the shortage also seemed related to the relative newness of the teaching field as a career option. Former teacher training requirements and adherence to oralism in Sweden made it almost impossible for Deaf people to become teachers. Before recent changes, the requirements specified that all teachers had to work for five years in a school for hearing children before training to become teachers of the Deaf. This is no longer the case. In addition to these variables, there was a shift among Deaf college students in the U.S. during the 1970s and '80s away from teaching (which was formerly one of the few professional career options for Deaf people) to a number of other fields that began to open up. According to Marie Jean Philip (personal communication, August 9, 1994), there were also more colleges for Deaf people to choose from in the 70's and 80's due to widespread interpreting, and many Deaf people turned away from teaching to go into fields where more money could be made. She feels this is changing now; that Deaf people are becoming very enthusiastic and interested in education due to the movement toward the recognition of Deaf children's languages and cultures and of the crucial role of Deaf adults in Deaf children's education.

In Sweden and Denmark, schools have tried to capitalize on the expertise of the Deaf teachers that are available. One strategy that provides both a popular and practical solution is to combine the classes within an age group, allowing two, three, even four teachers to work together (see section in this chapter on larger class size). Teams of Deaf and hearing teachers provide one way to have experts in both languages and cultures present, and to model Deaf/hearing cooperation and teamwork. Other Deaf teachers, of course, have their own classrooms. Strategies for capitalizing on the expertise of Deaf teachers also include having some Deaf teachers "float," visiting a number of classrooms on a regular basis to give lessons on specific topics. While Deaf teachers are often asked to teach or team-teach the lessons when the subject is Sign Language or Deaf Studies, I observed a junior high level lesson on World War II in which the discussion among students and the visiting Deaf teacher was clearly fast-moving and intense. Hearing teachers there often tried to schedule the Deaf floating teacher for content lessons in a variety of subjects, as it was clear to them that the students' discussions with her were often more open and substantive. Deaf teachers in this situation, however, sometimes feel scattered and overworked, as they are called upon for many age-groups, subjects, and settings in any given week, and are generally in high demand for both classroom teaching and special events (L. Gallimore, personal communication, December 2, 1994). The California School for the Deaf in Fremont recently converted its English Resource Center to a Bilingual-Bicultural Resource Center, one possible model for capitalizing on the expertise of Deaf teachers.

My contact with a number of programs moving in the direction of educating Deaf children bilingually indicates that bringing on more Deaf teachers and staff, or re-assigning those who are there to positions that impact on early language development, is partly a question of commitment—of simply finding ways to make it work. As an example, the Indiana School for the Deaf has greatly increased its percentage of Deaf staff in less than five years. As of the writing of this book, more than 1/3 of the school's staff is Deaf. In the preschool, 100% of the teachers and aides are Deaf, and preliminary outcomes of studies of the language development of Deaf, hard of hearing, and hearing children (children of Deaf adults) in this preschool appear very positive (Gallimore, 1994).

Sign Language as an Academic Subject

One area of study that has meant a great deal to students is the study of their own language, which includes the study of Deaf people's lives, history, and accomplishments (sometimes known in the U.S. as Deaf studies). According to an informal survey, learning about their own language, heritage, and strategies for day-to-day living has become many students' favorite subject (Lewis, 1994; Lewis, Madsen, Ravn, 1992).

In this area, Deaf teachers play a very significant role. One hearing teacher summarized her students' feelings about this subject, acknowledging the unique role a Deaf teacher can play:

There are more lessons in Sign Language and about being deaf for the younger children, but we have two or three hours a week [in ninth grade], and the students really love that subject now. As part of the reflection for our book on the bilingual project, I asked the students, what do they think of Sign Language, what is their attitude about the language and their lessons in that language. I had a whole range of reactions—all positive: "We like having Sign Language lessons because we talk about people and things and subjects from our own culture that we're interested in." "We like having deaf teachers who understand everything we say right away." It can be very difficult to discuss things with hearing teachers, because they say 'yes, OK, I agree with you,' but then the students don't really feel like we understand them. So they often feel they can never really get a good group discussion with a hearing teacher. "We like Sign Language because it is a language that we are capable of. Many other subjects we have to learn and learn and learn and there are many frustrations. With Sign Language, it is pleasant and it is easy and it is relaxing."

I—and the deaf teacher agrees—think that it is sometimes important to have a hearing teacher in Sign Language lessons as well, because the children are learning about their own culture in the context of the larger society, and the hearing teacher can help them make cultural comparisons about hearing and deaf, and link things up. Sometimes they start making generalizations and think it is only deaf that feel that way. Also the hearing teacher learns a lot.

BUT, it is very important that the hearing teacher doesn't take up any time in the class. And if she doesn't understand something, she must wait until after class to find out because there can be no time to interpret anything. The hearing person must not be a hindrance to anything that is going on in the class. This is a very special time. It is not only the amount of minutes the hearing person would take up, but it interrupts the whole thing that is going on because, for many students, this class represents their opportunity to search deeply for their own solutions to many problems (W. Lewis, personal communication, March 9, 1992).

The presence of Deaf teachers is critical to this educational model. While acknowledging an immediate need for more Deaf teachers, educators in Sweden and Denmark also seem aware that the transition to bilingual education will not be considered complete until there is a new generation of Deaf teachers in the system. Such individuals have the potential to be even better qualified as bilingual educators than today's Deaf teachers, because they will have grown up in a system that respected their language *and* educated them about the structure of that language; and because they had many positive experiences developing literacy in the majority language by learning about it from a new perspective.

Expertise

One very important attribute for hearing or Deaf teachers (especially those who teach young children), is a highly developed level of understanding and skill in both languages, as noted in the following quote:

> *The bilingual ambition emphasizes even more the need of mastery of Swedish Sign Language for teachers....*
>
> *To be able to teach a subject as abstract and intellectual as a written language to someone that has no access to the spoken form also requires more than good communication skills. That teacher needs to know a lot about the grammar of the language he teaches as well as the language he is teaching in (Ahlgren, 1989, draft version, p. 3-4).*

Knowledge of the Structure of Both Languages

Study of the grammar of both languages is an important component in the training of both Deaf and hearing teachers. Teachers from the most successful bilingual classes in Denmark and Sweden have worked to learn as much as they can about current research in Sign Language grammar, Swedish grammar, and teaching second languages. They have continued to expand their understanding of linguistics and language acquisition, and have applied their knowledge in ways that allow their students to proceed on a schedule that seems developmentally appropriate.

Because whole language, rather than simplified text, is used in the teaching of reading, writing, and other subject matter, Svartholm points out that:

> *The approach thus demands special knowledge not only of Swedish Sign Language but also about Swedish as a second language. The teacher of the deaf, just like any teacher of Swedish immigrants and the like, must be prepared to explain grammatical differences that seem natural or are not even noticed when teaching the language to native speakers....*
>
> *Even at the very early stages, the teacher must be able to explain textual matters; e.g., varying expressions for reference, or the functions of different sentence types....This calls for the teacher to have considerable knowledge of grammatical rules based on text linguistics. Such rules are of a different kind from those usually presented in elementary grammars, where short simple sentences out of context are used as examples. Although some rules of this kind may be useful for guiding writing activities (i.e., language production), they are not especially helpful for understanding real language usage....(Svartholm, 1993, p. 326).*

In order to ensure broad-based competence in this area among teachers, the responsibility ultimately lies with the educational system to provide teachers with adequate training and materials. In addition to programs of Sign Language instruction for teachers, some schools in Sweden have started in-service training in Swedish grammar, breaking it down from a second-language teaching point of view. (This was started after they found that, in many ways, they were better at teaching English to their Deaf students than Swedish—in part because the teachers had all had a chance to analyze it as a second language during their own learning process.)

Ahlgren (1992) points out that there are also important differences in the attributes of *spoken/signed* languages ("s-languages") vs. *written* forms of language ("w-languages"). Back in 1982, she pointed to the need to disentangle the teaching of the written form of the language to Deaf children ("Silent Swedish") from the sounds of that language. This requires that teachers of Deaf children must also be able to analyze and explain forms of the written language completely independent of their spoken representation:

> For anyone who cannot hear, Swedish is first and foremost a system of squiggles arranged from left to right in rows, and formed into groups. To define these squiggles as consonants and vowels, referring to how they sound, is pointless in this context. They have no sound, any more than "!" or "?". Instead, we have to describe each of the squiggles "!," "?," "m," "n," "a," etc. with reference to the function they have in the system. We must give rules for how the squiggles are combined into groups, such as "file," "life," "-ing," "-es," and so on. After that, we must describe how these groups can be combined into new groups, such as "filing," "files," and "lifetime" or "Peter files it" or "Eva loved life."

> A description of such combinations at all levels is not, however, sufficient. We must also be able to say what the different combinations mean and why we sometimes have to have groups of squiggles that mean nothing, like the "It's" in "It's raining."....

> When faced with the task, in the teaching of English to hearing children, of explaining such grammatical oddities as "Do you drink tea?", we do it by a comparison with the way in which Swedish expresses the same thing, "Dricker du te?". Similarly, in teaching Swedish in the School for the Deaf, we must be able to explain Swedish grammar by reference to how things are expressed in sign language....We therefore need a description of the differences, in order that we should be aware of what is not self-evident to the student.

Another way the Swedish system implemented their responsibility to teachers was to publish a handbook for teachers as a supplement to the national curriculum (Svartholm, 1990). The manual discusses aspects of written Swedish grammar that can be predicated (based on a contrastive analysis of the structures of the two languages) to be somewhat difficult for Deaf learners of Swedish. Svartholm (1993) acknowledges that, while linguists' contrastive analyses of Swedish Sign Language and Swedish have been helpful in predicting Deaf learners' difficulties, there is still inadequate knowledge of the two languages from this perspective. She suggests that it is important, therefore, for teachers to study and utilize already existing grammatical descriptions of Swedish (English, Danish, etc.) designed for general second language teaching purposes as a complementary source of knowledge. This Danish teacher's quote shows her own awareness of how the difference in the grammar of the two languages can be taken into account in our early expectations and our evaluation of students' competence:

> We have these two little words in Danish, "et" and "en." They would be like "the" in English, except you use a different one depending on the word it goes with. The rules for which one to use with any given word are totally unpredictable. They just have to be memorized. This comes easily for hearing children, who acquire the article right along with the noun when they are learning to talk. So this production is somewhat taken for granted in Danish lessons for hearing children and is one of the things hearing children master early in their writing.

> Danish Sign Language and written Danish handle some constructions in similar ways. But, in the same way Danish lacks many of the attributes of Sign Language, Sign Language does not have anything like "et" and "en." When Danish is not approached as a second language and deaf children are asked to master such tasks at the early stages, they often throw up their hands and say, "This is Danish and it is VERY hard."

> Now, as our analysis of Sign Language linguistics increases, and we are looking at Danish from a different perspective, we are becoming more sensitive about which Danish constructions are likely to come easily and which ones we should not expect our students to master in their writing till much, much later—when they have had time to acquire the structure by seeing it again and again in text (T. Ravn, personal communication, March 14, 1993).

While such contrastive analysis is in its very early stages, this kind of thinking has already proven important both for the explanation of concepts and the evaluation of skills acquired.

Many educators are aware that standardized testing has traditionally not proven to be a good tool for evaluating the emerging English competence of Deaf children and children of other cultures for whom English is acquired as a second language (Anderson-Logie, 1993). Failure to capture a clear picture of a Deaf child's growing competence in written English seems in part due to the fact that the skills expected of monolingual hearing children at a given age may be among those that would be learned much later by users of another language, especially a language one has not heard. Evaluating performance first in the kinds of structures that are similar to the children's own language gives them a sense of confidence with the majority language. Formal instruction and testing can be structured to account for some of the predictable problems in learning a second language. This also gives students time to develop the cognitive maturity they will need to acquire the less similar kinds of constructions later in their education after being exposed to them often in print.

Being a fluent, or even a native, speaker of Sign Language does not necessarily give one the expertise to explain grammatical structures and compare and contrast their production in both languages. When I asked about their "wish list," many teachers wished to have more research about Sign Language grammar and more opportunities to study in this area. They felt it was very helpful for teaching structures in the grammar of the majority language. This is one aspect of implementation that will simply take time. However, many, many discoveries have been made by linguists around the world about Sign Language grammar that have not yet been made available to teachers in a form that supports incorporating these findings into classroom instruction. Linguist Brita Bergman, for example, recalled a workshop where she was explaining about relative clauses in Swedish Sign Language. Later, one of the teachers of the first experimental class in Sweden, thanked Brita. This teacher said she had been trying to get the concept across to her students, most of whom hadn't been able to grasp the idea—until she was able to discuss with them how relative clauses were handled in their own Sign Language.

Along the same lines, Gallaudet University has recently added to its teacher training curriculum a course in contrastive analysis of ASL and English. The course consists of two sessions per week. One session looks at structures in ASL, the second at structures in English. Based on the experience of Swedish/Danish teachers, such expertise will be extremely valuable in teaching English as a second language to Deaf students.

Knowledge of the Language of the Deaf Community

> Writing activities can be conducted in the classroom from early on in several ways and for several purposes. For example, teacher and child can create texts in cooperation, where the children express content in Sign Language and the teacher renders their utterances into written Swedish....

> Needless to say, this is impossible to carry out properly if the teacher cannot fully understand what the children are conveying in signs. Of course, this puts demands upon the teacher's knowledge of Sign Language. But the responsibility for in-depth communication in the classroom must be placed on the teacher, not on the children (Svartholm, 1993, p.314).

It is clear to me that these countries have come to recognize that the responsibility extends even further than to the teacher; that it is really the responsibility of the larger system to provide adequate opportunities for teachers to become more fluent in Sign Language.

For hearing teachers who have been in the field for years and have devoted themselves to learning and using other methodologies, learning Deaf Sign Language[1] presents a very different challenge from that facing parents. In Sweden and Denmark today, many parents' first orientation to deafness often includes the clear suggestion that Deaf Sign Language will be the parents' life-line for communication with their child. Teachers, however, often began during the time of oralism and then moved into sign-supported Swedish, but were rarely expected to understand the Sign Language students used among themselves. Many teachers explained to me that if there was a communication breakdown, the burden has usually fallen on the children to slow down or state their thoughts in more Swedish-like signing, since the teachers did not necessarily possess the skills to understand them.

When criticisms regarding their skills were leveled at educators in Sweden in the early 1980s, many teachers felt very defensive. They knew they had contributed to many successes using a particular communication mode for years, and that they had done their very best as teachers. While most understood the rationale for changes in philosophy, there was still little *time* allotted in a teacher's day to devote to the development of new skills. Talk of increased scrutiny of teachers' Sign Language skills left many teachers feeling that the quality instruction and the caring attention they had given their children over the years was being nullified or at least grossly devalued.

Some related to me how hard they had worked to master what they had always *understood* to be Sign Language, only to find out later—as the descriptive research emerged—that Deaf people's language was quite different from what these teachers had been taught. Commenting on the experiment where she worked with a Deaf teacher to translate and analyze videotapes of Deaf children's signing, Britta Hansen discusses both her successes and her frustrations:

> *Another interesting fact was that by immersing myself in the [videotapes of] children's signing, I found that after three months I was able to understand most of the children's signing in the playground, and for the first time could relax and fully participate in the deaf adult's conversation.... This raised many questions about how I had been taught Sign Language over the past eight years. I felt frustrated and cheated by the traditional teaching I had received from both deaf*

1   The term "Deaf Sign Language" was often used by parents and educators in Sweden and Denmark to differentiate it from other forms of manual communication (see Appendix A, "Author's Note: Terms Used.")

and hearing people. My perceptions of Sign Language had been shattered and my thoughts reverted to all the clients I had worked with as a social worker, and how I had struggled to understand them. I had thought all the time that they were signing incorrectly and that their Sign Language skills were inferior to my own (Hansen, 1980a, p.249).

My interviews with hearing teachers revealed that many had experienced a period of intense turmoil and soul-searching, particularly in the early and middle 1980s. Some had considered leaving the field. However, most references to such feelings were in past tense. Teachers I spoke with seemed fairly secure now, having found their niche in the new system. Increased interaction and team teaching over the past eight years seems to have yielded an appreciation among both hearing and Deaf teachers of the respective contributions each can make. While most hearing teachers commented to me that they felt their Sign Language skills fell short, I didn't find any who still questioned or resisted the validity of striving toward more "Deaf" Sign Language. And both Deaf teachers and students were clearly appreciative of some of the hearing teachers who may not have been the best signers, but who were, nevertheless, sensitive communicators who were very skilled at imparting knowledge of their subject matter.

The intense early pressures on teachers seem to have diminished as the schools and the National Board of Education took increasing responsibility for facilitating a change they began to realize would not truly come about without some expenditure of resources. All schools I visited have in-service training in Sign Language for teachers, and many teachers have taken some of the intensive two-week courses at the Deaf club. Videotaping of their actual classroom communication and self-study with the help of a skilled signer has also been cited as beneficial to those teachers who are willing to open themselves to scrutiny (Edenås & Battison, 1989). This individualized analysis takes into account the fact that experienced teachers may all be at different skill levels (i.e., material in classes may be redundant) and that visual communication strategies can be as important as skills in the language. Such study can also bring some realism to the picture, as noted by Britta Hansen in her comments about the hearing teachers in the first bilingual project in Copenhagen:

Not being native signers, they asked for consultative evaluations of their own DSL skill. They presented videotapes of their signing in the classroom to the Centre for Total Communication in order to learn more. These evaluations resulted in some teaching of DSL to the teachers, but more importantly, it resulted in the teachers' total acceptance of not being able to be "adult models of DSL." Ever since, the project has had Deaf adults involved in the teaching and in the production of teaching tapes. (Hansen, 1987, p.85).

In Sweden, the National Association of the Deaf and the national parents' organization have worked hard to achieve two policy changes designed to improve teachers' Sign

Language skills, both of which went into effect early in 1990: 1) Entrance requirements have been changed so that individuals entering the training program to become teachers of the Deaf must first pass a rather stringent Sign Language test. 2) A five-year federal grant was given to Stockholm University to set up a one-semester Sign Language program for individuals who are already teachers. Every spring, twenty teachers, four from each of the five schools for the Deaf, are released for one semester to follow a full-time course of study in Sign Language at the University. Similarly, as of 1990, basic education of all prospective teachers of Deaf children in Denmark includes the requirement that teachers receive 19 weeks of Sign Language instruction (or 520-580 hours [Bergmann, 1994]).

Now that a high level of fluency in Sign Language is a prerequisite for entrance to the teacher training program in Sweden, the education itself differs little from that of teachers training to teach hearing children, except for a focus on the grammar of the student's languages from a first or second language perspective. In a recent correspondence, Kristina Svartholm of Stockholm University described the current training as follows:

> It's a new teacher training program—four years in all.[2] It gives authorization to teach children in grades 1-7. There are two main subjects: Sign Language and Swedish for the Deaf. Besides those, everything else in the programme is the same as in our ordinary teacher training programmes. i.e., for teachers in any school. Other subjects include different forms of math, art drama, history, etc.

> In other words, no "special education," but an "ordinary" education. Most of the lessons will be interpreted into S.L. [Sign Language] (because of the lack of signing teachers in these regular courses) but as much as possible will be given in S.L. The Department of Sign Language is very pleased with the level of fluency of students entering this first program, and since they are fluent in S.L. whether they are deaf or hearing, there is no proficiency training included (personal correspondence, October 2, 1994).

Training for Teachers of Sign Language/Deaf Studies as an Academic Subject

Officials in Denmark have instituted special training—a 170-hour course—for current teachers selected to teach Sign Language/Deaf Studies as a subject—teaching which requires a high degree of fluency in and knowledge of Sign Language to function as a linguistic role model and to teach about the grammar of the language and its usage in society. Ritva Bergmann summarizes the course as follows:

2   The reader will note that the equivalents of education preceding these four years may vary from the U.S. and other countries.

Both deaf and hearing teachers of deaf children will study more deeply what bilingualism in the education of deaf children means, what the culture of the deaf is, Sign Language grammar, and how they can analyze and evaluate deaf children's Sign Language (Bergmann, 1994, p. 90).

Clearly, there is a wealth of information and expertise that Deaf and hearing teachers need to know to address the linguistic and educational needs of Deaf children in an environment where they are expected to excel. Teachers of Deaf children in the U.S., most of whom grew up monolingual, could be much better prepared to keep the focus on subject matter teaching if their years of education provided them with an understanding of the nature of bilingualism/biliteracy, language contact, diglossia, and multilingualism/multiculturalism; as well as knowledge of the structure of both languages, of Deaf studies, child development, first language acquisition, second language teaching, and, of course, the subjects they are expected to teach. It will be important to incorporate state-of-the-art knowledge of findings in related fields, and to regularly seek out resources and expertise that do not necessarily exist among educators in today's teacher training programs.

Respect for Both Languages

Teachers in this context need unshakable respect for both languages. Recognition of both languages as equal in status (as languages), but different in function and value in the children's lives allows children to develop their fullest potential with regard to both languages and their many uses.

Swedish linguist Brita Bergman's words back in 1978 made people think about what they were doing—how they were approaching the children, and the consequences of their insistence on using signed Swedish and speech, rather than accepting and capitalizing on the fact that there existed a real language that was fully accessible to the children:

As I see it, it is impossible to discuss the choice between different systems of education as long as teacher and child cannot communicate with each other on more equal terms than is the case.

How does it affect children to find that they cannot express themselves in their own language because the grown-ups in their surroundings either do not understand it, or insist that they express themselves in another way? What attitude toward their own language, which they will continue to use later in life, is in this way conveyed to the deaf children during their entire school career? (Bergman, 1978, p. 2).

If this respect for Sign Language and its indispensable place in the childrens' lives is reflected in their attitudes toward themselves and their community, Deaf children can proceed to take full advantage of school. If, however, it is not present in the system, even children who develop a first language early—in a home where they are accepted and Sign Language is available to them—will run into many barriers when they reach school. This has been the experience of the parents in Michigan whose children had excellent early exposure to ASL and to English through text. When the children were ready to enter school, parents had difficulty finding educational settings where ASL was seen as a resource rather than a liability.

Good News

Changing the system is exciting work. It may, however, be easy to become discouraged by the magnitude of changes that need to take place in our current system in order to conduct successful programs of bilingual education for Deaf children. The good news is that, from both a theoretical and an experiential perspective, those who have written about the process of transition toward bilingual education seem to agree: Change in attitude toward the children and their language is the crucial ingredient for success. It may mean more than all the rest. The bad news is that attitudes may be the hardest thing to change.

Good teachers don't simply tolerate the existence of Sign Language, but embrace it— take full advantage of it—which can mean a great deal in the education and upbringing of young children. Valuing the childrens' language and those who use it may be one of the most important variables for success in educating children whose first language is other than the majority, according to this expert on bilingual education:

> In bilingual programs where mother-tongue instruction seems to be the causal factor in school achievement, it is presumably not for linguistic reasons; but for the changed attitudes on the part of students and teachers that go with recognizing the status of the native language, normally stigmatized, as worthy of school use. (Paulston, 1974, p. 24, as quoted by Woodward).

Skutnabb-Kangas (1994) described a continuum to gauge the extent to which educational policies reflect support for minority languages—and whether the intent is to maintain them or have them assimilated into the majority culture. The chart she and Robert Phillipson designed represents two dimensions:

- *degree of overtness* (the degree to which policies and laws express open support of the rights of minority languages in education) and

- *degree of promotion* (the extent to which a language is prohibited, tolerated, or actively promoted).

The first dimension ranges from overt to covert support of the rights of linguistic minorities and acceptance and use of minority languages in schools. The second dimension names some of the degrees on the continuum (from left to right): prohibition, toleration, non-discrimination prescription (where discrimination against the people who use the language is prohibited, either overtly or covertly through legislation), permission, and finally *promotion.*

Sweden and Denmark have moved far on the continuum in both official policy and practice toward overtly supporting Deaf people's right to be educated using Sign Language and toward promoting levels of proficiency in Sign Language as a language to be maintained. The more these attitudes and practices become part of the everyday operation of the school, the more this level of respect also extends to monitoring the language rights of Deaf children whose natural first language is spoken, or who have aptitudes for developing their speech and auditory skills. Once teachers overcome their fears that one language will somehow sabotage the other, and begin to recognize Deaf children's uncomplicated capacity for multilingualism, they will use their intuitions to individualize instruction and work to see that the rights and preferences of all the children are protected.

Commitment to Individualization

Finally, teachers who are educating Deaf children bilingually must possess a strong commitment to individualization—to finding ways to let each child take his/her own path to becoming a bilingual adult. In commenting on this manuscript, Marie Jean Philip, of The Learning Center for Deaf Children in Framingham, Massachusetts (one of the earliest programs in the United States to move in the direction of bilingual education) stressed that this concept was central to good teaching:

> *Teachers can't stick to a set formula for all children. They MUST follow each child's lead. If something is wrong, teachers must NOT assume the problem is with the child. I believe every child can learn. If they're not learning, then something is wrong with the teacher, the methodology, the environment. We have to look at ourselves. Teachers sometimes come to me and say "This strategy isn't working with _____." I tell them, "Try something else." We can find the thread that makes a meaningful connection for each child, but we have to be looking. It's all based on a strong belief in each child's abilities (M. Philip, personal communication, August 9, 1994).*

The teacher quoted at the beginning of this chapter (and the team teacher she worked with) displayed a strong commitment to individualization by videotaping, studying, and observing their students often to understand their difficulties, strengths, and differences. After some time using the teaching method for reading Swedish that was described earlier

(*Adam's Bøk*), they noted that some of the hard of hearing children in their class were lagging behind in reading, while the others were doing very well using the Sign Language videotapes and parallel study of Swedish text. The teachers then experimented with a separate reading group and some different techniques for the hard of hearing children. They discovered that these children needed to approach reading in a way that reinforced their auditory processing of the text, relying more on their knowledge of spoken Swedish. So they tried an approach like Language Experience, in which the children dictate to the teacher and then read back their own words aloud. These particular children progressed more quickly after they began reading aloud familiar texts such as the stories from *Adam's Bøk* or sentences they had generated themselves, later becoming fluent enough to read silently and independently.

These teachers' commitment to letting each child follow his or her individual path to becoming a bilingual adult meant recognizing that there was not one monolithic approach for success with all children. Likewise, this did not automatically become their method of choice for all hard of hearing children. Some of the children excelled with more visual strategies. This reading group continued to work with the whole class during most of their activities, including viewing and discussing the *Adam's Bøk* videotapes. It was clear to me that another part of these teachers' commitment to individualization included making sure that no grouping was allowed to dictate a child's entire identity (as "hard of hearing," "good at reading," "good at speech," "children of Deaf parents," or any of the other rationales for grouping—of which children quickly become aware).

Larger Class Size:
An Important Strategy for Individualizing

Teachers and school administrators in Sweden and Denmark have come to believe strongly that large class sizes are an important component in their ability to implement the goals described in this book. They have found creative ways to allow children to receive more individualized instruction and to learn cooperatively from their peers through small group work, while still experiencing their identity—including coming to recognize their strengths and weaknesses—as part of a larger group. While it doesn't always work for every class or school, combining smaller classes into one has also allowed Deaf and hearing teachers to work together more often as a team, which seems to affect the dynamics of the system as a whole.

Larger classes are an outgrowth of teachers' open-mindedness and commitment to finding ways to individualize. Their willingness to begin working together was part of their effort to find ways to allow their students to have an upbringing that includes a diverse group of children with all its social and academic dynamics. With large enough classes, students can be placed in changing working groups based on learning styles and skills in different areas of subject matter, not relegated to static groupings throughout their school career according to speech or reading skills only, as in the past.

The class of six students who were the first to be taught bilingually in Stockholm were later combined with the other groups of students their age. At the time of my visit in 1990, they were part of a large seventh grade class that included all their agemates at the school. Their teacher explained:

> *In this group, there are 24. And very often we are all together—for geography, history, sociology. Really everything except Swedish, English, math, and chemistry. And Swedish—we have one lesson when we are together and that is when we study Swedish authors or literature. It is just when we have grammar, like today, that we split up. (H. Björneheim, personal communication, May 20, 1990).*

In *Unlocking the Curriculum*, Johnson, Liddell, and Erting (1989) discuss the cost-effectiveness of combining classes and utilizing teams of Deaf and hearing teachers. Carol Padden, faculty member in the University of California, San Diego, Department of Communication, reinforced these authors' suggestion, saying that creating larger classes was more than just a way to deal with practical/fiscal considerations in implementing a model similar to the one described here. Padden (1990a) referred to the usual preference for small classes with 4-6 children as part of the traditional pathological view of these children, that the "poor deaf children" needed more special attention than other children. She observed that deaf children who are products of today's education in the U.S. often lack some inner substance; qualities that Swedish educators have found are, in part, born of diversity of experience and of dealing with the many challenges in a dynamic and diverse classroom. Padden also stressed the need to let children learn from each other, rather than supporting the notion that the teacher was the source of all information and control in the classroom. Having a large enough class that children can work in changing groups depending on the task seems to foster children's problem-solving skills independent of the teacher. Björneheim, quoted above, continued:

> *When there are only four or five students, as a teacher you feel like you have to do some work. So you go there and you help and you help and you help; and they never get the chance to think for themselves. But if you have 24, it is impossible for you to help everyone and the students realize that you can't, so they have to try.*

Ideally, every child in large class has full access to the classroom discussion through Sign Language, if the teacher utilizes strategies for presenting information visually in a way that keeps the children engaged. The prerequisite for this, of course, is that all children have the competence in Sign Language to understand the lessons presented, and feel comfortable asking questions when they miss something. When these circumstances are present, much less one-on-one instruction is needed. Teachers seem to get a better sense of each child's academic and social strengths and weaknesses, because there are more children to serve as a norm.

A common complaint of today's teachers in classrooms for Deaf children in the U.S. is that, in almost any grade, one can find children who were taught Sign Language only after failing with spoken communication. These children—from later in preschool through high school—are not in a position to sit back and comfortably comprehend a normal-paced classroom discussion in Sign Language; therefore the pace of a large class is often slowed, these children are left out, or smaller groupings/one-on-one arrangements are formed to allow them to do the work.

Until consistent early exposure to Sign Language becomes the norm, such children may need some remedial work in Sign Language before being expected to function in a large group, as stated in the 1983 Swedish Special School Curriculum:

> *Pupils whose Sign Language is substantially defective when they enter the special school must be given individual support for their linguistic development (p. 9).*

By configuring larger classes with Deaf and hearing team teachers, and promoting cooperative learning and creative groupings, schools can facilitate teachers' efforts to support each child's individual path to bilingualism. With fewer total classes, it also becomes possible for support staff (speech therapists, physical therapists, psychologists, Sign Language tutors, etc.) who work with some children, to have involvement with the whole class. This configuration seems to foster closer cooperation with teachers and helps to keep support professionals' individual work grounded in each child's everyday interests and interactions with peers. Interestingly enough, it seems large classes with teams of teachers and aides, working closely with support staff, can offer a *better* way to individualize instruction than the conventional approach of individualizing by placing children in very small classes.

Clearly, the study of what bilingualism means for Deaf and hard of hearing students, and how best to facilitate it, is just beginning. But teachers' willingness to investigate various responsive strategies and individualization has allowed them to accommodate children's differences in visual vs. auditory learning, as well as other attributes that affect learning. Rather than making the either-or choices that many approaches to education of Deaf children imply, teachers whose approach to education is based on awareness of the value of a strong first language can capitalize on the strengths of various teaching tools at the times when they are most beneficial, without threatening that first language.

A Team Effort

Teachers...are learning to see the strengths deaf students demonstrate and appreciate the glimpses into the language process afforded by the miscues and experimentation that are so valued in the whole language approach. Teachers are beginning to mistrust traditional testing methods and to trust themselves as learners and observers of their deaf student's process (Ewoldt, 1993, p. 4).

Teachers who have the commitment, expertise, and attitude discussed in this chapter are on the 'cutting edge' of learning what Deaf children can do, constantly seeking better ways to give each child the input he or she needs. Critical components for developing new models involve partnerships between teachers and researchers to better understand both the processes and results that are not likely to be revealed through simple standardized testing. A partnership between teachers and outside researchers is crucial for describing and observing what is working and what is not. Developing this new model must be a team effort.

Such a team effort really paid off in the first experimental class in Copenhagen. While the law passed in Sweden in 1981 required that Deaf children have the right to be educated bilingually, there was no such law in Denmark. Nevertheless, the level of sophistication in Denmark also rose somewhat simultaneously with that of the Swedish system. This was not because of formal changes in the curriculum. It was, at least in part, because the teachers in the experimental bilingual class wrote four books that were widely-read among teachers in Denmark about their methods, successes, failures, and outcomes as their students in the "bilingual project" progressed through the grades (Lewis, 1994; Lewis, et al, 1992; Sörensen, et al, 1983, 1984, 1988[3]

These teachers worked closely with linguists and psychologists, which gave them the theoretical underpinning to understand what they were seeing, the benefit of outside observation, and the ability to better explain the rationale for their methods to others. In addition to being part of the team in the development of successful models, the best teachers must be given time to document and share their methods and insights. Such cooperation is now taking place between teachers in the preschool research classes at Kendall Demonstration Elementary School (utilizing both ASL and English at an early age) and researchers in the Gallaudet Research Institute's Culture and Communication Studies Program.

---

3   These teachers have received a grant to produce a version of their final book in English. For more information, write to Döveskolernes Materialelaboratorium, Kollegievej 1, DK9210 Aalborg SØ, Denmark.

One of the biggest attributes for success of a changing system seems to be trusting teachers to do what all good teachers do: individualize instruction as they see it is needed. However, without sufficient orientation, training, and support from the system, not all teachers can be expected to be sensitive enough to each child's linguistic needs and preferences; that is why consideration of the "teacher attributes" discussed above is so important. Just because a school proclaims its intention to educate Deaf children bilingually, teachers do not all evolve overnight to the requisite respect for both languages, commitment to individualization in each child's path to bilingualism, and expertise in the structure and use of both languages. Schools must plan plenty of time for educating teachers about the theoretical rationale for such a change and working through cultural conflicts that arise as part of the process (Titus, in press).

As programs discuss change, *the classroom goals they set must be for the children.* If the goals defined by a program are *not* to dictate teacher behavior, but are child-centered (ultimate bilingualism, grade level achievement, high self-esteem, etc.) then teachers—provided they get training—will carry out these goals in a way that respects the linguistic needs and preferences of each child. It is the system's responsibility to see that the teachers understand the theoretical basis for the changes; this may include a great deal of education and orientation for all teachers to make the transition. In addition to providing inservice training, the system can promote this sensitivity to the children's needs by giving teachers opportunities for ongoing study of their students' progress through videotapes and collaboration with researchers or other teachers who are skilled observers.

Finally, it is very important during times of transition to make the best use of those teachers who already possess the attributes described above in dealing with young children and their parents. It is crucial to choose excellent teachers for preschool and the early years of school, when children's attitudes are being formed toward themselves and their languages—toward reading, writing, signing, and speaking. And then to trust those teachers to utilize the natural interplay between the two languages in a way that respects the language rights of each child and optimizes academic performance.

CHAPTER FIVE

Change the System, Not the Children

Meeting Deaf Children "Where They Live"

It is worth repeating that in this model Sign Language is not looked upon as a means for deaf children to achieve educational goals. Instead, Swedish Sign Language is looked upon as a language in its own right, indispensable to its users. Teaching it as a mother tongue, the interrelationship between such teaching and second language teaching, and its use in all kinds of educational settings—these matters have not been stressed because, in this model, such use of Sign Language is a matter of course.

This core principle, acceptance, brings with it a certain view of deaf people. Here they are not looked upon, as in other educational models, as defective human beings. Instead, they are seen as belonging to a minority group with its own conditions and requirements. As a whole, this group does not need remedial teaching. Instead, they need an educational system, and teaching, in which their special linguistic situation is taken into consideration. It is with such a system that their rights to equal participation in society can be realized, a participation which implies bilingual proficiency (Svartholm, 1993. p. 328).

This quote, by a linguist who specializes in Scandinavian languages, communicates a great deal about the attitudes I encountered during my two studies in Sweden and Denmark, and is meant to set the tone in this final chapter for discussion of change. In order to move toward an education that ensures Deaf children equal participation in society through proficiency in both the Sign Language and the majority language of a country, it is important to realize:

IT IS NOT DEAF CHILDREN THAT NEED REMEDIATION,
IT IS THE SYSTEM THAT EDUCATES THEM.

If the system considers Deaf children to be healthy, whole, human beings—if we assume a posture similar to that described in the quote above—then our job is to get better at meeting these Deaf children "where they live."

This placement of responsibility applies especially to decisions that dictate a course of action in dealing with infants and very young children who are deaf. The English idiom, "meeting them where they live," means it is *we* who are asked to change, not the children. We find out what's going on in their heads; we learn about their world; we discover how to make contact on their level. We let each child instruct us regarding the forms of linguistic input he or she finds readily available. Then we configure the system to give each child the tools he or she needs to grow up on schedule.

There is nothing inherently lacking in the children, only in the environments in which they find themselves. Given this perspective, the system's main responsibility becomes that of providing the kind of environment Deaf children need to be themselves and to learn; an environment that capitalizes on their strengths and allows them to build their inner resources with a minimum of pressure and a minimum of unnecessary experience with failure. *The earlier we can provide such an environment, the more happily and successfully Deaf children will function in their homes, in society, and throughout their education.* This seems to be the most important lesson learned by those who have worked to change their own systems in the direction of educating Deaf children bilingually.

Those who have successfully shaped the environment to meet the child's "specifications"—whether naturally in homes with Deaf parents, or through changes in the system—have extremely valuable information to share. Their insights and observations can serve in describing optimal theoretical models (separate from practical constraints created by our current system) and can guide us in our own decision-making processes.

Moving toward educating Deaf children with the goal of fluency in both Sign Language and the language of the majority is possible. But it will become necessary to assume a more child-centered perspective in examining our assumptions. In other words:

> If these children do not have full access to my language,
> then I need to learn theirs.

There is no evidence indicating that Deaf children should not, as a matter of course, function cognitively and linguistically on a par with hearing children. The idea of remedial teaching for deaf children usually works this way: proceed with the system, as is, and if things aren't working out well, give the child lots of specialized help later. In order for real change to take place, this approach needs to be completely turned on its head. Instead, the system could be configured to give Deaf children the best possible chances early to learn with tools that come naturally for them. Rather than withholding the tools they need (and reluctantly accepting that deaf toddlers will have a long, hard struggle comprehending their world), we *could* freely offer the kinds of language and socialization that come easily to them. One parent who reviewed this manuscript added, at this point:

> *Yes, the first message I received was 'Don't let him take the easy way (sign). He'll never adapt to hearing society.'*

Meeting the children where they live in the early years (happily letting them take "the easy way") allows them to build the cognitive and linguistic abilities—as well as the confidence—they will need to handle academic and societal challenges later. If children who are deaf are not functioning on a par with children who hear, we need to look hard at the system: *Is it providing an early education that attends to deaf children's linguistic realities?*

To assume it is the system, not the children, that needs remediating requires taking a long, hard look at what's happening—and what isn't happening—as noted by Liddell and Johnson (1992):

> *...the system has been notably reluctant to examine its own outcomes and to consider that such outcomes may in fact be the result of structural deficiencies in the system rather than of personality or cognitive defects of the students or of defects in the efforts of the parents. It is time for the system to undertake a critical self-examination, without fear of finding deficiency. Only through such self-examination can the system begin to make the kinds of changes needed to prevent the deficiencies from occurring.... (p. 22).*

Educational reform comes slowly. Ralph Fletcher, impatient for transformation in the New York City Public Schools, compared those involved in a changing educational system to the "walking trees" in one little girl's fantasy about the Florida marshlands—trees she claimed lift their roots one at time and take one step every hundred years. In the following quote, Fletcher equates the walking trees to his work in educational reform and to what he described as "the tremendous amount of effort implicit in even the smallest amount of growth in the teachers I worked with. And in myself." He describes such change as follows:

> *Walking trees. The phrase articulates the idea I have so far been unable to articulate to myself. It occurs to me that this is precisely what I have been trying to do all year long: to encourage big and ponderous trees to lift up their roots and take a step, even if it would be the only step they would take the entire year. This was my job: to take those rough old trunks by the hand, to coax them to uproot themselves from that tired dirt they'd been stuck in, to leave their familiar terrain, to take a chance, to go someplace new (Fletcher, 1991, p. 203)[1].*

Taking those steps is not easy. It will take a long time before changes are complete. But there are many people who work with Deaf children who have been ready for a long time and who carry with them a wealth of momentum and creativity. Certainly, there will be obstacles. But my perception is that the biggest thing keeping us "stuck" is our adherence to the old system and our unwillingness to accept that we have something to learn. According to Marie Jean Philip:

> *The process is painful and emotional, but enriching and inspiring. You may have to dismiss three-fourths of your earlier training. (M. Philip, 1990., p.47)*

"Yes, but..."

We have a great deal to learn from each other. When I share news from Sweden and Denmark, some people in the U.S. are ready to embrace the ideas and try to figure out how to make them work for us. Others (both Deaf and hearing) are full of doubt :

"Yes, but those countries have a more socialistic system of government and high taxes. We could never do that here."

Funding such a model may be no more costly than the current system—if we were willing to undertake a major redirection of priorities in the allocation of resources. Placing the most emphasis on early natural language acquisition (in which the children need few special services or tools, just regular contact with users of the language), yields benefits later in terms of student/teacher ratio and fewer remedial services. It seems providing these early services is not only effective, but *cost* effective.

Additionally, by creating many more centralized locations where Deaf children are educated together, our system could capitalize on available Deaf teachers, and more students could be with their Deaf peers and be in closer proximity to their homes. This would create a win-win situation where both the child's education and the family's needs are concerned, and would decrease the current cost of residential schools by allowing more Deaf children to live at home and still have access to Deaf language and role models.

Sweden is primarily a rural country—mostly small towns. Even Stockholm would be considered only a mid-sized city in the U.S. Geographically, Sweden is about

1   Thanks to Dave Schleper for bringing this wonderful analogy to my attention.

the size of California, with far fewer people (8 1/2 million people live in Sweden as opposed to 33 million in California). Yet Sweden has five central residential-type schools for educating Deaf children, while California only has two. Denmark is a very small country, smaller than Massachusetts and with a much smaller population, but has four central locations for teaching deaf children. Based on the approach in Sweden and Denmark—that the majority of children live within a 1 1/2 hour commuting distance from these schools—California, for example, would have *many* more large, centralized schools for the Deaf. In Sweden and Denmark, the few children whose homes fall outside the established radius live at the school or in nearby neighborhoods during the week (see Introduction for description of residential housing for Deaf students in the community).

Since there are far fewer residential students, schools save money. Any residential students go home on weekends. In this way, even children who live at the school get to see their families often. With fewer residential students, transporting those students home on weekends is considered more cost-effective than housing them at the school and paying staff around the clock to care for them. The same is true of transportation home each night for day students, which is still considered more cost-effective than feeding and housing all the students every night.

Of the Deaf children surveyed in the U.S. through the 1992-93 Annual Survey of Hearing Impaired Children and Youth (see Prologue), 66% are mainstreamed in classes with hearing children, with approximately 8% in small self-contained classrooms for Deaf and hard of hearing students within public schools. If these children were educated together, with their local school districts transferring funds to a more centralized location, the idea of more centralized locations would not only be feasible, but practical. Costs for interpreters, itinerant teachers, home speech therapists and sign language tutors, special resource teachers, and many other support and remedial services that are currently provided on an individual basis to Deaf and hard of hearing children who attend public schools in the U.S. could be reduced by serving a greater number of students in one place.

In the Denver area, for example, unpublished estimates of the average cost to local school districts of educating students in the public schools is $12,000 to $16,000 per year (G. Webster, personal communication, September 24, 1994), a cost that greatly exceeds the standard per pupil operating revenue (PPOR) for the area (in other words, much of this cost cannot be recouped by the schools from the operating funds they receive). The projected cost per student for a proposed Denver Magnet School of the Deaf (MSD) will be a little over $10,000 per student (MSD Core Committee, 1994).

This new *magnet* school's goal is to provide a high quality, alternative placement to current choices in the Denver area, which are now much like the choices for parents in other states. Parents currently have the difficult decision of whether to place their Deaf children in local schools with hearing children or to send them away to the state residential school for the Deaf in Colorado Springs. While there are many desirable benefits for Deaf children living in residential schools, this decision can still be hard on the family.

The Colorado Association of the Deaf (CAD), therefore, working as a team with some hearing parents in the Denver area, has proposed a charter school under Colorado state law—a publicly-funded school that is independent of normal school district administration (MSD Core Committee, 1994).[2] This school will be a place for Deaf children from the entire Denver/Boulder area to learn together, as well as a resource on deafness for the larger Denver Metro community, and for information and training for parents of Deaf children. Furthermore, the charter application states that "the Deaf community will be a key resource in determining what is needed to maximize learning on the part of Deaf children." The proposal states that the director will be Deaf, and a majority of the board of directors will be deaf. All members of the school staff will be fluent in ASL, and ideally, more than 50% of the teachers will be Deaf. Instructors will be certified in a Montessori approach to learning, using ASL and English as the languages of instruction in employing a student-directed learning style. One very important goal of the founders is to work with the medical community to identify Deaf children earlier, and to give the children and their parents the earliest possible support and services.

The idea of *more* central or magnet locations where there is a critical mass of Deaf children and adults is not only vital in educating Deaf children bilingually, but may be feasible as a long range solution to some of the current problems in educating Deaf children in the U.S. (Andrews and Covell, 1993). Another magnet school is already operating in the Minneapolis area. With creativity and some reallocation of resources, it seems a win-win situation is not totally out of reach for many Deaf children and their families.

Regarding the offering of American Sign Language learning "blocks" (week- or weekend-long courses) for parents, what looks to some like an expensive and impractical venture could become a cost-effective, practical solution, given a shift in priorities and funding. A great deal of time, money, and effort is *already* being

2   A copy of the Magnet School of the Deaf charter proposal can be obtained from the address
     in Appendix C.

expended by parents themselves, those designated to serve them, and the health care system that supports counseling, multiple medical opinions, and efforts to improve Deaf children's hearing.

Many mothers of Deaf children in the U.S. quit their jobs or take off large amounts of time, as advocating for their child, conducting one-on-one speech or manual English training, seeking medical treatment, seeking emotional support through what is often a long-lasting crisis, and learning about the confusing array of approaches to educating Deaf children in the United States can be a full time job. Many families already spend their summer vacations attending family learning retreats to find out more about raising a Deaf child, study sign language, and meet other families with Deaf children. Others don't have the luxury of time or money for these pursuits, but deserve no less support. For some families, early childhood is a virtual parade of regular visits from a variety of state- or county-funded speech-language therapists, sign language tutors, audiologists, and social workers.

Clearly, a great deal of time, money, and effort is already going in the direction of remedying the perceived problems of the deaf child and the family, while the most efficient early solution may be a positive, linguistic one. In other words, *the parents need to learn a new language.* The focus of this expenditure builds on a well-documented 'sure thing' in creating a strong foundation for the Deaf child's future academic and social success, and moderates expenditure in the direction of some well-documented 'unknowns.' In Sweden and Denmark, it is felt that there are both immediate and self-sustaining payoffs when family members are given the language, an understanding of Deaf children's potential, and the example and training to configure their family life to include their Deaf child in the kinds of interactions other children experience.

"Yes, but Sweden and Denmark don't have to deal with all the varied socioeconomic factors that we do here in the U.S."

Socioeconomic factors can truly impact on parents' time and money for learning the language and being actively involved in their children's education. Socioeconomic and cultural factors have a big impact on how children approach their world. As Padden (1990a) stated:

> *Hearing parents, for example, are not all alike, but come from different socioeconomic classes....and different ways of raising children. At school, it is sometimes assumed that deaf children are not influenced*

*by their families' backgrounds because they are deaf, but of course
many aspects of how these children are raised have important effects,
and the curriculum must take into account the resulting class
differences....We also need to understand differences between middle
and working class deaf parents' ways of raising their children.... For
the school to meet the needs of the different socioeconomic groups.... it
should assume that not all deaf children are the same (p. 28).*

The standard of living in Sweden and Denmark is shared somewhat equally by all citizens. This is probably one of the biggest differences that has impact on the model I have described. Clearly, the varied socioeconomic situations of Deaf children in the U.S. cannot be ignored. There is a great deal of evidence indicating that socioeconomic status is related to academic achievement. Trybus (1980) rates this factor as second in its influence on the average hearing impaired child's level of reading comprehension or other academic skills. Yet, while the socioeconomic statuses of hearing parents is, on average, superior to that of Deaf parents (Corson, 1973; Moores, 1987; Rodda & Grove, 1987), evidence continues to show Deaf children of Deaf parents to be superior in language, academic achievement, and social development—indicating that early accessible language and acceptance may outweigh the importance of socioeconomic status in the upbringing of Deaf children.

The existence of children's unequal socioeconomic status or lack of time in their parents' demanding schedule is likely to have an impact on outcomes of the system. It does not, however, constitute justification for *not* attempting to model the system to provide Deaf children with the best linguistic and academic input possible, which will ultimately affect the child's (and the family's) overall well-being. In fact, the existence of such variables is even stronger justification for the system to accept more responsibility for providing Deaf children with the early linguistic environment they require. Such an important variable as acquiring a first language should not be left to chance. *Even in the poorest of families, hearing children have full access to the language spoken in their homes as a model for developing their first language.*

The same socioeconomic variables that impact on some Deaf children's ability to get early services today would still be there under a bilingual system. However, such a system would, ideally, provide financial assistance and childcare to support parents in taking the time to learn Sign Language. Providing the parents and children opportunities to learn would be considered not just important, but an integral part of what it means to provide an appropriate education to Deaf children—an investment that would have later payoffs. Given this view, some of the socioeconomic factors that currently deprive low-income Deaf children of critical early language and socialization would become more equalized.

"Yes, but in Sweden and Denmark, they don't have to deal with all the cultural diversity we have here in the U.S."

In regard to consideration of cultural factors and home language differences in educating Deaf children, my impression is that the services and attitudes of a school district, state, or country as they relate to *all* children are likely to influence cultural attitudes toward Deaf children. Those schools in the U.S. who have worked with cross-cultural mediators to recognize such oppression have been able to raise sensitivity, standards, understanding, and awareness. In other words, while they cannot solve the problems prevalent in society, schools that have the consciousness required to conduct a well-designed program of bilingual education for Deaf children will be *more*—not less—likely to care for the needs of children of varied linguistic and cultural backgrounds than is the current monolingual system. Gallimore (1994) asserts that bilingual/bicultural education of Deaf children *can* flourish in a multicultural society, given sufficient awareness. Discrimination does exist toward Deaf and hearing children of different minority groups, within both Deaf and hearing society. But the same understanding and awareness of human languages and cultures that promotes acceptance of American Sign Language and the culture shared by Deaf people in the U.S., can also promote respect for the languages and cultural backgrounds of all peoples, including Deaf children of varying cultures.

The right to formal instruction in the home language is also a desirable goal in any educational system. The Swedish government has mandated support for maintaining the home language skills of all children. By law, all immigrant children are entitled to one hour and forty minutes a week of instruction in the language of their parents, if it is other than Swedish. When I visited the mid-sized city of Örebro in 1990, for example, there were 62 home language teachers that taught a total of 42 different languages. Clearly, ethnic, cultural, and linguistic minorities do exist in Sweden and Denmark. It was explained to me that when more immigrants began coming to Sweden 25 years ago, policy-makers decided that the culture would be much richer and the country would ultimately benefit if these children kept both languages. It is felt to be important for children to have a sense of pride in the language of their parents, rather than be ashamed of it because it is different.

Furthermore, the Swedish viewpoint seems to be that good family life—which ensures a more contented society—depends largely upon good communication between parents and children; hence, the commitment to support that connection by recognizing the home language of immigrant parents. One parent I interviewed felt strongly that all people—this includes Deaf children and parents from another culture—need to be able to express themselves in their first language when emotions are running high, as they often do in families.

> *Your first language is like your skin. It's what holds your thoughts and feelings together. Without it, you would fall apart.*

This level of consciousness among citizens about the importance a first language in establishing one's identity has influenced not only attitudes toward children of minority cultures, but also toward Deaf children. Respect and sensitivity for the culture and language of each family is crucial in the education of all children. The idea that a multilingual home is a positive asset, as well as the fact that all children in Sweden and Denmark learn second and sometimes third languages as an ongoing part of their school curriculum, contributes to the national sentiment that learning other languages is just part of life.

A number of teachers and parents felt that the law giving concrete support for maintaining the home language had an effect on attitudes toward minority languages, including Sign Language. Such attitudes also seem apparent in parents' willingness to learn their child's language, since the Deaf child in a hearing family doesn't have full auditory access to the home language—regardless of which language is spoken. It is recognized among many educators in the U.S. that, no matter what the language of the home—whether it is English or Spanish or Zulu—if it is a spoken language, many Deaf children will have little or no access to it as a comprehensive model for first language development. Therefore, given access to it, the language of the child's Deaf peers and teachers is likely to become the true first language for many Deaf children, regardless of what is spoken at home.

Despite this limited access, Deaf children may possess varying degrees of knowledge of the written or spoken form of their home language. It is crucial to evaluate and recognize whatever home language competence the child possesses (which is often coupled with gesture systems for communication). By school age, almost any child will have developed some kind of communication system with family members. This system must not be minimized or disregarded, as it is an indispensable resource—a bridge for making contact with the child (meeting the child "where he lives"), and the child's starting place for learning the language of the school or preschool (Gerner de Garcia, 1991).

Again, while some obstacles can be surmounted, financial and political support for educating Deaf children of varied cultural backgrounds will be subject to the disposition of current lawmakers and public opinion. As Harlan Lane asserts,

> We need not worry about the school's readiness to present and espouse mainstream culture and values. What we need to ensure is that its curriculum reflects minority cultures and values that are validating for the minority deaf child who is doubly oppressed. In many educational programs for deaf children, what is called for is a multilingual/multicultural curriculum that capitalizes on the knowledge and sense of self that the deaf child brings to the school (Lane, 1992a, p. 174).

"Yes, but how will educating Deaf children from a bilingual perspective impact on minority Deaf children in our multicultural society?

There are very serious concerns in the U.S. about achievement, acceptance, support, and equal access for Deaf children of various cultures within our educational system and within the Deaf community itself. This has been true under a monolingual system, and—due to societal factors—is likely to persist to some degree under a system that provides early access to American Sign Language. Yet, whether in the U.S., Sweden, or Denmark, many *minority Deaf adults* assert that concerns about access to language supersede all other forms of cultural oppression they have experienced. Discrimination against them because they were Deaf throughout childhood, school, and career is at the very heart of their experience of denial of human or civil rights, especially the still-common denial of an accessible first language and comprehensible class-room instruction (Gallimore, 1994).

Laurene Gallimore, program director at the Indiana School for the Deaf and Ph.D. candidate at the University of Arizona, describes her frustration at being told (as recently as 1986) that she could not teach preschool Deaf children because she, herself, was Deaf. Despite Gallimore's outstanding qualifications, a hearing person—a *Black woman*—was hired for the position. Gallimore also discussed the difficult English proficiency exams she was required to pass in order to go on in each higher level of education; exams that many Deaf people, regardless of their ethnic background or socioeconomic status, cannot pass because their education has not fostered high enough levels of literacy. Low levels of literacy and lack of access to information keep Deaf people of all colors and ethnic backgrounds at arm's length from countless opportunities. She points out that if you ask a group of monolingual hearing children in the United States—whether black or white—to describe an experience where they could not understand their teacher, could not take in the conversation going on all around them at a family gathering, or could not make themselves understood in their own home or classroom; most would have trouble coming up with examples. But if you ask a group of Deaf children the same question, their hands will shoot up. Such experiences can be a daily occurrence for Deaf children, regardless of their culture or the color of their skin. While it is reasonable to assume that access will be a problem in society at large, lack of access to language and information *in their own classrooms and homes* is still common in many areas of the U.S.

Gallimore explains that many preschool Deaf children, while surrounded by a rich cultural heritage at home, have not been provided the language to make sense of it, to develop a strong self identity, and to truly become part of that culture—to become more than just an observer. In other words, in the fight for Deaf children's rights, concerns about racial and ethnic discrimination should not be allowed to overshadow Deaf children's very basic needs for access to communication in the family and the classroom. Supporting children's right to develop solid early language competence and high levels of literacy, which will be each child's real ticket to effectively functioning in the larger hearing and Deaf society, as well as in his or her own home culture, must be given top priority.

"Yes, but the dynamics between Deaf and hearing cultures are too difficult."

The oppression Deaf people have experienced throughout history creates a major trust issue. And when Deaf people begin to assert their right to language, culture, and opportunities, their well-justified anger can, at first, feel threatening to hearing employees or parents involved in educational settings. These hearing people's resistance to change or denial of the problem further fuels the fire. As anger and fear grow, the chasm between Deaf and hearing staff members in a school program that is trying to make a transition toward bilingual education can widen. Those programs that endured the roughest part of the transition have often spent many hours processing anger, resentment, and fear on both sides under the direction of someone with skills in cultural mediation (Titus, in press). These emotions are already likely to be present, but they tend to be brought into the open as discussions of linguistic and cultural dynamics in the classroom, school, and society begin to flourish.

Before there was adequate training and support to carry out the goals named in the 1983 curriculum, teachers in Sweden and Denmark also went through a rough transition. When the schools first began moving in the direction of bilingual education, there were almost no Deaf teachers. In implementing bilingual education and recognizing Sign Language in the classroom, it was necessary to place a great deal of emphasis on hiring Deaf teachers and on skills in Sign Language, with hearing teachers feeling devalued and lacking in the skills or resources they needed to do what many agreed seemed best:

> . . . *when I started, it was total communication. That was the "thing" and that was still quite new. Then you had Brita Bergman's linguistic*

> *research and recommendations and things were starting to change. You knew about "bilingual," but you didn't dare try. Everyone was very scared of this new thing. And then we got the new curriculum in 1983 [see Appendix E] and that curriculum said the education was supposed to be bilingual—Swedish and Sign Language as equal languages. And the goal was to learn the Swedish language through the written form, and that was a whole new viewpoint on everything. So everything that you had done before was kind of turned upside down, and everyone was very confused. And there was a lot of criticism from parents, from the linguists, from the deaf association. Everyone said the school for the deaf was so worthless. It was a hard time, but it did get the process rolling . . . .*

Hearing teachers were not the only ones who had trouble during the early stages of transition. I interviewed a Deaf ex-teacher who had felt equally oppressed by the sudden recognition of her rapport with the students. She explained to me:

> *After a long struggle, I left teaching. I was simply worn out. I was team teaching with a hearing teacher who had come to recognize that her Sign Language skills needed a great deal of improvement. She recognized that I was not only better at communicating with the children, but much better at understanding them once we started to open the classroom up for more discussion. She said they listened better to me and looked up to me. EVERY time there was a problem, discipline or otherwise, she would ask me to handle it. I felt that I was carrying the entire burden of the class, and couldn't seem to get the dynamics to change, so I finally left. (name withheld, personal communication, April 15, 1990.)*

While the transition can be difficult, something very important happens when the Sign Language of the Deaf community is truly respected. When Deaf people are hired into administrative roles, the complexion of the organization changes. Decisions tend to take into account a Deaf perspective, which has long been overlooked. When hearing people put to use their best effort to produce the language, the dynamics in meetings and classrooms begin to change. Many communication situations among professionals with varying skills remain some-what tricky; however, increased sensitivity, recognition that significant resources must be devoted to in-service training, and hiring practices that take Sign Language skills into account gradually contribute to a changing make-up in the attitudes and skills of staff and faculty (Evans, et al, 1994; Titus, in press).

The biggest breakthroughs often take place when Deaf-hearing teams or friend-ships develop—when both individuals truly value their differences, which seems to free them to discover their similarities. I especially observed this cooperation among research and teaching staff at Stockholm University and Copenhagen's Kastelsvej Center, where Deaf and hearing staff work together in the study of Sign Language. I have also seen it among Deaf and hearing parents (in a variety of settings in the U.S. and abroad) who have worked together for political change, or to organize fundraisers or activities for their children.

Some Deaf-hearing teams don't work out. But neither do some hearing-hearing or Deaf-Deaf teams. I have met Deaf-hearing teams of teachers, both here in the U.S., and Scandinavia, that have worked together beautifully for many years. When the members of a team come to not only respect their differences, but see beyond them to the person, many problems can be worked through. Problems in a team should not necessarily be ascribed to Deaf or hearing cultural differences. Compatible philosophies about teaching as well as compatible personalities are important ingredients in any Deaf-hearing team (Erting, L. & Stone, 1992; Weinstock & Erting, L., 1994; Wischmeyer, 1994).

At the 1994 TESOL (Teachers of English to Speakers of Other Languages), one discussion group was devoted to the dynamics between Deaf-hearing teams. While it was clear that the participants barely scratched the surface in discussing the cultural and linguistic complexities, it was also clear that the teams that were "making it" were made up of two people who were very honest with each other, and who were both assessing their own contribution—not simply blaming the other or looking to a convenient Deaf-hearing stereotype—in solving problems. Even for those who had worked together many years, it was clearly a process of mutual discovery about differences and similarities, of having to rebuild trust at various turning points, and of looking past "Deaf" or "hearing" to "human." Many had become friends, which was the thing that got them through difficult times.Evans, et al (1994) offer a list of questions the staff at the Sign Talk Centre ask themselves when a conflict arises:

> *Have both Deaf and hearing people had equal input? Are all*
> *individuals being shown respect? Are people content with who they are*
> *or acting to meet an unhealthy need? Is the action/decision motivated*
> *by fear? Can people change their judgements of others to curiosity and*
> *desire to learn more about them? Is it safe for all involved to be honest?*

Is each individual striving to become more bilingual and bicultural—to learn more about themselves and others? Have people tried to find what they have in common or only focused on their differences? (p. 52).

Such questions, viewed in a broader sense, might also be helpful in looking at any classroom or program for Deaf children.

As schools and programs truly begin to recognize Sign Language—through practice, not just rhetoric—as a language equal in status to the majority language, the dynamics do change. Change also occurs as trust grows, as Deaf professionals' input is sought at every turn, as research about Sign Language continues to formalize descriptions that facilitate teaching, and as the benefits of having hearing parents who know the language of the Deaf community become more apparent. In environments where Deaf people are freed from the ongoing fight for recognition of their language and their status in the education of Deaf children, a peaceful coexistence seems possible, at least in settings that have made these efforts.

The following quote, from Dr. Harvey Corson's preface to the *KDES Deaf Studies Curriculum Guide*, sums up the attitude I observed in such settings:

Some people may believe that formalizing Deaf Studies will further separate deaf people from hearing people by defining how we, as deaf people, are different. If learning and teaching are conducted collaboratively in a community where deaf and hearing people work side by side to challenge assumptions and ways of thinking, then such separation will be less, rather than more, likely to occur. As we discover and share knowledge and recognize the richness of our diversity, as well as the depth of our similarities as human beings, a new partnership begins to grow. (In Miller-Nomeland and Gillespie, 1993, p. vii).

"Yes, but will Deaf people really share the language with hearing people?"

Deaf people, like other linguistic minorities, have traditionally exercised both conscious and unconscious mechanisms that restrict members of the majority community from certain aspects of their language and culture (Markowicz & Woodward, 1978). As long as oppression of Sign Language continues, such dynamics are likely to continue, and will have an impact on relationships between Deaf and hearing professionals. However, those Deaf professionals who have studied the grammar of their language—and are aware of the need to make it available to hearing parents and professionals who come into contact with Deaf children—have worked to overcome deep-seated code-switching mechanisms (i.e., the automatic switch to a more English/speech-based variant of Sign Language when encountering a hearing person). Whether in Sweden and Denmark, or in settings in the U.S., Deaf Sign Language teachers and other professionals working in culturally sensitive environments, as well as Deaf consumers whose goal is to support Deaf children of hearing parents, evidence an openness and willingness to share more and more of the language as it is used among Deaf people.

"Yes, but hearing parents who want to give their child Sign Language and Deaf culture do not always find a supportive or welcoming community."

The dynamics just described also enable members of the Deaf community and hearing parents who share a belief in the importance of ASL in the classroom to work together toward their common goals. Trust, however, takes time.

My observation is that three kinds of interactions are optimal in helping both Deaf and hearing parents develop good relationships and get the support they need: 1) Deaf and hearing people working together toward a common goal, 2) each group having separate time for support, socialization, or work toward a goal, and 3) Deaf and hearing families socializing and having fun together.

The group of hearing and Deaf parents in Denver, Colorado who are founding the Magnet School of the Deaf (discussed earlier) are an example of Deaf and hearing people working together toward a common goal. In the process of conceptualizing, proposing, and establishing a charter school, the Colorado Association of the Deaf attracted local hearing parents of like minds (some who were experienced signers, others who were relatively new) for both their steering committee and their smaller working group. This core committee (made up of at least half Deaf members) has been an extremely productive unit. This small committee has conducted working meetings once a week for almost three years—twice a week when there were deadlines to meet with their proposal to the state. Through the necessity of devoting their Sunday afternoons and Tuesday evenings to this job, they have built a strong, cooperative relationship because of their common goals: founding a school that would provide Deaf children and their parents in the Denver area with the early language and support they need, as well as a quality education throughout their school years. This group provides an example of how well Deaf and hearing parents/advocates can work together. Time spent together and a common goal seem to be important ingredients in building trust and making communication work within a group of individuals who are bound to have varying skills in Sign Language. It seems that in such a situation, if the attitude of mutual acceptance and respect for Sign Language and Deaf people is there, individuals and groups will find a way to deal with discrepancies in communication skills and approaches to problem-solving as they work to achieve their common goals.

Whether the goal is to work for educational reform, to advocate for the rights of Deaf children, to serve on the board of a school, or to plan a picnic or a school party, having a common goal and a job to get done is one of the best ways to work out communication strategies and to build mutual trust and respect. In addition to being able to work productively for educational change, the Deaf and hearing parents I have met who have worked to listen and learn from each other about their differing challenges and perspectives have reaped many other benefits for themselves and their children. Again, trust takes time.

In some cases, interactions have gone more smoothly when participants are unaware of traditional fears and Deaf/hearing stereotypes. Inger Ahlgren conducted an experiment in the early 70s that brought Deaf and hearing couples together. She comments as follows:

> We organized courses in sign language for a group of 6 hearing couples here in Stockholm... and deaf people volunteered as teachers, and took care of the children. So these were sort of boarding courses, where they could bring their children. That was the first time in Swedish history that anyone brought deaf people to be teachers for hearing people. It was such a small thing to do, but had such dramatic consequences. We did this in 1976 and -77 with this one group of 12 parents, a one-week retreat each year. During the year that passed between those 2 week-long gatherings, we met regularly on Saturday afternoons in each others' homes. Both parents could come because they could bring their children.
>
> So we pushed together 2 groups of people that were equally scared of each other. There again, I didn't know enough to be careful, because if I had known, I wouldn't have dared to do this, I think.
>
> ....that experience taught them some of the things that I wanted them to know. Just by being together....(Ahlgren, personal communication, May 14, 1990)

The experiment was so successful that all the parents continued to work together for educational reform (See Ahlgren [1989] or Davies [1991b] for a more complete description.)

If work toward changing the educational situation for Deaf children is to proceed as a team effort, it is important that activists not stereotype either group. Each individual's viewpoint is complex and brings with it a variety of factors that deserve to be heard. Individuals, given a chance, typically overcome stereotypes. Hearing parents, for example, are among the best advocates I know in the fight to maintain a range of educational placement options, or in advocating for their Deaf child's right to ASL in school; yet they are often dismissed as potential allies because of continuing stereotypes among the Deaf community that the only thing hearing parents care about is speech. Likewise, while "Deaf culture" has taken on a scary connotation for some people, hearing parents who have actually gotten to know Deaf parents and professionals have often found them to be the most giving, caring, and sensitive to hearing parents' needs and fears.

When it comes to achieving political aims, advocates may not always agree on all fronts (whether they are Deaf or hearing). In order to effect change, the process cannot wait for everyone to be convinced. Those who are ready can forge ahead. Individuals or groups do not need to see eye-to-eye on everything to get something done. They can learn to "agree to disagree" about three political goals in order to work together toward the one or two goals they *do* agree on. This is how the cooperation in Sweden and Denmark started.

In discussing the historic achievement of one significant political milestone—the 1991 order by the Danish Ministry of Education that all deaf children should have the opportunity to study Danish Sign Language as an academic subject— Deaf researcher, teacher, and parent, Ritva Bergmann, describes the importance of ongoing dialogue among those involved with Deaf children:

> *How did we reach this wonderful goal? We are convinced that the strength of the deaf community in Denmark is that we—like our friends in the Nordic countries—have a very long tradition of effective dialogue between three key groups: Deaf adults, parents of deaf children, and teachers of deaf children. Of course we often have different views but by interacting with each other we are able to listen, argue, and discuss in an informal way. We understand each other better, so now we have a common goal: Bilingualism for deaf children.*

Regarding this willingness to start working together, it often becomes clear that some change is better than none—and that no change will take place unless Deaf and hearing people find ways to work together. In any country, state, or school district, there are always some common issues on which hearing parents and the Deaf community can work together for needed change. If they can determine that the goals they do share are a reasonable starting place, they may begin work on them immediately—even if there are other areas they have not yet worked out.

In the U.S., parents are the only people with true rights under the law when it comes to making educational decisions and demands for their own Deaf children; real change will not occur without parents' understanding and acceptance of the rationale for that change. Therefore, the ability Bergmann mentions of individuals who are Deaf and parents of Deaf children to "listen, argue, and discuss in an informal way" is a crucial ingredient in change. While dialogue and cooperation must take place. it seems they cannot be imposed on the Deaf community by hearing parents. In the same way the Colorado Association of the Deaf were the prime movers for the formation of the Magnet School, the Deaf communities in Sweden and Denmark have accepted the responsibility to initiate this joint work to meet the needs of Deaf children.

In order to sustain this kind of cooperation and to bring on new recruits from within the parent or Deaf contingency, it is also very important for each group to have work time or social time when they are *not* together with the other group. This second kind of support parents need is with parents who are similar to them. They deserve to have some times when the talk is comfortable, in their own language, and geared to their common issues. This is the place to vent their frustrations, to comfort and empathize, to teach each other, to convince those who aren't yet convinced of certain political goals—in an environment that feels safe. The importance of hearing parents having other hearing parents who have learned Sign Language and accepted their child's deafness is discussed in Chapter Three. Deaf and hearing parents face some very different issues in raising their Deaf children, and often need time to process them separately.

One Deaf parent (in the U.S.) explained that, in the past, she had tried to offer support by entering into discussions with hearing parents of children the same age as hers, but often felt their issues about their children were so different than hers that she was getting "dragged down." In groups, the hearing parents wanted to discuss basic issues about access to Sign Language, while she was concerned at that time with reading skills. While she was trying to meet the needs of the hearing parents, this Deaf parent began to feel that she had to put all her own issues aside. She also needed the support of other Deaf parents and time to discuss her own issues. In addition, communication can be slow and tedious at first, and Deaf people in educational settings have often had the experience of being used in conversations largely for the "practice" of new hearing signers.

For these reasons, the entire Deaf community and the parents organization must get involved. The burden to meet both group's needs for interaction and support—and meet the children's needs for exposure to Deaf families and Sign Language in social settings—should not fall on a handful of parents whose children happen to be about the same age. Those parents—Deaf or hearing—

have enough to handle, especially in the early years. That is why regular events (not once a year) need to be planned that include hearing parents who have already been through various stages of raising their Deaf and hearing children, Deaf adults who may or may not have children, Deaf grandparents, and all the Deaf and hearing children in the families.

While work and learning groups are important, regular opportunities for relaxation and play may be even more important. While it is not necessary for them to do all the work, the Deaf community, ideally, must play a big role in initiating or sponsoring various events, and for making sure hearing parents are really included—not left standing together. Hearing parents who try to get this kind of interaction for their children and themselves cannot force themselves on the Deaf community—that quickly becomes clear to them. If this interaction and support, then, is going to take place, it must be initiated by the Deaf community out of their commitment to Deaf children of hearing parents.

There are a lot of energetic, "ready," hearing parents out there who want their children to have regular contact with Deaf peers and adults but aren't given the opportunity, and often feel rejected if they try to go after it. I was recently at a discussion group where Deaf parents were criticized for congregating away from the hearing parents at an all-day information-sharing event. The hearing parents were frustrated because they had made long-term efforts to involve their child with the Deaf community and to learn Sign Language, but did not feel included or supported. In response, some of the Deaf parents admitted they hadn't really realized that it was up to them to approach hearing parents or that these hearing parents were unsure if they were welcome. Others have explained that these perceived "rejections" are often a misinterpretation of deference to hearing parents. Marie Philip talks about the ambivalence among Deaf people who do want to be of help and support, but who likewise don't want to force themselves on hearing parents:

> It seems to happen often that my Deaf colleagues or friends and I feel unsure about approaching hearing parents who are talking together. We often discuss among ourselves whether to approach these parents or to let them have the time to themselves. These events are sometimes hearing parents' only opportunity for support from each other, and I don't want to interrupt those dynamics. Sometimes I go over and briefly say "Hi," but I'm not sure whether the parents really want to pursue a long conversation with me, so I back off (M. Philip, personal communication, August 9, 1994).

If these joint work or social assemblies are the only opportunity parents have to be together, then they *are* likely to congregate with those from whom they can get the most comfortable and available support. Again, that is why other opportunities for socialization within their own group are important for the processing of fears, frustrations, questions, needs for information, etc. Each group can then be free to truly socialize and become more comfortable with each other when the two groups get together.

Clearly, individuals on both sides are concerned about forcing themselves in where they are not welcome, concern that is sometimes misinterpreted. Mistrust can be lessened somewhat by keeping in mind that, in most cases, we are talking about honest, caring individuals who wish each other well and have the best interests of Deaf children at heart, but who often may have culturally different approaches to social interactions or who are not aware of the other groups' needs and expectations.

While the system is moving in the direction of hiring more Deaf professionals, it is clear that—at this time—hearing parents' interactions with Deaf families and adults must often come as a result of volunteerism. There are a lot of Deaf consumers out there who *are* concerned about the welfare of all Deaf children, but also need to be provided a structure within which to give of their time. One example of how this has worked was in the "Bridges" program, which started as a summer camp in North Carolina with the intent of providing Deaf role models for the children, largely through the help of Deaf "grandparents" (Saylor, 1992). Deaf teen clubs can raise money by babysitting groups of children while parents socialize, or provide hearing parents with the addresses of Deaf teens who would like to babysit in their homes. The strong Deaf athletic associations could occasionally serve as a network for spreading the word about events to support parents or need for political activism to change educational policy. The Deaf clubs and associations in Sweden and Denmark, working with local and national parents organizations, have been very creative in "making things happen" for Deaf children of hearing parents by sponsoring activities, potlucks, family camps, etc.

Chapters of parent organizations and Deaf clubs who have this awareness can be the catalyst to bring people together and make it possible for each of the three kinds of interactions to take place for those who need it. Parents' organization meetings, for example, are housed in the Deaf club in Stockholm. In addition to hearing parents meeting together with Deaf parents to discuss issues in raising their Deaf child, this club has sponsored meetings for Deaf parents with hearing children who want to learn more from hearing parents about raising a hearing child. Even for those parents who have to drive a distance to get there, these various forms of support and camaraderie can be well worth the time and effort.

"Yes, but we don't have the expertise to undertake this task."

Regarding our understanding and level of expertise in using ASL to teach, it *is* reasonable for programs trying to implement bilingual education to be aware of the magnitude and long-term nature of this undertaking. It is wise to realize that, while it will make a big difference, simply adding ASL as a language for instruction in the classroom will not be enough.

Much of the theory is clearly laid out in the literature and actual practice is getting underway in a few places in the world. Yet, it will be necessary here in the U.S. to build more expertise in teaching American Sign Language to hearing parents and teachers, in teaching English as a second language to Deaf children, in testing the competence of Deaf children in both English and ASL, in training more Deaf teachers and early care providers, and in organizing support from the Deaf community. Many attributes need to be in place before we will see Deaf children realize their full potential. Study of how best to educate Deaf children bilingually is still ongoing in Sweden and Denmark. There is also a level of realism about the long-term nature of such a basic change in approach. While it takes time, their successes seem to increase their commitment to making these theoretical ideals a reality, even if there is still much to do.

A great deal can be learned from other bilingual educators, second language teachers and researchers, child development experts, and child language and literacy specialists—not to mention the wealth of untapped information possessed by Deaf professionals and the children themselves. These sources of information must be assimilated and modified to conform to the kind of bilingualism to which Deaf people aspire. Clearly, we are in an ongoing process of understanding what it means to present the best possible education for Deaf children. While we haven't got it all figured out, it seems we have enough information to get started right now.

"Yes, but Sweden and Denmark are such small countries. We could never make that kind of change in our educational system here."

Deaf consumers and hearing parents in Sweden found the power in their unity when they worked together to block the growing tide of mainstreaming. Now they are consulted on all decisions that affect Deaf children. Changes in the laws in Sweden and in the services for parents and children in Denmark did not come down from the top; they originated with what Lars Wallin (Bergman & Wallin, 1989) calls the "Three cornerstones:" *deaf consumers, parents, and linguists* working together (the association for hard of hearing adults also became part of the fight). As noted earlier, these groups did not always see eye-to-eye on everything, but they were willing to come to an agreement on many issues and present a very strong, unified front to the lawmakers, in order to meet the goals for the children that they held in common. They were diligent about working together to prioritize their political goals and assign work needed to achieve them, yet it was also significant that each consumer group also continued to function separately. While they did some work together, it was also necessary for them to have time to sort out their views from their own group's perspective, to process information and make decisions in a safe environment where they could communicate easily, vent their anger, learn from each other, and support each other in the hard work they were doing to achieve the goals. Now that they are through that transition, they function more like branches of a single unit (R. Bergmann, personal communication, August 18, 1993). While the system has now been reshaped to meet many of their goals, it still is not perfect. They are continuing to learn as they go, and some schools/areas in Sweden and Denmark—like in the U.S.—have evolved further in this direction than others (see Strong, in press, for a review of programs in the U.S.).

Even in a country as large as the U.S., where sweeping changes in the entire system are slow in coming, each state already functions as a unit politically, economically, and often philosophically. Many changes can be made at the state and local as well as national levels that move Deaf children's education in a new direction. Just a few examples are listed below of the many instances of important movement on a variety of levels:

- Some states have adopted a "deaf childrens' bill of rights" that highlights the importance of a critical mass of Deaf peers and of access to classroom communication as crucial variables in making placement decisions (contact NAD's political liaison on education for more information).

- A special task force of the Council on Education of the Deaf (CED), the national body that certifies teachers of the deaf, is developing guidelines for teacher training programs whose goal is to prepare teachers to work in bilingual/bicultural programs for Deaf students throughout the U.S. The proposed evaluation guidelines are patterned after the professional standards for the preparation of bilingual/multi-cultural teachers established by the National Association for Bilingual Education (NABE).

- There is some very exciting work being undertaken by the National Association of the Deaf, working with the Office of Bilingual Education and Minority Languages Affairs and the Office of Special Education and Rehabilitation, to consider how deaf children's educational and linguistic needs can be best served under current laws.

- The Indiana School for the Deaf conducted a National Training for Bilingual-Bicultural Educators and is in the process of publishing the proceedings of this meeting, as well as other documents that share the information and cultural mediation processes that facilitated their revolutionizing of their own system (Nover & Ruiz, in press; Titus, in press. Also contact the school about future training workshops and other upcoming publications).

- A discussion was started at California NAD conference about how to involve the grass-roots Deaf community in offering support and socialization to parents and their Deaf children.

- The Communication Academy in Issaqua, Washington, has developed both weekend workshops and a University-level course to orient parents to aspects of human communication as it relates to their own communication, with the goal of giving parents the theoretical and practical knowledge to make well-informed choices about their Deaf or hard of hearing child.

- The Bicultural Center in Riverdale, Maryland publishes a newsletter for Deaf people, parents, interpreters, and others interested in education and other bilingual/bicultural issues. Staff from the center also provide orientation, training, and cultural mediation for schools in transition, as well as courses and weekend workshops in American Sign Language and interpreter training. Acknowledging that early exposure is the key, the Oakland Society of Deaf Children, a parent group near Detroit, has sent a packet of articles and information to medical professionals in their area, notifying them of the existence of the Deaf community and of their parents' organization as important sources of support and information for parents whose infants are found to be deaf. They have also collected a library of articles and developed an annotated bibliography of materials they feel are helpful to parents in various stages of decision-making.

- Some of the parents in this group have also demanded that the local schools present an education in both ASL and English for their children, and are working with the schools now to investigate tools for evaluating their children's skills in ASL and in English as a second language.

- This same group has also formed an alliance with the Deaf community to sponsor social and educational gatherings for Deaf and hearing families with Deaf children on monthly Saturdays.

- A national coalition is being discussed that would create an information-sharing network for organizations and individuals in each community/state who are working to make changes, allowing them to capitalize on the successes and strategies of others (see reference to Coalition on Equal Education for Deaf Children (CEEDS) in Appendix C).

- In the fall of 1993, Kendall Demonstration Elementary School inaugurated three preschool research classes in which American Sign Language and English are used as the languages of instruction. These classes are part of a longitudinal collaborative study[3] of the development of language and literacy skills. Innovative instructional and assessment strategies will also be described.

- Central North Carolina School for the Deaf has received a 3-year grant from the state to set up a bilingual developmental day-care program for Deaf and hearing children. At least 51% of the children will be Deaf. The others accepted will be children with Deaf families, or whose parents are interpreters or CNCSD staff. All teachers will be fluent in ASL, and research will be conducted on the language and development of the 20 children in the program.

- The Indiana School for the Deaf is now enrolling hearing children of Deaf parents in its preschool, which is currently staffed by 100% Deaf teachers and aides. Language development of the Deaf and hard of hearing children in the classes will be monitored as part of a federal grant.

- A checklist was recently published by the Sign Talk Children's Centre Development Project that describes developmental stages for basic assessment of the language development of both Deaf and hearing preschoolers in bilingual environments using ASL and English (Evans, et al, 1994).

A great deal is possible. Information from those parents, teachers, and schools in the U.S. and abroad who have already made progress in updating their own educational systems is extremely valuable. Until the status quo changes, each locale will have to find its own way, at first. But there is no reason to keep re-inventing the wheel when many of the battles have already been fought.

---

3   This research is a collaboration between Gallaudet University Pre-College Programs and the Gallaudet Research Institute.

Turning the World Upside Down

Through this approach to instruction in the classroom, there exists the potential to put to rest the "impassioned debate" which has adversely affected the lives of deaf people for at least two centuries (Dyer, 1992, p. 251).

A bilingual approach to education—if structured toward fostering ultimate fluency in both languages as a goal—can accommodate vast differences in Deaf children. The idea that we might eliminate the confusing myriad of "choices" and incorporate the best of each into a theoretically-sound, individualized education for all Deaf children represents a major upheaval in current practice in the U.S. In order to configure the system to allow Deaf children just to be children, in some ways, it will be necessary to "turn the world upside down." Turning the world upside down means recognizing that some very real problems have been the result of viewing Deaf children from a framework that has made the simple too complex, and the complex, too simple.

True change won't occur until we work toward a theoretical model that capitalizes on what we know about language/child development, what can be discovered from studying Deaf children who *do* have the optimal conditions for normal development, and what can be learned from Deaf children and adults about what works for them. Practical solutions will follow; the logistics of implementation should not be allowed to interfere when formulating a theoretically-sound model to strive toward. Education about the theoretical underpinnings for such changes is crucial, so that informed, meaningful dialogue between Deaf and hearing parents, researchers, and teachers can take place.

Making a Transition

While none of the countries/programs that have moved in the direction of this child-centered model has had a smooth road, there are clearly some common elements that have contributed to success for the parents, the teachers, and the children. There are many observations and cautions that can be shared by those who are in this process of change. A few are summarized below:

- If support, training, and example are not given to parents *early*, and Deaf children are not allowed to spend time with other Deaf children and Deaf adults *early* (well before age 3), significant results are not likely. The choice to place resources in this direction will have payoffs in children's cognitive, social, and linguistic competence, which will affect all learning that follows. No amount of excellent programming later will make up for losing this crucial time in the development of Deaf children and their relationship with their parents and with the languages in their environment.

- Providing early exposure to Sign Language and Deaf adults would constitute the biggest change in the system (and the hardest to implement) in the United States and most other countries. However, evidence from Sweden and Denmark indicates that it can be done—even in rural areas—if it is recognized as a priority. Systems that wish to see real change must recognize this early component as the most crucial element in giving Deaf children a free and appropriate public education.

- Many of the changes toward bilingual education for Deaf children have started with a group of very small children and their parents. The success of these groups has convinced others that such a change is desirable. Many aspects of these children's programming can be moved toward the goal of bilingualism as they progress through school.

- At the same time, important changes must take place at all levels: in knowledge about and attitude toward Sign Language as a language for classroom instruction; in the hiring of more faculty and staff who are Deaf; in supporting the solid development of American Sign Language and recognizing its role in acquisition of the majority language and academic achievement in students of all ages; and in the implementation of Deaf Studies and American Sign Language as part of the curriculum.

- Those caught in the middle of such a major transition need a clear theoretical orientation to the rationale for change—and some recognition for what they have been trying to do all along—before they can be expected to accept this departure from former ways. While parents and others may feel angry about earlier guidance they received, or frustrated at being asked to invest themselves in something new, it is important to note that events and experimentation over the past 30 years have all been part of a gradual move toward meeting Deaf children 'where they live.' It is also important to acknowledge the frustration of many Deaf and hearing staff who are tired of dialogue and impatient for long-awaited change.

- Recognition that this is a *major* transition will add some realism to the process. The changes required are great. There are deeply-entrenched monolingual attitudes that will require some re-education, as well as staffing and placement practices that do not currently occur in many places. Some things can be changed very quickly; others simply take time.

The decision to move in a new direction may be the most important decision of all. The next step is to identify short-term and long-term goals, and to map out the steps that will be needed to begin making them happen.

There is likely to be a significant period of transition. For this reason, it is potentially dangerous for programs to claim they are offering a full-fledged bilingual education when they do not yet have all the tools, expertise, and personnel to offer comprehensive instruction in Sign Language and the majority language, the support and involvement of the Deaf community, and crucial early support for parents and children immediately after diagnosis. As Woodward noted in 1978:

> *Again, I want to stress the uselessness and danger of setting up poorly-designed bilingual programs (p. 198)...If bilingual education programs are not set up carefully, they will probably fail. The result could be a very swift and drastic reactionary shift to oralism within fifty years and possibly less time.*
>
> *The reason for this should be clear. If there are no substantial changes in programs, research evaluations will show no significant improvement. Programs that call themselves bilingual that are not really bilingual will damage evaluations of good bilingual programs (p. 184).*

With these cautions in mind, plenty of wisdom about what is needed is available. Those interested may start by going back to the proceedings of a conference in 1978 entitled "ASL in a Bilingual, Bicultural Context" (Stokoe, 1978). More currently, a number of schools that have been implementing bilingual-bicultural education for Deaf students have documented the stages of their transition, which involved school-wide (parents, teachers, administrators, kitchen staff, etc.) education and processing of intercultural issues (for example, Evans, et al, 1994; Nover & Ruiz, in press). Some schools for Deaf children around the country have published a mission statement or philosophy describing their educational aims for the children with regard to both English and ASL as languages of instruction. Most of these statements were drafted through a careful process that elicited feedback from parents, teachers, students, and members of the community. Others have worked to develop testing and orientation materials through their process of moving toward educating Deaf children bilingually. Deaf-hearing team teaching, support for parents, transition models, and many other issues are discussed in the proceedings of conferences sponsored by Gallaudet's College for Continuing Education and Pre-College Programs. Many related topics are discussed annually by the TEDS (Teachers of English to Deaf Students) interest section of TESOL (Teachers of English to Speakers of Other Languages).[4]

---

4   See Appendix C for addresses of schools, organizations listed here.

In other words, a helpful amount of information is available. But there is no road map. The practical aspects of implementing a change toward educating Deaf children bilingually will differ for every country, local area, and school. While some of the problems thought to be insurmountable in earlier writings are solving themselves as a result of changes in attitude and knowledge; other challenges will appear as our expectations for Deaf children and the people who teach them continue to evolve. There are many pitfalls that *might* be avoided by learning from others, and many common attributes for success.

But there is no *quick* fix. While it would be optimal if attitudes, perceptions, knowledge, and laws could change immediately, actual implementation still would not happen overnight because some of the attributes that must be developed simply take time. Even so, my own observation is this: If attitudes and some practices even begin to change in this direction, Deaf students and their parents will be better off than they are now. As Woodward (1978) predicted:

> *Bilingual education is a very desirable alternative in the education of deaf students, however, there are a number of very large and important problems for most schools in setting up bilingual education programs for deaf students. Core members of the deaf community (not just hearing impaired individuals) must share equally in the control, administration, and teaching in any bilingual program or track for deaf students. The bilingual program must allow the free use of American Sign Language in and for itself and not merely as a temporary tool for teaching English. Negative attitudes on the part of teachers, parents, administrators, students, and the local deaf community must be overcome....*

> *Certainly, bilingual education, while desirable, is not going to be an easy or cheap proposition. In fact, most schools will probably not be able or willing to make the necessary commitments to research, teacher training, etc., that a shift to bilingual education would mean. This however, does not mean that the schools can do nothing.... (Woodward, 1978. p. 198).*

While change has been very slow in coming since Woodward stated these cautions, many things *have* changed since 1978, especially regarding attitudes toward Sign Language and recognition of the value of Deaf adults' presence in programs that educate Deaf children.

It is my hope that schools who wish to implement bilingual education for their students will not have to make the transition in isolation, as Woodward implies, but will collaborate in their efforts and—more importantly—will be supported by higher level changes (state and federal) that result from honest self-study of the efficacy of our current approach to Deaf children's education.

Mas (1994) describes the obstacles faced by an organization of Deaf citizens and parents who started pilot bilingual classes in France in the early 80's—without such higher-level support. He summarizes the significant difficulties they encountered in four categories: political, financial, educational, and philosophical. While this consumer organization did have an inspiring level of commitment to the attributes Woodward describes, it has been extremely difficult for them to create and sustain—without higher level support—the fundamental components needed for long-term success in bilingual programming.

Building the attributes needed for a comprehensive program that fosters high levels of achievement and bilingualism (or multilingualism) in Deaf children will take time and will require broad-based support, but we will *never* get these attributes in place if we don't at least identify them as important goals. We can no longer look the other way when we know there is a logical, humane, theoretically sound approach to Deaf children and their parents that is consistent with the things that make all human beings thrive. As Robert and Weiss (1988) said in "The Innovation Formula: How Organizations Turn Change into Opportunity":

> *Of all the alternatives, not innovating is the riskiest course of action of all.*

It is possible to develop a theoretical model shaped, not by the restrictions of the current system, but by envisioning a system that will someday be truly responsive to the needs of Deaf children. It may appear overwhelming, but deciding to start is half the battle. Reflecting on this decision, Britta Hansen of Denmark summarizes some of the early challenges and the crucial elements they determined were necessary to move forward:

> *Many problems have arisen during the first experiments, for example "What is bilingual education?," "How do hearing teachers support DSL usage, not being fluent signers of the language themselves?," "What is the role of deaf adults in the education and upbringing of deaf children?'" "How do we describe and analyze deaf children's DSL skill at different developmental stages?" I have discussed some of the solutions to these issues, and although we have no simple answers, we have concluded that a bilingual approach can be developed even if the optimal conditions are not yet present. It is more a question of a positive attitude to DSL and Danish as two languages with the same status, combined with a close cooperation between teachers, parents, researchers, and deaf adults (Hansen, 1987, p. 88).*

Whatever you can do—or dream you can do—begin it.
Boldness has beauty, power, and magic in it.

Goethe

APPENDIX A

Author's note: Terms Used

A new consciousness often gives rise to a new discourse
(Jankowski, 1994, p.15).

Many schools are at a critical juncture in their views of children who are deaf or hard of hearing, which may ultimately affect how they refer to these children. For these reasons, choices about terminology for this book have required extensive re-evaluation, and therefore merit extensive explanation.

Rationale

For the past two decades, the upper case "D" spelling of Deaf has been used in the U.S. to refer primarily to Deaf adults and children who use American Sign Language for everyday communication; and who share common values, rules for behavior, traditions, and views of themselves and others (Padden, 1980).

The ideal described in this book is one in which every deaf and hard of hearing child has the right to grow up with access to this language and community. Terms used in the part of the book that describes this model (starting with the Introduction) are based on the premise that Deaf people are defined not by their hearing status but by their sharing of a common language and a visual approach to communication. Swedish linguist Kristina Svartholm (1993) describes this perspective:

> *Here they [deaf people] are not looked upon, as in other educational models, as defective human beings. Instead, they are seen as belonging to a minority group with its own conditions and requirements (p.328).*

What is confusing for Americans, then, is that—while Scandinavian Deaf people and educators view Deaf people as a linguistic minority, these countries nevertheless use lower case "d"—as this is how they would refer to other linguistic groups.[1] From an editorial perspective, it was *very* tempting to simply adhere to the Swedish convention and use the

---

1   It is important to note that this convention (capitalizing the "D") is not used in Sweden and Denmark. However, it is also important to note that references to languages and groups of speakers are generally not capitalized in these countries. For example, the adjective "svenska" which refers to both the "Swedish" language and "Swedish" people is NOT capitalized, nor is the word "dansk" in Denmark. Therefore, to maintain the integrity of verbatim utterances or written excerpts, a lower case "d" will appear in most quotations.

---

small "d" throughout this book.[2] However, because this book is written in English and will be disseminated largely in the U.S., I have attempted to adhere to American spelling conventions, while trying to capture the perception that is clear in Sweden and Denmark, and has been made official in the European Economic Community: *Deaf children and adults, as a group, function like other linguistic/cultural groups* (Andersson, Y., 1994; Svartholm, 1993).

The American convention is to capitalize the names of such linguistic minority groups; i.e., those people whose roots are in a culture that shares a language other than English (Hispanic, Italian, Cajun, Navajo) whether it is an indigenous[3] or a foreign language. In the United States, use of a capitol "D" has symbolized an important turning point in how Deaf people view themselves, and how they are viewed by others—as a cohesive group of people who share a common language and a culture based on seeing, rather than as disparate individuals who are lacking in something. As Bahan put it:

> *American Sign Language was developed not because Deaf people can't hear, but because they can see....All people share basic needs such as love, food, and shelter. But Deaf people also have a need to make maximum use of their vision. Everything we learn, everything we do and move on is done through seeing. For us, we capitalize the "D" to mark this difference. We see ourselves as a noun, not an adjective (1988, p. 1).*

Conventions Used

In establishing a convention for this work, I have tried to attend less to labels currently used, and more to what might be appropriate given the consciousness this model represents. Once the reader is familiar with the conventions used throughout the book, they should become straightforward and predictable. For those who wish to understand the basis on which terms were applied, conventions for their use are described in detail on the following pages:

---

2   Special thanks to my colleague, Marie Jean Philip, who challenged me *not* to go the easy route.

3   American Sign Language has been recognized by a number of scholars as one of our country's indigenous minority languages (Lane & Grosjean, 1980; Wilbur, 1987; Van Cleve, 1986.)

General references:

There are many variables present in even a small sample of deaf children who arrive at school. While these variables are of prime importance in dealing with each child on an individual basis, they cannot be discussed in every reference to deaf children in this context. Throughout this book (starting with the Introduction), I will use the term "Deaf"[4] in general references to all children and adults *for whom the primary receptive channel of communication is visual.*[5]

More specific references:

1) *Deaf adults/professionals/teachers:* "Deaf" will be used when referring to Deaf adults/professionals as language models and teachers for Deaf children. It is of paramount importance that such individuals are part of the linguistic minority of people who use a natural Sign Language as their primary language (see section on natural language), and who view being Deaf from a linguistic or cultural perspective.

2) *Deaf children:* In addition to being used as a general reference (described above), "Deaf" will be used in more specific contexts to refer to any child or group of children who use manual communication.

Many young deaf children of hearing parents in the U.S. today are not exposed regularly to American Sign Language, but rather to other forms of manual communication meant to represent the majority language. However, it is well-documented that signed language production and use in children who have various models for manual communication eventually gravitates toward the Sign Language of the Deaf community, as a function of physiological naturalness and/or socialization (Gee & Goodhart, 1988; Gee & Mounty, 1986; Hoffmeister & Bahan, 1991; Hom, et al, 1994; Lane, 1992; Livingston, 1983; Schein, 1989; Supalla, 1986; Singleton & Newport, 1987).

Furthermore, in the model described here, the goal for all Deaf children is to become bilingual in order to function optimally in family and society. In addition to becoming proficient in the language of the majority, these children (and their parents) would have ample opportunities to learn the Sign Language of the Deaf community and to communicate freely with others who share the language.

3) *Hard of hearing:* There are also references throughout this document to Deaf children whose auditory perception is sufficient to acquire some of the spoken language through natural interaction (not training), in some cases as their first language. Many children that are typically described as hard of hearing are among the children that are the focus of this book, and are included here under the term, "Deaf." These children will be referred to

---

4   The 1988 report of the U.S. Commission on Education of the Deaf states in their notes on terminology: "We also use the term *Deaf* to refer to all persons with hearing impairments, including those who are hard of hearing, those deafened later in life who are profoundly deaf, etc." (C.O.E.D, 1988, p. xii).

5   Magnet School of the Deaf Core Committee, 1994.

specifically as "hard of hearing" only in some discussions in the book that refer to spoken or written language acquisition or educational placement issues in which their ability to comprehend spoken language is the salient factor in the discussion.

Use of the label "hard of hearing" in these contexts is not necessarily meant to differentiate educational approaches to deaf vs. hard of hearing children. In fact, separating the two groups can *minimize* our ability to meet each child's individual linguistic and educational needs by lumping him or her into one group or another, then applying the currently accepted methodologies for that group. The objective of the model described here is that each child's *individual* path to bilingualism be supported and facilitated. This educational approach is based on each child's behavior with regard to the languages in his/her environment, not predetermined by a label that is based on audiometric criteria.

Even if they acquired some spoken language early, the children referred to in this book as Deaf still rely heavily on vision, rather than audition, in receiving information, whether it is through lipreading or signs. That is, those who do not perceive the spoken language—an auditorily-perceived language—through their hearing, would be educated in such a way that they will also have early opportunities to acquire a language that is *intended* to be perceived visually.

There are two other instances in which the term "hard of hearing" is used in this book:

a) "Hard of hearing children" is used occasionally in what I consider to be its true sense: to refer to children whose hearing is sufficient that they do not rely primarily on vision as their receptive channel for communication, and who therefore may function well in a classroom of hearing children without an interpreter. Such children, while mentioned in some contexts, are not intended to be the primary focus of this book.

b) "Hard of hearing adults" is used in reference to members of the association of adults in Sweden who consider themselves hard of hearing and whose primary language is Swedish, many of whom have advocated for today's hard of hearing children to become bilingual, learning both spoken Swedish and Swedish Sign Language.

4) ***deaf:*** Lower case "d," deaf, will be used only in two instances in this book: a) when the term "deaf" refers strictly to a child's audiological status, especially when discussing the medical discovery and description of a child's deafness, 2) to refer to deaf children who are addressed by their parents or educators only through spoken language. For example, "deaf" will be used to refer to deaf infants of hearing parents who were recently discovered to be deaf. In most cases, these children have been (and could continue to be) exposed only to oral means of communication, so it cannot be assumed that they will develop linguistic or cultural ties with Deaf people who use Sign Language.

5) Finally, in this model, being Deaf is an important and valued attribute; therefore, saying "Deaf children" (as opposed to "children who are Deaf") is completely acceptable in the Swedish, Danish, and American Deaf communities.[6] Keeping the focus on Deaf children being "just children" and celebrating their growing up Deaf are *both* important parts of this model (see Chapter Two).

Sign Language(s):

This book will follow the convention used by Danish educators and linguists of capitalizing the term "Sign Language" when it is used to refer to the natural language used for interaction in a Deaf community.[7] Of course, one would expect to capitalize the proper nouns American Sign Language, Danish Sign Language, etc. in written English. But since this book crosses international boundaries and there are more general references to the language used by Deaf people, the term Sign Language—used alone—will likewise be capitalized to indicate reference to the language of the respective community. In Sweden and Denmark, most interviewees referred to this language as "Deaf Sign Language," to differentiate it from other manual systems that have also been referred to colloquially as 'sign language' (see Chapter Three on natural language and sign-based codes).

The term "signed language(s)" (used by linguists in the U.S. and abroad), is also used in contexts where a more general reference to the visual/gestural languages used by Deaf communities is intended (i.e., "signed" is used in the same way as "spoken" or "written" when talking about language). It is not intended to refer to signed codes or systems invented to manually represent the majority language.

---

6   Spencer, Bodner-Johnson, and Gutfreund (1992) explain the preference of the mothers in their parent-infant study to describe themselves and their children as *deaf* rather than *hearing-impaired,* and to place the adjective *deaf* first: "Because both the participants and the authors think of deafness as a cultural descriptor rather than a disability, we have placed the word *deaf* before, rather than after, the adult or child descriptor when referring to these members of the Deaf community" (1992, p. 66).

7   The Sign Languages in use by Deaf communities around the world are grammatically distinct languages (distinct from the spoken language of the country in which they are used, and, like spoken languages, distinct from the Sign Languages used by people in other countries). They are linguistically equivalent in complexity to other languages of the world, be they signed or spoken. (For a summary of research, see Petitto, 1993b.)

Appendix B:

Summary of Procedure and Limitations of this Study

Well in advance of the visits to Sweden and Denmark, a number of contacts were established in each country. Rationale and design for the study was discussed with each of these individuals when they were in the United States for the DEAF WAY Conference in July, 1989. Each suggested names of key individuals in the schools, consumer organizations, and the government who were considered important sources of information as a place to start. When the study began, primary contacts assisted with logistics and initial introductions to prospective interviewees. The first study, which took place from March through June, 1990, was primarily based in Stockholm, Sweden, with a little over two weeks spent in Copenhagen and Fredereccia, Denmark. During the second study, I spent a little over one week in each country in March, 1992.

All respondents in my study were asked a series of standard questions regarding interviewee's name, address, current position in the system, his or her history with Deaf children and experience with the current approach. Interviews were designed to elicit not only a description of the history and current state of affairs with regard to bilingual education, but also to obtain information about the individual's own role, attitudes, and feelings about recent events, as well as insights and strategies. Although this project was intended to be descriptive and not evaluative, all interviews with professionals included a question regarding methods of evaluating the success or failure of the new approach. Other standard questions concerned what interviewees saw as the biggest problems during these years of transition, how they have addressed those problems, what challenges they are currently facing, and, in a related vein, what would constitute their "wish list" if they could have a more perfect situation for Deaf children in their city or their country. They were also asked to name the most positive—and the most negative—aspects of the situation as it exists now. Questions in the second study related more to specific methods, experiences or insights, and results in certain environments, not to general trends or history.

As the first study progressed, the nature of the interviews changed. Based on repeated tellings of events or general agreement from a variety of sources regarding the issues discussed, I came to regard a number of premises as the "facts" of each country's situation. The interviews then served to verify these "truths" and seek perceptions which contradicted or varied from the more widely-accepted views. In other areas, previous interviews had not yielded general consensus, had exposed discrepancies, or had raised new questions; hence, subsequent interviews served to seek clarification and identify conflicting perceptions regarding a situation, event, or methodology. Interviews generally ranged from 30 minutes to 3 hours, depending on the amount of information the individual possessed and—most often with teachers—on constraints in schedule. Although some interviews took place with the children present during a classroom or home observation, one-to-one sessions with teachers or parents separate from observation times were arranged in most cases. Follow-up meetings were conducted with a number of key figures in order to address further questions and new issues that came to light as the study progressed.

Some of the Limitations of this Study

Within the time constraints and financial limits of this study, I was primarily limited to interviewing those Deaf professionals and consumers who knew some American Sign Language. It is possible that their level of education and knowledge of ASL as common variables may have biased or predisposed these respondents in some ways. Also, interviews were primarily limited to Deaf and hearing professionals and parents who have involvement with the current educational system. While I did glean some information from Deaf adults outside the educational system about what their own education was like, the scope of the study was not intended to cover that area.

Interviews with Deaf children individually or in groups were usually a spontaneous event, as there was rarely an opportunity to meet with teachers or parents *before* observing a class or home to determine if the children's comments would be available. Therefore, the parents and teachers, although they hardly represent unbiased third parties, often acted as interpreters at these times when I could not understand beyond my rudimentary Swedish/Danish Sign Language skills.

Interviews with hearing people—who still constitute the majority of parents and professionals in the system—all took place in English, a language widely spoken in both countries. Only in one instance did an individual's mastery of English result in his declining to be interviewed (a reason I learned of after the study was over.) Most interviews with hearing individuals were audiotaped and later transcribed.

Interpreters who translated from Swedish/Danish Sign Language to English were almost impossible to obtain, especially with the type of flexibility I needed to follow me around schools. When interviewing Deaf persons, my own rough sign-to-voice synopsis of the interviewee's ASL comments was recorded in most cases, in addition to my notes, which I transcribed in greater detail soon after each interview. Due to these limitations, it was difficult to reconstruct exact quotes from my notes or tapes of interviews with Deaf individuals. While I communicated the information and perspectives these individuals shared to the best of my abilities, I regret that there are not more direct quotes from Deaf people throughout the book.

As stated in the Introduction, it is important for the reader to keep in mind that I, the author, am neither Swedish nor Danish; more importantly, I am not Deaf. (A joint project with a Deaf researcher was discussed, but because the study entailed taking a leave of absence and living abroad, the other researcher determined that it was not feasible.) Ideally, more in-depth information will someday be gathered by a Deaf researcher with conversational skills in both Sign Languages to get a clearer picture—from a Deaf perspective.

APPENDIX C: Addresses

The addresses of most schools and organizations named within the text are listed below as possible resources for those interested in learning more about the transition to bilingual education for Deaf children, networking to improve services, or participating in the political work to ensure that Deaf children have access to placements where they can be educated together.

UNITED STATES AND CANADA:

The Bicultural Center (TBC)
5506 Kenilworth Avenue, Suite 105
Riverdale, MD 20737-3106
301-277-3944 (TTY)
301-277-3945 (V)
301-277-5226 (Fax)

The California School for the Deaf
30350 Gallaudet Drive
Fremont, CA 94538
510-794-3666 (TTY/V)

The Cleary School
301 Smithtown Road
Nesconset, NY 11767
516-588-0530 (TTY/V)
516-588-0016 (Fax)

The Communication Academy
240 NW Gillman Blvd., Suite H
Issaqua, WA 98027
(workshops for parents/professionals)
(206) 391-7305 (TTY/V)
(206) 391-6728

Gallaudet University Pre-College Outreach
800 Florida Ave, N.E.
Washington, DC 20002
(202) 651-5340 (TTY/V)
(202) 651-5708 (FAX)

Indiana School for the Deaf
1200 East 42nd St.
Indianapolis, IN 46205-2099
317-924-4374 (TTY/V)

The Learning Center for Deaf Children (TLC)
848 Central Street
Framingham, MA 01701
508-875-5110 (TTY/V)
508-875-9203 (Fax)

Madonna University
Sign Language Studies Department
3600 Schoolcraft Rd
Livonia, MI 48150-1173
313-591-9266 (TTY)
313-591-5131

Magnet School of the Deaf
c/o Clifford Moers
2305 Pearl Street #5
Boulder, CO 80302
Fax 303 556 8100
e-mail moers@spot.Colorado.Edu (Deaf chairperson),
or Glenn Webster gwebster@cudnvr.Denver.Colorado.edu (hearing parent), 303-220-9277 (TTY only)

Maryland School for the Deaf
P.O. Box 894
Columbia, MD 21044-0894
410-418-8660 (TTY)/8661 (V)

Sign Talk Children's Centre
285 Pembina Hwy, 2nd Floor
Winnipeg, MB, Canada R3L2E1
204-475-8914 (TTY)
204-475-8906 (V)

The National Clearinghouse for Bilingual Education (NCBE)
1118 22nd Street, N.W.
Washington, DC 20037
202-467-0867
1-800-321-NCBE

The Oakland Society of Deaf Children
(Address of current president may be obtained from Madonna University, listed above).

The Office of Bilingual Education and Minority Languages Affairs (OBEMLA)
U.S. Department of Education
600 Independence Ave (MES Bldg.—OBEMLA), S.W.
Washington, DC 20202
(202) 205-9700

The Sterck School, Delaware School for the Deaf
620 E. chestnut Hill Rd.
Neward, DE 19713
302-454-2301 (TTY/V)
302-454-3493 (Fax)

Teachers of English to Speakers of Other Languages (TESOL)
1600 Cameron St, Suite 200
Alexandria, VA 22314-0774
703-836-0774 (V/TTY)

Teachers of English to Deaf Students (TEDS)
(contact through TESOL address above)

Political Action/Networking:

ACTION (Action for Children to Include Options Now)
PO Box 70-1280
Flushing, NY 11370
718-899-8880 (V)
718-899-3030 (TTY)
718-889-1621 (Fax)

American Society for Deaf Children
2848 Arden Way, Suite 210
Sacramento, CA 95825-1373
916-482-0120 (TTY/V)
916-482-0121 (Fax)

Coalition on Equal Education for Deaf Students (CEEDS)
5569 Gloucester Street
Churchton, MD 20733

Louder than Words
PO Box 90934
Washington, DC 20090
202-526-8806

The National Association of the Deaf
814 Thayer Ave
Silver Spring, MD 20910-4500
301-587-1789 (TTY)
301-587-1788 (V)
301-587-1791 (Fax)
301-587-6282 (Bookstore)

SWEDEN

NOTE: The following numbers in Sweden and Denmark are voice numbers as TTYs are not compatible with their text telephones. Some organizations may have Fax machines or be connected to e-mail but I did not gather that information. These addresses and phone numbers were compiled as part of the 1990 IDEAS study.

Department of Educational and Psychological Research
Lund University
(C/O Kerstin Heiling)
School of Education
Malmö, Sweden
46-8-040-32-0259

Department of Sign Language
Stockholm University
106 91 Stockholm
46-8-16-2349/2330#

Dövas Hus or Stockholms Dövas Förening ('Deaf Club/Local Deaf Association')
Storagatan 23
114 53 Stockholm
46-8-24-9190 (V/Texttelephone

Institute of Scandinavian Languages
Stockholm University (Same address as above. Also conducts Sign Language research and has a major in bilingualism for deaf students)

Manilla School for the Deaf
Manillavägen 32-36
115 21 Stockholm
46-8-783-2770

Östervägen School for the Deaf
Lund, Sweden
46-8-11-7140

Skeppargatan Preschool
Dövas Hus (Stockholm Deaf Club)
Storagatan 23
114 55 Stockholm
46-8-66-231-38 (V)

Sveriges Dövas Riksförbund (SDR) 'Swedish National Association of the Deaf'
Friedhemsgatan 15
Bix 122 85
102 27 Stockholm
46-8-5200-7570 (Texttellephone or voice)

DENMARK:

Bonaventura Parents' Association
c/o Danske Döves Lansförbund
Fensmarksgade 1, Box 704
2200 Copenhagen, Denmark

Danish Association of the Deaf
(Dansk Döves Lansförbund
Fensmarksgade 1, Box 704
2200 Copenhagen, Denmark

Center for Total Communication (Kastelsvej Center)
Kastelsvej 58
2100 Copenhagen, Denmark
45-31-42-3828

Kastelsvej School for the Deaf
(Same address as above)

THE SWEDISH NATIONAL BOARD OF EDUCATION•INFORMATION SECTION• S-106 42 STOCKHOLM

The Swedish School System

All children in Sweden start school the year they are seven. Before this they may have attended pre-school, which is voluntary. Compulsory schooling lasts for nine years, after which 90 per cent of school-leavers go on to upper secondary school, from which about 25 per cent proceed to some form of post-secondary education. Several million Swedes over the age of 18 also take part in various forms of adult education.

Pre-school education

All children aged 6 and over are eligible for pre-school education, which is optional for the children but compulsory for municipal authorities. Responsibility for pre-school education is vested in the National Board of Health and Welfare.

Compulsory school

Roughly one million pupils, i.e. all children between the ages of 7 and 16, attend the nine-year compulsory school, which is divided into three levels: junior, intermediate and senior. The great majority of these schools are run by municipal authorities and are free of charge. Nor is any charge made for teaching materials, school meals, health care or school transport (for children living a long way away from school).

There are also a very small number of private schools.

Upper secondary school

Upper secondary school is divided into 25 lines of two, three or four years' duration. Some of these are vocational, while others lead on to further education. Upper secondary school also includes more than 500 directly vocational specialised courses of varying duration.

About 25 per cent of upper secondary school-leavers go on to higher education. The remainder enter employment, possibly entering higher education or some form of adult education later on in life.

Adult education

There are many different forms of adult education in Sweden, viz municipal adult education (conferring essentially the same qualifications as compulsory school and upper secondary school), folk high school, labour market training or some form of study circle activity. Adult education is often free of charge.

APPENDIX E

EXCERPT FROM THE SWEDISH CURRICULUM (1983)

(AUTHOR'S NOTE: This document has recently been revised (1994) but had not been translated to English when this book was printed. My understanding is that the spirit of the revised curriculum is basically the same as this historic 1983 version. Since 1990, this document has also been accompanied by a supplement discussing the teaching of Swedish as a second language for Deaf students. The reader is asked to keep in mind that this is a 1985 verbatim translation of a 1983 document. Some spellings and translations of terms may differ from that used in the U.S., may currently have different connotations from the intended meaning in the original version, or their usage may have changed since 1983. [Swedish National Board of Education Information Section, S-106 42, Stockholm.])

Pupil categories

The Special Education Ordinance defines a deaf, hearing impaired or speech-disturbed pupil as a pupil prevented, by deafness, hearing impairment or speech disturbance from assimilating the instruction provided in ordinary compulsory schools.

The question as to which pupils are to be provided with special schooling for these reasons has to be decided on an individual basis. Each pupil's total situation must be taken into account, and especially the pupil's need of the bilingual environment of a special school.

The identity of the deaf is based on sign language constituting their primary language and vision their principal means of communication, whereas the hearing-impaired have Swedish as their primary language and hearing - often with the support of technical aids - as their principal means of communication. The factors determining group identity can vary from one individual to another. Each individual must be given the opportunity of choosing his own identity.

Deaf and severely hearing-impaired need to belong to a sufficiently large group of coeval, older, younger and adult deaf and hearing-impaired persons who also use sign language, so as to give them access to positive, realistic models for the identification process.

The prelinguistically deaf or "childhood-deaf" are regarded as deaf pupils in the true sense. Pupils belonging to this group have a congenital or early-acquired hearing injury which has resulted in such a degree of hearing impairment as to preclude speech and language development through the medium of hearing, even with the use of a hearing aid. The linguistic development of these children has to proceed with the aid of vision. They are dependent on sign language communication and need early access to sign language if their linguistic and social development is not to be seriously delayed.

The term "hearing-impaired" or "hard of hearing" is applied to those who, in spite of hearing impairment, have been able to develop speech and language with the aid of their hearing. They are usually dependent on hearing aids and favourable outward circumstances, good lighting and acoustics and the absence of disruptive background noises in order to be able to utilise their residual hearing. It is essential that existing residues of hearing be utilised in the work of developing Swedish language.

Special school pupils with residual hearing enabling them to assimilate instruction via speech and hearing when using technical aids in suitable surroundings ought if possible to form teaching groups of their own. Special attention should be devoted to the need of these pupils to use both sign language and the spoken language.

The teaching languages in school are sign language and Swedish. Where deaf pupils are concerned. Swedish as a teaching language means writing, while hearing-impaired pupils, given hearing aids and good surroundings, can also make use of speech. They should be given as much training and stimulus as possible in the use of speech as a form of expression.

Communication opportunities for deaf and severely hearing-impaired pupils in a sign-language environment are essential for their cognitive and personal development. Schools, therefore, must try to ensure that their staff achieve a good knowledge of sign language, which will put them in a good position to understand their pupils.

Schools must help pupils to come into contact with associations of the hearing-impaired and deaf and with various cultural activities.

Teaching materials

The deaf and many hearing-impaired persons are mainly dependent on their vision as a means of obtaining information and knowledge. Visual aids, therefore, have an important part to play in teaching. Special attention should be paid to the development of working methods in which visual aids are employed. Video technology affords great opportunities of producing and using handy and up-to-date materials for teaching, and it also enables pupils to produce their own programmes, conduct interviews and "correspond" with other deaf/hearing-impaired persons in Sweden and further afield.

Aids to speech and hearing

Hearing damage can vary a great deal from one pupil to another as regards the magnitude of hearing impairment and the frequencies affected. Tone-audio programmes, however, yield incomplete knowledge of the pupils' ability to utilise residual bearing and amplified sound. Hearing impairments described similarly in audiograms can in reality constitute very different kinds of damage having different effects on the individuals concerned.

The support provided by audiotechnological equipment can very often make it possible for the spoken language to be used in teaching. In this and other contexts, schools should keep close track of technical progress and enlisted support where necessary.

When deciding how much use a pupil has of his hearing aid, great importance must be attached to his opportunities of apprehending speech and monitoring his own speech. It is also important to take into account the pupil's own opinion.

The hearing and speech aids used in teaching should be based on the pupil's personal hearing aid.

When teaching pronunciation, various possible ways should be tested of using technical aids which can give the pupil a visual, auditive or kinesthetic feedback of his speech and in this way augment his understanding of the speech process.

Syllabi: The Language Block

The language block deals with sign language and Swedish and with the appurtenant bilingualism, sign language in other countries, English and the elective subjects French and German.

The language block constitutes a subject (block) in special school in order for every school to be able, in this context, to adapt its teaching to the aptitudes and needs of individual pupils. In local working plans, each school must specify the allocation of teaching periods between the various subjects making up the language block. This allocation must be constructed in such a way as to ensure that the pupils develop in the direction of bilingualism.

BILINGUALISM, SIGN LANGUAGE AND SWEDISH

Sign language and Swedish are separate languages. The bilingualism aimed at for deaf and many hearing-impaired pupils is not absolutely comparable with other bilingualism. The bilingualism of the deaf is monocultural since both languages convey essentially the same culture.

Bilingualism does not occur spontaneously. Sign language is learned naturally and spontaneously, as part of the child's general development, in the environment where it is used, while acquisition of the second language - Swedish - is more dependent on instruction.

The two languages - sign language and Swedish - perform different functions for the pupil. Sign language is the deaf pupil's primary means of acquiring knowledge and is the language used by him in direct communication with others. It is by way of sign language and in his contacts with parents and others that the pupil develops socially and emotionally. Swedish has primarily the function of a written language, but lip reading and speech, of course, are also important elements of this subject.

In the course of teaching, names and contexts which are important in order for the pupil to assimilate the content of reading passages must be given both in sign language and in Swedish. Information about the Swedish language, however, must not be given such prominence as to relegate the content of subject teaching to second place.

The pupils' language learning must be supported by comparisons between the various linguistic expressions of sign language and Swedish and must be based on language being an implement used in handling perceptions, experiences and knowledge etc.

SIGN LANGUAGE AND SWEDISH

Sign language and Swedish are included in special school teaching because

- Every pupil must realise that language is our most important means of achieving contact with other people, close to us or far away, in our own time or in past ages, and as a means of receiving and supplying information.

- The pupils must develop their ability to read sign language and their ability to read so as to apprehend and understand what other people mean.

- The pupils must develop their ability to use sign language and their ability to write clearly, regularly and expressively, so that other people can apprehend and understand what they mean.

- Pupils who are capable of learning to speak must develop this ability so as to facilitate contact with hearing persons who do not know sign language.

Goals

The pupils' ability to understand and use sign language and Swedish is to be developed. They are to learn to read and write. Compared with hearing pupils, who learn to read and write the language they speak, deaf pupils have to learn these skills without yet having mastered any other form of expression in Swedish. Hearing-impaired pupils doing this have to contend with hearing and speech deficiencies. Consequently both deaf and hearing-impaired pupils may need to spend more time on the various teaching items.

All children must feel that their language is good enough and that they can make use of their experience and their words when learning to read and write. Accordingly, common reading and writing instruction must relate to events and everyday work in the class and to the common ideas and interests which the children develop there. In addition, the children must be given time, support and encouragement for individual work.

A person's language is closely connected with his personality and situation in life. If that connection is severed, the development of both language and personality is blocked. An important objective in the teaching of sign language and Swedish, therefore, is to strengthen the pupils' self-confidence so that they will have the courage to express themselves and stand up for their opinions. Work should therefore be based on the language and the experience which the pupils have already acquired.

The pupils must experience literature as a source of knowledge and enjoyment. They must be encouraged to make creative use of all their expressive resources - signs, words, pictures, movements, facial expression, role play and drama. They must also learn the hallmarks of good language, so as to be able to work deliberately on improving their own language.

By the time they leave compulsory schools pupils must have achieved the confidence to express themselves in the linguistic situations confronting them in the family, together with their friends, in voluntary associations, at work and in subsequent education. They must have had an opportunity of meeting and using official written language. They must be given preparation to read well enough to have a solid foundation on which to acquire knowledge, information and experience for themselves through the medium of newspapers and periodicals, reference works, and works of fiction and nonfiction. Pupils who are capable of developing intelligible speech must be given individualised instruction to this end.

Language grows with experience of the outside world, and pupils must therefore constantly acquire new knowledge and experience through direct observations and investigations of the world around them in conjunction with other subjects, through studies of mass media and literature and in joint creative work. In doing so they must acquire an increasingly diversified repertoire of signs and words and clear conceptions and images of the reality which those signs and words represent.

Starting with discussions of their own and other people's ways of expressing themselves in sign language and in speech and writing, the pupils should acquire a knowledge of the way in which language changes according to the purpose, situation and social context involved and of ways in which language can be used to influence one's own situation and linguistic development in society at large. Grammar teaching must contribute towards the pupils' linguistic confidence.

Schools must support pupils to enable them to create good children's and juvenile culture which will satisfy their needs for social participation, knowledge and experience.

Teaching should put particular emphasis on literature, and the reading of literature at school and at home must be aimed at creating an abiding interest in books and reading. In their reading, the pupils must be enabled to encounter reality as other people experience and interpret it. They must acquire an insight into material and social conditions in different periods and in different parts of the world. Their encounters with people in literature must give them enjoyable experiences of beauty, humour and excitement but must also enable them to view themselves in perspective, in relation to their own lives and other people's.

The pupils must familiarize themselves with people and scenes in a large number of books for children and young persons and also, in senior grades, with adult literature of both recent and earlier vintages. They must familiarise themselves closely with books, authors and libraries and must get into the habit of borrowing and reading fiction.

The pupils must get to know the linguistic situation of the Nordic countries with regard to sign language and writing. They must gradually acquire sufficient knowledge of Norwegian and Danish to understand easy reading passages in those languages.

SIGN LANGUAGE—Main teaching items

All levels

The pupils must develop their ability to penetrate other people's conditions, understand their purposes and adapt their own language and behaviour to the requirements of different contexts. They must learn to study other people's opinions and values, to stand up for their own and to subject their own arguments and other people's to critical scrutiny. The pupils must also acquire a knowledge of the structure and grammar of sign language. They must learn the rules applying to different conversational situations and they must also learn that these can be influenced and improved. Video technology provides opportunities for the pupils to work with their own sign language and other people's.

Pupils whose sign language is substantially defective when they enter special school must be given individual support for their linguistic development.

Dramatic activities must form an important ingredient of school work. Through improvisation and role play, the pupils must penetrate and test various roles, situations and modes of action. They must convey experience, ideas and opinions to others in dramatic form, with a view to informing and involving their audience. They must attend theatrical performances, live or via TV, and be encouraged to take part in drama games, role play and theatrical activities during the school day.

By making video recordings the pupils must learn to document and convey information and cultural activities. The pupils must be given practice in using interpreters in various situations.

They should also acquire knowledge of the international sign alphabet and sign language in other countries, especially within the Nordic area. General information on national and international organisations of the deaf should be included.

Over and above the indications given for all levels, work at the individual school levels must also include the following:

Junior level

The pupils must develop their ability to use conversation as a working method and must accustom themselves to narrative discourse.

They must

- Talk and converse, spontaneously and after preparation, about their own experiences and adventures, about events and people in stories, books, films and plays, and they must talk and converse using impulses from pictures.

- Describe and discuss observations and inquiries and develop ideas and suggestions, test values and attitudes.

- Discuss current events, problems and conflicts (e.g. in class committees).

- Gradually learn to plan. report and evaluate common work.

- Investigate signs and manifestations to see how they correspond to what they can observe or want to say and, by doing so, acquire a knowledge of language and usage.

Intermediate level

Over and above the activities of junior level, the pupils are to further improve their ability to use conversation as a working method. They are also to learn the use, as working methods, of interviews, discussions and reports and formally organized debates, class and pupil committee meetings, and conferences.

Senior level

The pupils must further develop what they have learned at Junior and intermediate levels. They must gradually learn to express themselves logically, to vary their sign repertoire and to express themselves clearly, concisely and concretely.

They must

- Consciously adapt their language to the requirements of different conversational situations.
- Analyse their own and other people's statements, contributions to debate etc.
- Learn something about human acquisition of language
- Learn something about the way in which language is constantly changing and why.

SWEDISH—Reading, writing, and speech

The goals - learning to read and write - are common to hearing, hearing-impaired and deaf pupils but they are achieved in different ways.

The teaching of Swedish to the deaf cannot be based on hearing and speech. The skills which deaf Pupils are to develop through Swedish teaching must emanate from what the pupils are capable of apprehending visually, through sign language and by means of written Swedish.

Some pupils have residual hearing which it is important to use when they are learning Swedish. With the aid of audiological amplification, they can assimilate instruction via hearing and speech, but they may still be dependent on visual support in the form of writing and signs for the consolidation of their skills.

Reading—Main teaching items

All levels

Reading is one of the most important ways of giving the pupils a knowledge of the Swedish language and making them aware of the written language as a means of augmenting their knowledge.

It is natural at junior level that the reading passages used for reading instruction should frequently be based on the teacher translating into Swedish the stories which pupils tell in sign language. Other reading passages have to be translated in the opposite direction and

---

explained in sign language. As the pupils' knowledge of Swedish improves, the amount of translation work done by the teacher should diminish.

The pupils should gradually practice using single-language dictionaries and the "dictionary" role of the teacher can be gradually transferred to dictionaries and other works of reference. When this happens, more emphasis can be put on analyzing the form and composition of the reading passages. The teacher's control of reading will diminish, focusing more on textual analysis as less translation comes to be needed. Practice in reading techniques, such as scanning and skimming, should be included. Comparisons between Swedish and sign language should be made from the very first grade.

Junior level

At this level the pupils must

- Learn to read and develop their reading ability on the basis of the language they have acquired before starting school.

- Get into the habit of acquiring knowledge, experience, stimulus etc. by reading modern and less modern picturebooks, nursery and other rhymes, poetry, stories and tales, children's books, children's non-fiction and newspapers and magazines.

- Be encouraged, by playing with words and meanings and talking about form and content, to observe and reflect on different ways of building up texts.

- Learn to use proper lists and reference works.

- Learn to present messages, poems, stories and tales of their own making etc. in various ways for purposes of information, amusement and involvement.

- Be acquainted with poems, tales, stories etc.

- Have an opportunity of conversing about events, situations, personal experiences and problems, e.g. conversing with classmates and teachers about what they read: summarizing the content, describing characters and events, any problems and conflicts, drawing conclusions etc.

- Have an opportunity of testing value and attitudes concerning, for example, sex roles, race and violence as reflected by books, newspapers, comics etc.

- Learn to use school and public libraries.

Intermediate level

At this level, over and above the activities specified for junior level, the pupils must

- Develop their ability to read and ponder reading passages of different kinds.

- Read books for children and young persons which will put their own circumstances and existential questions into perspective and give them a knowledge of the world they are living in.

- Learn to make use of non-fiction written for children and young persons, and also of handbooks relating to relevant interests and cognitive needs.

- Develop their ability in the course of conversation to analyse and scrutinize the way in which reading passages of various kinds, comics and other mass literature included, are related to the reality they can observe or otherwise learn about.

- Get into the habit of using reference works, word lists and dictionaries as an aid to their studies.

- Learn librarianship and bookmanship in a practical fashion in the school library.

- Be encouraged during the school day to utilise and develop school library services to pupils and staff and to compile reportages, newspapers, poetry collections etc.

Senior level

At this level, over and above the activities specified for junior and intermediate levels, the pupils must

- Develop their interest in and capacity for using literature as a source of knowledge about the world they are living in and as a means of putting their own circumstances and existential questions into perspective. A wide selection of literature must include poetry, novels, short stories, non-fiction and other reading passages shedding light on phenomena, circumstances and human relations in such contexts as the home, school, leisure and working life.

- Learn to adapt their mode of reading to the nature of the reading passage and their purpose in reading it.

- Develop their ability to observe and reflect on different ways of building up texts, so that form and content will contribute towards the purpose of the text.

- Develop their ability both independently and by talking to others, to analyze and critically scrutinize reading passages of different kinds, including comics and other mass literature.

- Learn to see how values concerning, for example, nationality, social status, sex roles and vocational roles are reflected by reading passages and how our own expectations and values govern the way in which we interpret what we read.

- Get into the habit of independently using word lists, dictionaries, catalogues and reference works as well as the school and public libraries.

Studies of mass media

Pupils at all levels must

- Use newspapers, television programmes and films as a source of information about events, people and existential questions in various social contexts.

- In conjunction with other subjects, produce and discuss film strips, videograms or comics, newspapers or films etc. in order to document facts, provide information, encourage debate or provide amusement.

- Acquire a knowledge of the social role of mass media in connection with a critical appraisal of the way in which they depict events, circumstances or problems.

- Material in Danish or Norwegian is to be included in the mass media studies, so as to enable the pupils to view current issues in a Nordic perspective and to accustom them to reading the languages of the neighbouring countries.

Writing

All levels

Pupils must be encouraged to express themselves in writing, even if the result is not grammatically correct. When pupils have spontaneously written messages or used the text telephone, this written activity should not be structured.

Pupils should learn to write correctly, however, when doing teacher-directed written exercises. They must gradually learn to write in agreement with accepted standards of orthography, declension, syntax and vocabulary. To this end they must be given grammar instruction which will enable them to understand the structure of the Swedish language. This more structured written instruction must already begin at junior level. It must be geared to the study of the structure of sign language and Swedish grammar and must be aimed at teaching the basic structure of Swedish words and sentences. The written exercises must be applications of rules at all linguistic levels, from grapheme to text.

The pupils' production of texts should constitute the main item in writing instruction. They must learn to process their texts together with classmates and teachers.

The pupils must learn to use writing as a means of coming into contact with other people. They must relate, inform and describe, through the medium of letters, notice boards and posters, convey news or debate conditions and problems with the aim of exerting influence and bringing about improvements. They must reflect and speculate about personal experience by writing poetry, diaries, letters, narratives, short stories etc.

The pupils must make notes and summaries, process and present in writing the knowledge they have acquired, as well as recording events and decisions by writing working plans, draft documents and minutes of proceedings etc.

Typing practice must fit in naturally with the pupils' other school work.

In addition to the activities already specified for all school levels, work at the various levels also includes the following.

Junior level

The aim of work at junior level is for the pupils

- To learn to print and write "longhand" and to get into the habit of writing distinctly.
- To learn to express thoughts, feelings, opinions and to present observations, questions, information, requests etc. by writing messages, stories, fairy-tales, poems, diaries etc.
- To learn to make their texts distinct and easy to read by dividing up what they write into sentences and paragraphs and by using capital letters and punctuation marks.

Intermediate level

Work at intermediate level should be concentrated on stabilizing and developing the pupils' writing ability. Above all this means that they must develop their ability to express what they mean, whether they are writing factual accounts, fantastic adventure stories and tales or poetic texts in verse or prose.

Work must also continue on imparting clarity of form to the pupils' texts by dividing them into sentences and paragraphs and by making use of capital letters and punctuation marks. The pupils also require continuing support in developing a distinct style of handwriting.

Senior level

Work at senior level is aimed at teaching the pupils to write well enough for writing to be a self-evident and frequently used means of coming into contact with other people and a viable aid to school work.

Above all this means continuing work in order to

- Apply the pupils' growing knowledge of the structure of the Swedish language.
- Express clearly what they mean.
- Adapt the content and form of language to the written situation, i.e. to the purpose of the text and to its intended readers, and at the same time to impart coherent structure to the pupils' written work.

In conjunction with their written output, pupils continue learning to satisfy formal requirements with regard to distinct handwriting, correctness of language and appropriate style, orthography and the observance of accepted standards of punctuation.

Grammar

All levels

In grammar teaching, special importance is attached to comparisons between sign language and Swedish which can improve the pupils' insight and their linguistic confidence.

As part of this work the pupils must

- Observe and discuss the ways in which sign language and Swedish vary from one situation or text to another.

- Compare sign language, spoken language and written language and different ways of drawing, speaking and writing.

- Learn to use such terms as word, letter, sound, vowel, consonant, syllable, stem, ending, word order, sentence, paragraph and punctuation when talking about words and texts.

- Learn the parts of speech, above all the commonest forms of noun, verb and adjective.

- Study the structure of the Swedish language as compared with that of sign language: parts of speech, sentences and clauses.

- Develop their ability to observe and discuss the ways in which sign language and Swedish are used in different connections and for different purposes.

- Investigate usage and linguistic differences and acquire a knowledge of the reasons for such differences: usage in different groups, colloquial language, written language, dialects, official language.

Speech and lipreading

All levels

The pupils must acquire a basic knowledge of the workings of speech, lip reading and the organs of speech.

Pronunciation teaching forms part of the teaching of Swedish and must be based on each individual pupil's aptitudes, must have individualized objectives and must emanate from the concepts and the language which the pupil has mastered.

It is important that other teaching items, e.g. the reading of texts for the sake of their content, should not be combined with pronunciation practice. The pupil is very liable to find such situations conflicting and involving disparate requirements.

The aim of pronunciation teaching must be to give the Pupil a feedback of their speech via vision, hearing or touch.

In the course of pronunciation teaching, the pupils supported by the manual alphabet and signs and with explanations in sign language must be given practice in using their voice and articulation. They must use meaningful sign language in rhythmic units. Special attention should be paid to the possibilities of the pupils having different capacities for using kinesthetic and/or auditive Control of their speech.

ENGLISH

English is included in special school teaching because

- Citizens of a small language area need to know a world language. English is spoken as a mother tongue or lingua franca in extensive areas of the world.

- Pupils must realize that language is expressive of different living conditions, different cultural backgrounds and different conceptual divisions in different countries.

- Proficiency in English will be useful to the pupils in their subsequent educational and vocational activity.

Goals

Through their English studies, the Pupils are primarily to develop skills which will enable them to:

- Read and understand texts of different kinds.
- Use the written language in various forms.

Skills based on hearing and speech must be adapted to the pupils' individual aptitudes. As a result of the instruction, the pupils should also:

- Be willing and prepared to use the English language.
- Acquire a knowledge of and interest in everyday life, working life, social conditions and culture, above all in English-speaking countries.
- Become aware of the importance of English as a vehicle of contact between people in different parts of the world.

Main teaching items—All levels

The primary aim of teaching English to deaf/hearing-impaired pupils is for the pupils to be able to read and understand texts of different kinds and to use simple forms of the written language. Listening and speech exercises must be adapted to the pupils' aptitudes.

Teaching must be based on the pupils reading and writing words, phrases and sentences. The content of their reading passages must be discussed in sign language. Grammar studies must be conducted in sign language.

Instruction should if possible employ sign language from English-speaking countries, especially American Sign Language.

TIME SCHEDULES

Regulations Concerning Time Schedules

Periods per week: The term period per week (ppw) refers to one lesson per week in a particluar grade. The time schedules specify for each level the total number of periods per week allocated for various subjects and groups of subjects. Junior level comprises four grades and the other levels comprise three grades each.

The headmaster decides how the totoal number of periods per week are to be allocated between the grades making up the level in question and, after consulting the working unit conference, the number of periods per week for the subjects constituting the language block. The number of periods per week allotted to the various grades must then be as follows:

Grade	1	2	3	4	5	6	7	8	9	10
ppw	25	28	32	34	34	34	35	34-35	34-35	34-35

The total number of periods per week for grades 8-10 (senior level) must be 103.

Sign language, Swedish, and mathematics must be taught in every grade. English is to be included in every grade from grade 5 onwards. If the school governing body has decided, pursuant to point 13, that English is to be taught from grade 4 onwards or in a superior grade, English is to be taught in every subsequent grade as well.

Optional subjects are to be made available in each of grades 8, 9, and 10 as provided in point 3. In addition to the activities specified in the time schedule, free activities are also to be included at intermediate and senior levels.

JUNIOR LEVEL (grades 1-4)	
Subject	Total Number of Periods/Week
Pictoral studies	4
Physical Education	12
Mathematics	18
Rhythmics/Drama*	6
General Subjects	24
Handicraft	5

Language Block
    Swedish
    Sign Language
	51

Total	120

INTERMEDIATE LEVEL (grades 5-7)	
Subject	Total Number of Periods/Week
Pictoral studies	6
Home Economics	3
Physical Education	9
Mathematics	15
Rhythmics/Drama*	3

General Subjects
    Social Studies
    General Science
	21
	(15)
	(6)

Handicraft	9

Language Block
    Swedish
    Sign Language
    English
	37

Total	103

* Music is also included for hearing pupils with speech and language disturbances.

SENIOR LEVEL (grades 8-10)	
Subject	Total Number of Periods/Week
Child Care	1
Pictoral studies	5
Home Economics	4
Physical Education	9
Mathematics	12
Rhythmics/Drama*	3

General Subjects
    Social Studies
    General Science
	28
	(15)
	(13)

Handicraft	6

Language Block
    Swedish
    Sign Language
    English
	24

Optional Subjects	11
Total	103

Appendix E: Swedish Curriculum

APPENDIX F

DEAF CHILDREN ARE CHILDREN:
The Bonaventura Model for the Conditions of Deaf Children in 1990-2000

THE BASIC ATTITUDES OF BONAVENTURA PARENTS' ORGANIZATION

The primary goal of this memorandum has been to maintain the basic attitudes, which have passed from mouth to mouth from "old parents" to "new parents" within Bonaventura. The reasons for the activity of the Parent Association politically and socially are the basic attitudes we wish parents with deaf children to understand and deal with in order to create the best conditions for their children.

- Deaf children are children
- Deaf children's language is Sign Language
- Deaf children are not ill
- Deaf children become deaf adults
- Deaf children should be together with deaf people
- Deaf children should be together with hearing people
- Parents of deaf children need each other
- The impact of a deaf child is on the family

Deaf children are children

The basic view of Bonaventura is that deaf children are normal children, who cannot hear. Typically they have normal intelligence, and they should have the same opportunities as hearing Danish children to play and learn, to grow up and to become complete and well-functioning adults. Options - both technically and socially - corresponding to their age should be available during their upbringing.

Parents should be allowed to be parents as well. They should not just be teachers and speech-therapists. The parents must understand their continuous right to make decisions concerning their child, and not allow external experts to take over just because of the deafness.

Deaf children's language is Sign Language

It is important for the self-image and identity as human beings to focus on what the children are able to do, and not on their hearing loss or difficulties in speaking Danish. Hearing handicapped children who speak insufficient Danish may easily look upon themselves as less valuable human beings. Sign Language is the language of deaf people. Sign Language is just as genuine a language as Danish is, but it is a visual language, where all the language-information is visual. It is the firm attitude of Bonaventura, that all children with a hearing loss and their respective families should be taught Sign Language. Formerly many people believed that teaching signs would make it more difficult for the deaf child to learn proper Danish.

More likely the opposite is true - the signs make it easier for the children to grasp words and concepts. Sign Language makes it easier for the parents to fulfill a great part of their natural wishes concerning the childhood of their child and future - wishes which parents with hearing children take for granted

Sign Language gives the parents the possibility to communicate with their deaf child in the same way as parents talking to hearing children about practical subjects, small-talk, comfort, wisdom, upbringing etc. Thereby the world of concepts and social behavior is developed corresponding to the age of the child.

Sign Language makes it possible for the deaf children to play on equal terms, to make friends, to compare experiences and to develop socially. Regardless of their degree of hearing loss Sign Language can be used by all hearing impaired children. By being together, the deaf children give strength to each other, and because of that, they dare to join activities for normal hearing children.

Sign Language makes it possible for deaf children to communicate with deaf adults. It is depressing to witness hearing impaired children and adults speaking together orally having immense troubles in understanding each other.

Sign Language makes it possible for the deaf child to learn Danish as far as concepts and speech are concerned. Important elements in future educational possibilities for deaf children are the newly-gained experiences in the field of bilingual education, the Experimental class at The Deaf School, Kastelsvej, Copenhagen, etc.

Sign Language makes it possible for deaf children to receive normal school-teaching on the same level as hearing children, and to sit for the necessary examination.

Sign Language makes it possible for young deaf to get information through the help of an assigned interpreter.

> "If I accept another person's language, I have accepted the person....if I refuse the language, I thereby refuse the person, because the language is a part of the self."

Deaf children are not ill

Very rarely is deafness a kind of disease, which can be cured in a hospital. Bonaventura takes the same line as many deaf: they might be impaired, but they are not HARD of hearing people, and they are not defective hearing people. They have another language: Sign Language, and that is why they look upon themselves as a language minority group. Our deaf children are neither weak nor ill— provided they are given the right conditions during their upbringing. It also means, that we as parents must protest against our children being tested, checked up, observed again and again by different professional people, just because they are deaf.

Deaf children become deaf adults

Deaf children should be viewed in the light of their lifetime and therefore it is essential that Bonaventura and The Danish Federation for the Deaf have a close relationship, so by that the parents can realize the kind of needs their children will have in the future. Furthermore it is very important that all deaf children and their parents should have personal contacts with adult deaf.

Deaf children should be together with deaf people

It is the definite attitude of Bonaventura, that deaf children should be together with other deaf, children as well as adults. That means Bonaventura opposes individual integration of a deaf child or some frail arrangement based upon a few children. Bonaventura advocates the central deaf school as a center of energy and power. Here small children with their families will have counselling, and here the children will be together in school. There ought to be deaf adults employed in all the environments which deaf children are frequenting.

Deaf children should be together with hearing people

There are only few deaf people, and therefore deaf children must know how to manage in society. There are more possibilities for spare time activities, if they can be together with hearing children, and later on most likely our children are going to work among hearing colleagues. But it is hard for a deaf person to be among hearing people, and it is Bonaventura's firm belief that the strength which the deaf children will need for that is acquired through building up a strong identity as deaf and by having a good social relationship with the deaf community. Furthermore is required an obvious - but unfortunately not a natural - consideration from the society in the form of a text-telephone, interpreters etc.

The parents of a deaf child need each other

In order to believe in their own intuition and common sense, the parents of deaf children need each others' support. This intuition and the common sense are also valid for their deaf child - even if the experts the parents meet on their way should disagree. One should think that there were objective, identical instructions for what parents with deaf children should do, instructions they just could carry on. But it is not like that. There are several views on what is good for deaf children, and even professional advisers don't agree on their message.

Like all other groups professional advisers are influenced by their working field. Audiograms, the anatomy of the ear etc. are the focus of the counseling at a Hearing clinic situated at a hospital. At another counseling situation they will focus primarily on the care for the parents and the speaking skill of the child. It is rare to get advice and counseling which applies to the ENTIRE child in the ENTIRE family, with the ultimate purpose that the deaf child and its surroundings should have a good life also when the child becomes an adult.

Talking to the parents, there are still many professionals who never use the word DEAF as a diagnosis. They cling to whatever might be left of the hearing and use a lot of different names, which from a distance seems as irrelevant: Slight hearing damage, marked hearing handicap, hard of hearing, a severe hearing loss, and they try to handle it with hearing-aids, speaking-to-the-ear-technique, etc. "If you as a parent keep on practicing, surely the child will learn to speak." "Oh, Sign language...The child is not *that* bad." By doing so they minimize the existing communication disability and convey to the parents a negative attitude towards deaf, the language and the culture of the deaf, instead of advocating just to accept the deaf child and overcome the communication disability by the use of the child's new mother tongue, Sign language.

Therefore it is important that each parent know, that they are the ones to choose, what they want for their child. "Old parents" possess a wide ranging knowledge and a lot of experiences. Of course the knowledge is subjective, but by collecting information from different sources, new parents can find a standing platform. The important thing is that the choice of the parents is based on a comprehensive and solid knowledge.

The impact of a deaf child is on the family

It is a major change to have a deaf child in a hearing family. It puts a heavy burden on parents, the hearing siblings, friends and acquaintances, and it is obvious that these families need all the support they can get.

It causes the families grief and suffering what they have to get through, and also it entails an enormous amount of hard work. Theoretically all family members ought to learn Sign Language, but very seldom all of them acquire such a high skill in Sign Language for the daily communication to proceed satisfactorily. A lot of impossible situations emerge, where parents have to consider both the deaf child and the hearing children and survive as human beings at the same time.

Parents of some deaf children can expect a daily fight to ensure the child an appropriate school attendance and appropriate activities in their spare time. They must also secure their rights as regards covering additional expenditures, different kind of aids and etc. Public authorities can be tough to deal with.

In return a new and exciting world is opening, a highly promising world for the future of our deaf children and their adult life, and on our way there are a lot of wonderful events with new people, whom we otherwise never would have met.

The Bonaventura can be contacted through Danske Döves Landsförbund, Fensmarksgäde 1, Box 704, DK-2200 Copenhagen N. Denmark

References

Ahlgren, I. (1978) Early linguistic cognitive development of the deaf and hard of hearing. In W.C. Stokoe (Ed.), *American Sign Language in a bilingual bicultural context: Proceedings of the National Symposium on Sign Language Research and Teaching* (pp. 167-172). Silver Spring, Md: National Association of the Deaf.

Ahlgren, I. (1980). *Projektet Tidig språklig kognitive utveckling hos döva och gravt hörselskadade* ('The research project in early linguistic cognitive development of deaf and severely hard of hearing children'). Stockholm University: FoT VI.

Ahlgren, I. (1982). Sign language and the learning of Swedish by deaf children. *School Research Newsletter, 2.* Stockholm: National Board of Education, Division of Research and Development.

Ahlgren, I. (1989). *Swedish conditions: Sign Language in deaf education.* Paper presented at the International Congress of Sign Language Research and Application, Hamburg, Germany, March, 1989.

Ahlgren, I. (1992, Spring). S-languages and W-languages from the learner's perspective. *Sign Post, Journal of the International Sign Language Research Association,* 13-17.

Ahlgren, I. (1994). Sign language as the first language. In I. Ahlgren & Hyltenstam, K. (Eds.), *Bilingualism in Deaf Education: Proceedings of the International Conference on Bilingualism in Deaf Education, Stockholm, Sweden.* International Studies on Sign Language and Communication of the Deaf. Vol. 27. Hamburg, Germany: Signum-Verlag Press.

Ahlström, M. (1991). *Inte en vanlig familj. 'An (un)ordinary family'.* Stiftelsen Familjesamverkan DHB, HRF, SDR.

Ahlström, M. (1994). Personal correspondence, September 29.

Ahlström, M. (In press). [contact Ahlström in Stockholm University Department of Psychology for titles and information about two publications not yet available at the printing of this book].

Akamatsu, C., & Andrews, J. (1993). It takes two to be literate: Literacy interactions between parent and child. *Sign Language Studies, 81,* 333-360.

Allen, T. (1986). Patterns of academic achievement among hearing impaired students: 1974-1983. In A. Schildroth and M. Karchmer, (Eds.). *Deaf children in America.* San Diego: College-Hill Press, 161-206.

Anderson-Logie, J. (1993). *Reading assessment and oral deaf/hard of hearing students. The 1982 Stanford Achievement Test for use with hearing impaired students vs. the reading miscue inventory.* Unpublished master's thesis, York University Department of Education, Ontario, Canada.

Andersson, R. (1994). Second language literacy in deaf students. In I. Ahlgren & Hyltenstam, K. (Eds.), *Bilingualism in Deaf Education: Proceedings of the International Conference on Bilingualism in Deaf Education, Stockholm, Sweden.* International Studies on Sign Language and Communication of the Deaf. Vol. 27. Hamburg, Germany: Signum Press.

Andersson, Y. (1994). Deaf people as a linguistic minority. In I. Ahlgren & Hyltenstam, K. (Eds.), *Bilingualism in Deaf Education: Proceedings of the International Conference on Bilingualism in Deaf Education, Stockholm, Sweden.* International Studies on Sign Language and Communication of the Deaf. Vol. 27. Hamburg, Germany: Signum Press.

Andrews, J., & Covell, J. (1993). Magnet schools: Future bilingual day schools for deaf students. *Deafness: 1993-2013: A Deaf American Monograph,* Vol. 43, pp. 1-10.

Andrews, J., & Taylor, N. (1987). From sign to print: A case study of picture book "reading" between mother and child. *Sign Language Studies, 56,* 261-274.

Armengaud, A., & Armengaud, J. (1979). "Itinéraire" d'un enfant sourd. *Rééducation orthophonique, 17* (107), 265-274.

Axelsson, M. (1994). Second language acquisition. In I. Ahlgren & Hyltenstam, K. (Eds.), *Bilingualism in Deaf Education: Proceedings of the International Conference on Bilingualism in Deaf Education, Stockholm, Sweden.* International Studies on Sign Language and Communication of the Deaf. Vol. 27. Hamburg, Germany: Signum Press.

Bahan, B. (1988). *Deaf culture: A preparation for the mainstream of life.* Keynote speech at the American Society for Deaf Children Convention, Indianapolis, IN, July 1-4. (summarized in *The Endeavor,* July/August, 1988 issue).

Baker, C. (1978). How does "sim-com" fit into a bilingual approach to education? In Stokoe, W. (Ed.), *American Sign Language in a bilingual bicultural context: Proceedings of the National Symposium on Sign Language Research and Teaching.* Silver Spring, Md: National Association of the Deaf.

Balke-Aurell, G. (1989). *The structure of intelligence and changes in intelligence factors in deaf students.* Poster presented at the Third European Conference for Research on Learning and Instruction, Madrid, Spain, September 4-7.

Barnum, M. (1984). In support of bilingual/bicultural education for deaf children. *American Annals of the Deaf, 129* (5), 404-408.

Barrs, M., Ellis, S., Hester, H., & Thomas, A. (1989). *The primary language record*. London: Center for Language in Primary Education.

Battison, R. (1974). Phonological deletion in American Sign Language. *Sign Language Studies, 5,* 1-19.

Battison, R. (1978). *Lexical borrowing in American Sign Language.* Silver Spring, MD: Linstok Press.

Barrs, M., Ellis, S. Hester, H., Thomas, A. (1990) *Patterns of learning.* London: Centre for Language in Primary Education.

Bellugi, U. (1980). Clues from the similarities between signed and spoken language. In Bellugi and Studdert-Kennedy (Eds.), *Signed and spoken language: Biological constraints on linguistic form,* pp. 115-140. Weinheim/Deerfiled Beach, FL: Verlag Chemie.

Bellugi, U. & Fischer, S. (1972). A comparison of sign language and spoken language: Rate and grammatical mechanisms. *Cognition,* (1), 173-200.

Bellugi, U., Fischer, S., & Newkirk, D. (1979). The rate of speaking and signing. In E. Klima & U. Bellugi (Eds.), *The signs of language.* (pp. 181-194). Cambridge. MA: Harvard University Press.

Bellugi, U., & Studdert-Kennedy, M. (Eds.). (1980). *Signed and spoken language: Biological constraints on linguistic form.* Dahlem Konferezen. Weinheim/Deerfield Beach, Fl: Verlag Chemie.

Bergman, B. (1975). Två språk med samma namn! ('Two languages with the same name!') *SDR Kontakt,* vol. 85, no. 10.

Bergman, B. (1977). *Tecknad Svenska.* Stockholm: National Swedish Board of Education.

Bergman, B. (1978, October). Current developments in Sign Language research in Sweden. Supplement to the *British Deaf News.*

Bergman, B. (1979a). *Signed Swedish.* [English version.] Stockholm, Sweden: National Swedish Board of Education.

Bergman, B. (1979b). Dövas teckenspråk - en inledning. ('Deaf Sign Language'). FoT III (43s).

Bergman, B. (1981). *Sign language: The primary language of the deaf minority.* Paper presented at the International Symposium "Communicatie bij doven" Gent-Gentbrugge, November 6-8. (Published in Flemish and English).

Bergman, B. (1982). *Studies in Swedish Sign Language (summary of doctoral dissertation).* Stockholm University Institute of Linguistics.

Bergman, B. (1994). Signed languages. In I. Ahlgren & Hyltenstam, K. (Eds.), *Bilingualism in Deaf Education: Proceedings of the International Conference on Bilingualism in Deaf Education, Stockholm, Sweden.* International Studies on Sign Language and Communication of the Deaf. Vol. 27. Hamburg, Germany: Signum Press.

Bergman, B., & Wallin, L. (1989). *Swedish Sign Language and Society.* Draft of Keynote presentation for THE DEAF WAY conference and festival, July 9-14, Washington, DC. (more recent version appears in Erting, C.J., Johnson, R.C., Smith, D.L., & Snyder, B.D. (Eds.). (1994). *The Deaf Way: Perspectives from the international conference on Deaf culture.* Washington, DC: Gallaudet University Press.)

Bergmann, R. (1994). Teaching sign language as the mother tongue in the education of deaf children in Denmark. In I. Ahlgren & Hyltenstam, K. (Eds.), *Bilingualism in Deaf Education: Proceedings of the International Conference on Bilingualism in Deaf Education, Stockholm, Sweden.* International Studies on Sign Language and Communication of the Deaf. Vol. 27. Hamburg, Germany: Signum Press.

Bienvenu, M. (1994). *Implementation of a bilingual/bicultural program: The obstacles and how to overcome them.* Panel presentation at the 28th Annual Convention of Teachers of English to Speakers of other Languages, Inc. March 8-12. Baltimore, MD.

Brown, H. (1980). *Principles of language learning and teaching.* Englewood Cliffs, N.J.: Prentice-Hall.

Blumenthal-Kelly, A. (1994). Fingerspelling in the interaction between deaf parents and their deaf daughter. In B. Snider (Ed.). *Post-Milan ASL & English Literacy: Issues, Trends, & Research* (pp. 95-104). Washington, DC: Gallaudet University College for Continuing Education.

Boothroyd, A., & Cawkwell, S. (1970). Vibrotactile thresholds in pure tone audiometry. *Acta Otolaryngol, 69,* 381-387.

Bosso, E., & Kuntze, M. Literacy for deaf students: Freire and Macedo's model. In B. Snider (Ed.). *Post-Milan ASL & English Literacy: Issues, Trends, & Research* (pp. 37-44). Washington, DC: Gallaudet University College for Continuing Education.

Bouvet, D. (1983). Bilingual education for deaf children. In W. Stokoe & V. Volterra (Eds.), *Sign Language Research.* Silver Spring, MD: Linstok Press.

Bouvet, D. (1990). *The path to language: Bilingual education for deaf children.* Philadelphia, PA: Multilingual Matters.

Bruner, J. (1983). *Child's talk: Learning to use language.* New York: Norton.

CCE (Gallaudet University College for Continuing Education) (In press). *Inclusion? Defining Quality Education for Deaf and Hard of Hearing Students. Proceedings of a conference at Gallaudet University, Washington, DC, October 26-28, 1994* . Washington, DC: Gallaudet University.

Charrow, V. (1975). Manual English: A Linguist's Viewpoint. *Proceedings of the Congress of the World Federation of the Deaf.* Washington, D.C.: Gallaudet University.

Christersson, G. (1990) *Adam's Bøk.* Stockholm, Sweden: SIH Läromedel.

Collier, V. (1987). Age and rate of acquisition of second language for academic purposes. *TESOL Quarterly, 23,* 509-531.

Collier, V. (1989). How long? A synthesis of research on academic achievement in a second language. *TESOL Quarterly, 23,* 3, 509-531.

Collier, V. (1994). *Promising practices in public schools.* Featured presentation at the 28th Annual Convention of Teachers of English to Speakers of Other Languages. March 11, Baltimore, MD.

Collier, V. (In press). *Promoting academic success for ESL students: Understanding second language acquisition for schooling.* Princeton, NJ: NJ TESOL-Bilingual Educators.

Commission on Education of the Deaf. (1988). *Toward Equality. A Report to the President and the Congress of the United States.* Washington, D.C.: U.S. Government Printing Office.

Corder, S. (1974). Error analysis. In J. Allen & S. Corder (Eds.), *The Edinborough Course in Applied Linguistics,* Vol. 3. Oxford: Oxford University Press.

Corson, H. (1973). *Comparing deaf children of oral deaf parents and deaf children using manual communication with deaf children of hearing parents on academic, social, and communicative functioning.* Unpublished Ph.D. dissertation, Northwestern University.

Crandall, K. (1978). Inflectional morphemes in the manual English of young hearing impaired children and their mothers. *Journal of Speech and Hearing Research, 21,* 372-386.

Cummins, J. (1979). Linguistic interdependence and the educational development of bilingual children. *Review of Educational Research, 49,* 222-251.

Cummins, J. (1980). The entry and exit fallacy in bilingual education. *NABE: The Journal for the National Association for Bilingual Education, 4* (3), 25-29.

Cummins, J. (1981). The role of primary language development in promoting educational success for language minority students. In *Schooling and language minority students: A theoretical framework* (p. 3-49). Los Angeles: California State University, National Evaluation, Dissemination, and Assessment Center.

Cummins, J. (1984). *Bilingualism and special education: Issues in assessment and pedagogy.* Clevedon, England: Multilingual Matters.

Cummins, J., & Danesi, M. (1990). *Heritage Languages.* Montreal, Quebec: Our Schools/Our Selves Educational Foundation.

Cummins, J., & Swain, M. (1986). *Bilingualism in education: Aspects of theory, research, and practice.* Essex, UK: Longman Group UK Limited.

Daniels, M. (1993). ASL as a factor in acquiring English. In W. Stokoe (Ed.). *Sign Language Studies, 78*, p. 23-29.

Davies [currently Mahshie] , S. (1990). *Bilingual education in Sweden and Denmark: Strategies for transition and implementation.* Unpublished report submitted to the World Institute on Disability.

Davies, S. (1991a) Two languages for deaf children in Sweden and Denmark. *IDEAS Portfolio II.* New York: Rehabilitation International and the World Institute on Disabilities.

Davies, S. (1991b). *The transition toward Bilingual education of deaf children in Sweden and Denmark: Perspectives on Language.* . Gallaudet Research Institute Occasional Paper 91-1. Washington, D.C.: Gallaudet University. (Also in 1991 *Sign Language Studies, 71*, pp. 169-195.)

Davies, S. (1992a, May). What they've learned: Revolutionizing education for deaf children. In *ASL and Deaf Culture/Minority Achievement and Mulitcultural Programs Newsletter of KDES/MSSD.*

Davies, S. (1992b). *Bilingual education in Sweden and Denmark.* Presentation at the Deaf Children in Two Worlds: Bilingual/Bicultural conference. Madonna University, Livonia, Michigan, October 24. (Also presented as part of the Sign Language Lecture Series, Gallaudet University, Washington, DC, October, 14.)

Davies, S. (1993). *Educating deaf children bilingually: Insights and applications from Sweden and Denmark.* Paper presented at the Convention of American Instructors of the Deaf/Conference of Educational Administrators Serving the Deaf, Baltimore, MD, June 26-30.

Davies, S. (1994a). *A first language: Whose choice is it?* Keynote presentation at the "ASL and English: A Winning Team" Conference, Greensboro, North Carolina, August 7-9, 1994.

Davies, S. (1994b). Attributes for Success: Attitudes and practices that facilitate the transition toward bilingualism in the education in Sweden and Denmark. In I. Ahlgren & Hyltenstam, K. (Eds.), *Bilingualism in Deaf Education: Proceedings of the International Conference on Bilingualism in Deaf Education, Stockholm, Sweden.* International Studies on Sign Language and Communication of the Deaf. Vol. 27. Hamburg, Germany: Signum Press.

De Avila E. & Duncan, S. (1980). The language minority child: A psychological, linguistic, and social analysis. In J.F. Alatis (Ed.), *Georgetown University Round Table on Languages and Linguistics, 1980: Current issues in bilingual education* (pp. 104-137). Washington, DC: Georgetown University Press.

Diaz, R. (1983). Thought and two languages: The impact of bilingualism on cognitive development. *Review of review of research in education, 10,* 23-54.

Doorn, D., Serna, I., Espinosa, C., Moore, K. & Hough, R. (1994). *Mentoring and recording bilingual children's language and literacy development.* Panel presentation at TESOL '94, Baltimore, MD., March 8-12.

Dyer, S. (1992). *Hermeneutics and deaf education: An analysis and critique of theories of language and communication.* Unpublished masters' thesis, University of Washington, Department of Speech Communication.

Edenås, C. & Battison, R. (1989). *Improving sign language skills of hearing teachers: A Swedish experiment.* In Erting, C.J., Johnson, R.C., Smith, D.L., & Snyder, B.D. (Eds.). (1994). *The Deaf Way: Perspectives from the international conference on Deaf culture.* Washington, DC: Gallaudet University Press.

Eilers, R., Vergara, D., Oller, K., & Balkany, T. (1992). Evaluating hearing impaired children's usage of tactual vocorders. In A. Risberg, Felicetti, A., Plant, G., & Spens, K-E. (Eds.) (1992) *Proceedings of the second international conference on tactile aids, hearing aids, and cochlear implants.* Stockholm, Sweden: KTH Department of Speech Communication and Music Acoustics.

Engberg-Pedersen, E. (1993). *Space in Danish Sign Language: the semantics and morphosyntax of the use of space in a visual language.* Hamburg: Signum-Verlag.

Erber, N. (1982). *Auditory Training.* Washington, DC: The AG Bell Assoc. for the Deaf, Inc.

Erber, N. (1972). Speech-envelope cues as an acoustic aid to lipreading for profoundly deaf children. Journal of Speech and Hearing Research, 15, 413-422.

Erting, C. (1978). *Language Policy and Deaf Ethnicity.* Sign Language Studies, 19, 139-152.

Erting, C. (1986). Sociocultural dimensions of deaf education: Belief systems and communicative interaction. *Sign Language Studies 19,* 139-152.

Erting, C. (1992a). Deafness and literacy: Why can't Sam read? *Sign Language Studies, 75,* 97-112.

Erting, C. (1992b). Partnerships for change: Creating new possible worlds for deaf children and their families. In *Bilingual considerations in the education of deaf students: ASL and English.* Washington, DC: Gallaudet University College for Continuing Education.

Erting, C. (1994). *Deafness, communication, social identity: Ethnography in a preschool for deaf children.* Burtonsville, MD: Linstok.

Erting, C., Prezioso, C., & Hynes, M. (1990). The interactional context of deaf mother-infant communication. In V. Volterra nd C. Erting (Eds.), *From gesture to language in hearing and deaf children* (pp. 97-106). Washington, DC: Gallaudet University Press. (Originally published in 1990 by Springer-Verlag: Berlin, Heidelberg.)

Erting, L., & Pfau, J. (1994). Becoming bilingual: Facilitating English literacy development using ASL in preschool. In B. Snider (Ed.). *Post-Milan ASL & English Literacy: Issues, Trends, & Research* (pp. 135-150). Washington, DC: Gallaudet University College for Continuing Education.

Erting, L., & Stone, R. (1992). Deaf and hearing team teaching: learning from each other. In *Bilingual considerations in the education of deaf students: ASL and English.* Washington, DC: Gallaudet University College for Continuing Education.

Evans, C., Evans, G., Hope, T., Zimmer, K. (1994). *Meeting the Challenge: Deaf and hearing children's language needs.* Paper presented at the 1994 Conference of Teachers of English to Speakers of Other Languages, March 8-12, Baltimore, MD.

Evans, C., Zimmer, K., Murray, D. (1994). *Discovering with words and signs.* Winnipeg, Canada: The Sign Talk Children's Centre.

Ewoldt, C. (1983). Research Reports - Text Simplification: A solution with many problems. *Perspectives for teachers of the hearing impaired, 1,* 23-25.

Ewoldt, C. (1985). A descriptive study of the development of literacy of young deaf children. In R. Kreschmer (Ed.). *Volta Review* [Special Edition]. *Learning to write and writing to learn.* Volume 87, 109-126.

Ewoldt, C. (1990). The early literacy development of deaf children. In D. Moores & K. Meadow-Orlans (Eds.). *Research in educational and developmental aspects of deafness.* Washington, DC: Gallaudet Press.

Ewoldt, C. (1993, Winter) Language and literacy from a deaf perspective. *Teachers networking: The whole language newsletter, 13,* p. 3-5.

Ewoldt, C., & Saulnier, K. (1992). *Engaging in literacy: A longitudinal study of three- to seven-year-old deaf participants* (Final Report). Washington, D.C.: Gallaudet University Center for Studies in Education and Human Development.

Fisher, C. (1994). *The Writers' Workshop.* Washington, DC: Gallaudet University Pre-College Programs.

Fletcher, R. (1991). *Walking Trees.* Portsmouth, NH: Heinemann.

Foss Ahldén, H., & Lundin, K. (In press). *Process signing/Process writing.* Stockholm, Sweden: SIH Läromedel.

Freeman, Y., & Freeman, D. (1992). *Whole language for second language learners.* Portsmouth, N.H.: Heinemann.

Frishberg, N. (1975). From arbitrariness to iconicity: Historical changes in American Sign Language. *Language, 51,* 696-719.

Frishberg, N. (1976). *Some aspects of historical development of signs in ASL.* Unpublished doctoral dissertation, University of California, San Diego.

Furth, H.G. (1966). A comparison of reading test norms of deaf and hearing children. *American Annals of the Deaf, 111,* 2. p. 461-462.

Gallimore, L. (1994). *Bilingual/Bicultural education in a multicultural society.* Presentation at, "Especially for parents: Everything you always wanted to know about bilingual/bicultural education but were afraid to ask." Gallaudet University, October 26, 1994.

Gee, J., & Goodhart, W. (1988). ASL and the biological capacity for language. In M. Strong (Ed.), *Language learning and deafness.* New York: Cambridge University Press.

Gee, J., & Mounty, J.L. (1986). *Nativization, variability, and style shifting in the sign language development of deaf or hearing children.* A paper presented at the Conference on Theoretical Issues in Sign Language Research, June, University of Rochester.

Gengel, R., & Foust, K. (1975). Some implications of listening levels for speech reception by sensorineural hearing-impaired children. *Language, Speech, and Hearing Services in Schools, 6,* 14-20.

Gentile, A. (1972). *Academic Achievement Test Results of a National Testing Program for Hearing Impaired Students: 1971.* Washington, D.C.: Gallaudet College Office of Demographic Studies, Series D. No 9.

Gerner de Garcia, B. (1992). Diversity in deaf education: What we can learn from bilingual and ESL education. In S. Martin and R. Mobley (eds.), *Proceedings of the First International Symposium on Teacher Education in Deafness.* Washington, DC: Gallaudet University.

Gibbons, P. (1991). *Learning to learn in a second language.* Portsmouth, N.H.: Heinemann.

Goodhart, W. (1984). *Morphological complexity, ASL, and the acquisition of sign language in deaf children.* Unpublished doctoral dissertation, Boston University, Boston, MA.

Goodman, K. (1986). *What's whole in whole language?* Portsmouth, N.H.: Heinemann.

Goodstein, A. (1988). *Fall, 1988 Admissions/Enrollment Summary.* Unpublished Memorandum. Washington, D.C.: Gallaudet University.

Graney, S. (1994). *Where does speech fit in to a bilingual approach?* Presentation at, "Especially for parents: Everything you always wanted to know about bilingual/bicultural education but were afraid to ask. Gallaudet University, October 26, 1994.

Grosjean, F. (1977). The perception of rate in spoken and sign languages. *Journal of Psychological Research, 22,* 408-413.

Grosjean, F. (1992). The bilingual and bicultural person in the hearing and deaf world. *Sign Language Studies, 77,* 307-320.

Hakuta, K. (1986). *Mirror of language: The debate on bilingualism.* New York: Basic Books.

Hakuta, K. (1990, Spring). *Bilingualism and bilingual education: A research perspective.* Occasional papers in bilingual education, 1. Washington, DC: National Clearinghouse for Bilingual Education.

Hansen, B. (1975). Varieties in Danish Sign Language and grammatical features of the original sign language. *Sign Language Studies, 8,* 249-256.

Hansen, B. (1980a). Research on Danish Sign Language and its impact on the deaf community in Denmark. In C. Baker and R. Battison (Eds.), *Sign language and the deaf community.* Silver Spring, MD: National Association of the Deaf.

Hansen, B. (1980b). *Aspects of Deafness and Total Communication in Denmark.* Copenhagen: Centre for Total Communication.

Hansen, B. (1987). Sign Language and bilingualism: A focus on an experimental approach to the teaching of deaf children in Denmark. In J. Kyle (Ed.) *Sign and School.* Clevedon, UK: Multilingual Matters, Ltd.

Hansen, B. (1989). *Trends in the progress toward bilingual education of deaf children in Denmark.* Copenhagen, DK: Center for Total Communication.

Hansen, B. (1990). Trend in the progress toward bilingual education for deaf children in Denmark. In S. Prillwitz & T. Vollhaber (Eds.), *Sign language research and application* (pp. 51-64). Hamburg, Germany: SIGNUM-Press.

Hansen, B. (1994). Personal correspondence, September 4.

Hansen B., & Kjær-Sörenson, R. (1976). *The sign language of deaf children in Denmark.* Copenhagen: The School for the Deaf.

Hanson, V. & Padden, C. (1988). The use of videodisc interactive technology for bilingual instruction in American Sign Language and English. *Quarterly Newsletter of the Laboratory of Comparative Human Cognition, 10,* 92-95.

Heiling, K. (1989). *Has anything happened in twenty years? Achievement level of Swedish deaf eighth graders in the sixties and now—a comparison.* Unpublished transcript of a lecture held at various schools in the U.S., September, 1989. Malmö, Sweden: Lund University Department of Educational Research.

Heiling, K. (1990). *Education of the deaf in Sweden.* Occasional paper written for a Lewis and Clark College (Portland, Oregon) world-wide survey of deaf education (working draft).

Heiling, K. (1993). The development of knowledge in deaf children [English translation of paper presented in Swedish] at the Nordisk Barnaudiologisk Kurs/Kongress, Örebro, Sweden, June 13-16.

Heiling, K. (1993a). *[Deaf children's development in a temporal perspective: Academic achievement levels and social processes.] Döva Barns utveckling i ett tidsperspektiv, Kunskapsbuva icg sicuaka processer.* Doctoral dissertation, Lund University Department of Educational Research, Malmö, Sweden.

Heiling, K. (1993b). *A psychologist's perspective.* Presentation at the conference on education of deaf children with cochlear implants: A new challenge for the teacher. Luxemborg, November 4-6.

Hester, H. (1990). *Patterns for learning.* London: Centre for Language in Primary Education.

Holdaway, D. (1979). *The foundations of literacy.* Portsmouth, NH: Heinemann.

Hoffmeister, R. (1990). ASL and its implications for education. In H.Bornstein (Ed.), *Manual Communication in America* (pp. 81-107). Washington, DC: Gallaudet University Press.

Hoffmeister, R. (1992). *Why MCE won't work: ASL forms inside signed English* (Working paper 16). Boston: Boston University, Center for the Study of Communication and Deafness.

Hoffmeister, R. (1994) Metalinguistic skills in Deaf Children: Knowledge of synonyms and antonyms in ASL. In B Snider (Ed.), *Post Milan ASL and English Literacy: Issues, Trends, and Research.* p. 151-176. Washington, DC: Gallaudet University College for Continuing Education.

Hoffmeister, R., & Bahan, B. (1991, February). *The relationship between American Sign Language, signed English and sim com in the language development of deaf children or why MCE won't work.* Paper presented at the annual conference of American College Educators of the Hearing Impaired, Jekyll Island, GA.

Hom, C., Laldee, J., Treesberg, J., Venturini, D., Venturini, P., & Wilson, A. (1994). *Parent perspectives on bilingual/bicultural education.* Panel presentation at, "Especially for parents: Everything you always wanted to know about bilingual/bicultural education but were afraid to ask." Gallaudet University, October 26, 1994.

Hudelson, S. (1984). Kan yu ret an rayt en Ingles: Children become literate in English as a second language. *TESOL Quarterly, 18* (2), 221-238.

Hudelson, S. (1987). The role of native language literacy in the education of language minority children. *Language Arts, 64,* (8), 827-841.

Hyltenstam, K. (1992). Non-native features of native speakers. In R. Harris, (Ed.), *Cognitive processing in bilinguals.* Amsterdam: Elsevier.

ISD position paper committee (In press). *Indiana School for the Deaf Bilingual/bicultural philosophy position paper.* Indianapolis, IN: Indiana School for the Deaf.

Israelite, J., Ewoldt, C., & Hoffmeister, R. (1989). *A review of the literature on the effective use of native sign language on the acquisition of the majority language by hearing impaired students.* Toronto, Canada: MGS Publication Services.

Jankowski, K. (1994). Reflections upon Milan with an eye to the future. In B Snider (Ed.), *Post Milan ASL and English Literacy: Issues, Trends, and Research.* p. 1-36. Washington, DC: Gallaudet University College for Continuing Education.

Johnson, R.C., & Cohen, O. (Eds.). (1994). *Implications and complications for Deaf students of the full inclusion movement: A joint publication by the Conference of Educational Administrartors Serving the Deaf and the Gallaudet Research Institute.* Gallaudet Reserach Institute Occasional Paper 94-2. Washington, DC: Galllaudet University.

Johnson, R.E. (1994). Possible influences on bilingualism in early ASL acquisition. *Teaching English to deaf and second language students: 1994.*

Johnson, R.E., & Erting, C. (1989). Ethnicity and socialization in a classroom for deaf children. In C. Lucas (Ed.). *The sociolinguistics of the Deaf community.* New York: Academic Press.

Johnson, R.E., Liddell, S., & Erting, C. (1989) *Unlocking the Curriculum: Principles for Achieving Access in Deaf Education.* Gallaudet Research Institute Working/Occasional Paper Series, 89-3. Washington, D.C.: Gallaudet Research Institute.

Kampfe, C., & Turecheck, A. (1987). Reading achievement of pre-lingually deaf students and its relationship to parental method of communication: a review of the literature. *American Annals of the Deaf, 132*(1), 11-15.

Kannapell, B. (1974). Bilingual Education: A New direction in the Education of the Deaf. *The Deaf American, 26*(10), 9-15.

Kannapell, B. (1978). Linguistic and Sociolinguistic Perspectives on Sign Systems for Educating Deaf Children: Toward a True Bilingual Approach. In: Frank Caccamise and Doin Hicks (eds.). *American Sign Language in a Bilingual, Bicultural Context. The proceedings of the Second National Symposium on Sign Language Research and Teaching.* Silver Spring, MD: national Association of the Deaf, 219-232.

Kelly, E., Bloechle, L., Esp, B., Van Hove, A., Ingrassia, M., Morseon, K. (1994). *Measuring ASL and written English development of deaf students.* Paper presented at the 1994 Conference of Teachers of English to Speakers of Other Languages, March 8-12, Baltimore, MD.

Klima, E., & Bellugi, U. (1979). *The signs of language.* Cambridge, MA: Harvard University Press.

Kluwin, T. (1981). A rationale for modifying classroom signing systems. *Sign Language Studies, 31,* 179-187.

Krashen, S. (1973). Laterlization, language learning, and the critical period: Some new evidence. *Language Learning, 23,* 63-74.

Krashen, S. (1981). *Second language acquisition and second language learning.* Oxford: Pergamon Press.

Krashen, S. (1982). *Principles and practice in second language acquisition.* Oxford: Pergamon Press

Krashen, S. (1991, Spring). *Bilingual education: A focus on current research.* Occasional papers in bilingual education, 3.

Krashen, S. (1994). *Beyond the input hypothesis.* Keynote presentation at the 28th Annual Convention of Teachers of English to Speakers of Other Languages, March 12, Baltimore, MD.

Krashen, S., & Biber, D. (1988). *On course: Bilingual education's success in California.* Sacramento, CA: California Association for Bilingual Education.

Kuntze, M. (1992). *Bilingual/bicultural approaches to deaf education and language policy.* Paper presented to the Fourth International conference on Theoretical Issues in Sign Language Research, San Diego.

Kuntze, L. (1994, August). Personal correspondence.

Lane, H. (1992a). *The mask of benevolence: Disabling the Deaf community.* New York: Alfred A Knopf.

Lane, H. (1992b). Educating the American Sign Language speaking minority of the United States: A paper prepared for the Commission on the Education of the Deaf. In S. Wilcox (Ed.), *Academic Acceptance of American Sign Language.* SLS Monographs. Burtonsville, MD: Linstok Press.

Lane, H. (1994) The cochlear implant controversy. In *World Federation of the Deaf News, 2-3.*

Lane, H., & Grosjean, F. (1980). *Recent perspectives on ASL.* Hillsdale, NJ: Lawrence Erlbaum Associates.

Lenneberg, E. (1967). *Biological foundations of language.* New York: Wiley.

Leone, B., et al. (1992). *TESOL statement on the role of bilingual education in the education of children in the United States.* Alexandria, VA: Teachers of English to Speakers of Other Languages.

Lewis, W. (Ed.). (1994). *Bilingual teaching of deaf children: Extracts from four reports, 1983-1993.* Aalborg, Denmark, SÖ: Döveskolernes Materialelaboratorium (DM).

Lewis, W., Madsen, J., Ravn, T. (1992). To-sproget Döveundervisning 4 ('Bilingual teaching of the deaf, 4'). Aalborg, Denmark: Döveskolernes Materialelaboratorium (DM).

Liddell, S., & Johnson, R. (1992). Toward theoretically sound practices in deaf education. In *Bilingual considerations in the education of deaf students: ASL and English,* pp. 8-34. Washington, DC: Gallaudet University College for Continuing Education.

Lightbown, P. (1983). Exploring relationships between developmental and instructional sequences in L2 acquisition. In H. Seliger & M. Long, (EDS.), *Classroom-oriented research in second language acquisition.* Rowley, Mass.: Newbury House.

Ling, D. (1976). *Speech and the hearing impaired child: Theory and practice.* Washington, DC: The AG Bell Assoc. for the Deaf, Inc.

Ling, D., & Nash, S. (1975). Threshold variations in repeated audiograms. *Volta Review, 77,* 97-104.

Long, M. (1990). Maturational constraints on language development. *Studies in Second Language Acquisition, 12* (3).

Livingston, S. (1983). Levels of development in the language of deaf children: ASL grammatical processes, Signed English structures, semantic features. *Sign Language Studies 40,* 193-286.

Lucas, C. (1989). English only: Bad news for the deaf community. *EPIC Events: Newsletter of the English Plus Information Clearinghouse 1.6:* 3.

Lucas, C., & Valli, C. (1988). Language contact in the Deaf community: Linguistic change and contact. *Proceedings of the 16th Conference on New Ways of Analyzing Variation. Texas Language Forum 30.* Austin: University of Texas, Department of Linguistics, pp. 209-215.

Luetke-Stahlman, B. (1988). Documenting syntactically and semantically incomplete bimodal input to hearing-impaired subjects. *American Annals of the Deaf, 133,* 230-234.

Maestas y Moores, J. (1980). Early linguistic environments: Interactions of deaf parents with their infants. *Sign Language Studies, 26,* 1-13.

McGarr, N. (1980). Evaluation of speech in intermediate school-aged deaf children. In J. Subtelny (Ed.). *Speech assessment and speech improvement for the hearing impaired.* Washington, DC: AG Bell, pp. 45-66.

McIntire, M. (1977). The acquisition of American Sign Language hand configurations. *Sign Language Studies, 16,* 247-266.

McIntire, M., & Groode, J. (1982). Hello, goodbye and what happens in between. In C. Erting & R. Meisefeier (Eds.), *Deaf children and the socialization process* (Working papers #1). Washington, DC: Gallaudet University.

Mace, A., Wallace, K., Whan, M., & Stelmachoica, P. (1991). Relevant factors in the identification of hearing loss. *Ear and Hearing, 12,* 287-293.

Magnet School of the Deaf Core Committee. (1994). *Magnet School of the Deaf: The charter school application.* Denver: Colorado Association of the Deaf.

Mahshie, J. (In press). The use of sensory aids for teaching speech to children who are deaf. In K. Spens & G. Plant (Eds.). *Speech Communication and Profound Deafness.* London: Whrrr Publishers.

Mahshie, S. (1994). *A look at 'sim-com' through new eyes.* Presentation at a workshop entitled, "Especially for parents: Everything you always wanted to know about bilingual/bicultural education but were afraid to ask." Gallaudet University, October 26, 1994.

Mahshie, S. (1995). *Educating Deaf Children Bilingually.* Washington, DC: Gallaudet University Pre-College Programs.

Markowicz, H., & Woodward, J. (1982). Language and the maintenance of ethnic boundaries in the deaf community. In J. Woodward (Ed.) *How you gonna get to heaven if you can't talk to Jesus: On depathologizing deafness.* Silver Spring, MD: TJ Publishers.

Marmor, G., & Petitto, L. (1979). Simultaneous communication in the classroom: How well is English grammar represented? *Sign Language Studies, 23,* 99-136.

Mas, C. (1994). Bilingual education for the deaf in France. In I. Ahlgren & Hyltenstam, K. (Eds.), *Bilingualism in Deaf Education: Proceedings of the International Conference on Bilingualism in Deaf Education, Stockholm, Sweden.* International Studies on Sign Language and Communication of the Deaf. Vol. 27. Hamburg, Germany: Signum Press.

Mather, S. (1989). Visually-oriented teaching strategies with deaf preschool children. In *The Sociolinguistics of the Deaf Community*, C. Lucas, (Ed.). San Diego:Academic Press.

Mather, S., & Mitchell, R. (1994). Communication abuse: A sociolinguistic perspective. In B. Snider (Ed.). *Post-Milan ASL & English Literacy: Issues, Trends, & Research* (pp. 117-134). Washington, DC: Gallaudet University College for Continuing Education.

Maxwell, M. (1983). Language acquisition in a deaf child of deaf parents: Speech, sign variations, and print variations. In K. Nelson, (Ed.), *Children's language, 4,* 283-297. Hillsdale, NJ: Erlbaum.

Maxwell, M. (1984). A deaf child's natural development of literacy. *Sign Language Studies, 44,* 191-224.

Maxwell, M. (1987). The acquisition of English bound morphemes in sign form. *Sign Language Studies, 57,* 323-352.

Maxwell, M. (1988). The alphabetic principle and fingerspelling. *Sign Language Studies 44,* 191-224.

Meadow, K. (1966). *The effect of early manual communication and family climate on the deaf child's development.* Unpublished doctoral dissertation. University of California, Berkeley.

Meadow, K. (1967). *The effect of early manual communication and family climate on the deaf child's development.* Unpublished doctoral dissertation, University of California, Berkeley.

Meadow, K. (1968). Early manual communication in relation to the deaf child's intellectual, social, and communicative functioning. *American Annals of the Deaf, 113,* 29-41.

Meadow, K. (1972). Sociolinguistics, Sign Language and the Deaf Sub-Culture. In: T.J. O'Rourke (ed.). *Psycholinguistics and Total Communication: The State of the Art.* Washington, D.C.: American Annals of the Deaf, pp. 19-33.

Meadow, K., Greenberg, M., Erting, C., & Carmichael, H. (1981). Interactions of deaf mothers and deaf preschool children: Comparisons with three other groups of deaf and hearing dyads. *American Annals of the Deaf, 126,* 454-468.

Miller-Nomeland, M., & Gillespie, S. (1993) *The KDES Deaf Studies Curriculum Guide.* Washington, D.C.: Gallaudet University Pre-College Programs.

Moores, D. (1987). *Educating the Deaf.* (3rd ed.). Boston: Houghton-Mifflin.

Mounty, J. (1986). *Nativization and the acquisition of American Sign Language.* Unpublished doctoral dissertation, Boston, University.

Mozzer-Mather, S. (1990). *A strategy to improve deaf student's writing through the use of glosses of signed narratives.* Gallaudet Research Institute Working Paper 90-4. Washington, DC: Gallaudet Research Institute.

Newport, E., & Meier, R. (1986). Acquisition of American Sign Language. In D.I. Slobin (Ed.), *The cross-linguistic study of language acquisition.* Hillsdale, NJ: Lawrence Erlbaum Associates, Vol. 1, pt. 2.

Newport, E., & Supalla, T. (1987). *A critical period effect in the acquisition of a primary language.* Unpublished manuscript.

Nielsen, B. (1991). *Use of the OS-400 reading test.* Working paper, Kastelsvej School, Copenhagen, Denmark.

Nober, E. (1964). Pseudoauditory bone-conduction thresholds. *Journal of Speech and Hearing Disorders, 29* 469-476.

Nordén, K, Tvingstedt, A-L., & Heiling, K. (1989). *A longitudinal study of deaf children.* Occasional paper, Lund University Department of Educational Research, Malmö, Sweden.

Nover, S. (1994). *Full inclusion for deaf students: An ethnographic perspective.* Keynote presentation at "Inclusion? Defining Quality Education for Deaf and Hard of Hearing Students." Gallaudet University, Washington, DC, October 26-28.

Nover, S., & Ruiz, R. (1992, June). *ASL and language planning in deaf education.* Paper presented at the "ASL in Schools: Policies and Curriculum" conference, October 28-30, Gallaudet University, Washington, DC.

Nover, S. & Ruiz, R. (Eds.). (In press). *Becoming Bi-Bi: A workshop for personal and Deaf school transitions.* Proceedings of the First Annual Bilingual Bicultural Conference, Indiana School for the Deaf, April 28 - May 1, 1994. San Diego: DawnSign Press

Olsen, R., & Leone, B. (1994). Sociocultural processes in academic, cognitive, and language development. In *TESOL Matters, 4,* 3.

O'Neill, J., & Oyer, H. (1981). *Visual communication for the hard of hearing: History, research, methods.* Englewood Cliffs, NJ: Prentice Hall, Inc.

Osberger, M., & McGarr, N. (1982). Speech production characteristics of the hearing impaired. *Speech and Language: Advances in Basic Research and Practice, Vol. 8,* pp. 221-283.

Ovando, C.J. & Collier, V.P. (1995, in press). *Bilingual and ESL classrooms: Teaching in multicultural contexts, 2nd edition.* NY: McGraw-Hill.

Padden, C. (1980). Deaf community and the culture of Deaf people. In C. Baker and R. Battison (Eds.), *Sign language and the Deaf community.* Silver Spring, MD: National Association of the Deaf.

Padden, C. (1990a). Response to *Unlocking the Curriculum* in *Access: Language in Deaf Education.* Gallaudet Research Institute Occasional Paper 90-1 (pp. 25-29). Washington DC: Gallaudet University.

Padden, C. (1990b). The acquisition of fingerspelling by deaf children. In P. Siple & S. Fisher (Eds.). *Theoretical issues in sign language research,* Vol. 2: Psychology, 191-210. Chicago: University of Chicago Press.

Padden, C., & LeMaster, B. (1985). An alphabet on hand: The acquisition of fingerspelling in deaf children. *Sign Language Studies, 47,* 161-172.

Paul, P. (1987). Perspective on using American Sign Language to teach English as a second language. *Teaching English to deaf and second language students, 5,* 10-16.

Paul, P. (1988). American Sign Language and English: A Bilingual Minority-Language Immersion Program. *CAID-News'N'Notes.* Washington, D.C.: Conference of American Instructors of the Deaf.

Paulston, C. (1974). *Language-Learning Theory for Language Planning.* Papers in Applied Linguistics, Bilingual Education Series.

Paulston, C. (1977). Research. *Bilingual education: Current perspectives, 2.* Washington, DC: Center for Applied Linguistics.

Petitto, L. (1987). On the autonomy of language and gesture: Evidence from the acquisition of personal pronouns in American Sign Language. *Cognition, 27,* 1-52.

Petitto, L. (1993a). On the otogenetic requirements for early language acquisition. In B. de Boysson-Bardies, S. de Schonen, P. Jusczyk, P. MacNeilage, and J. Morton (Eds.). *Developmental neurocognition: Speech and face processing in the first year of life.* Kluwer Academic Press. 365-383.

Petitto, L. (1993b). *On the linguistic status of natural signed languages.* Manuscript distributed by the cognitive Neuroscience Laboratory for Language, Sign, and Cognitive Studies, Department of Psychology, McGill, University. Montréal, Québec, Canada.

Petitto, L. (1994a). Personal correspondence, March 11.

Petitto, L. (1994b). On the equipotentiality of signed and spoken language in early language ontogeny: What we have learned since the Congress of Milan. In B. Snider (Ed.), *Post-Milan ASL & English Literacy: Issues, Trends, & Research* Keynote address (pp. 195-224). Washington, DC: Gallaudet University College for Continuing Education.

Pettito, L., & Bellugi, U. (1988). Spatial cognition and brain organization: Clues from the acquisition of a language in space. In J. Stiles-Davis, M. Kritchevsky, & U. Bellugi (Eds.), *Spatial cognition: Brain bases and development.* Hillsdale, NJ: Lawrence Erlbaum Associates.

Petitto, L., & Marentette, P. (1991). Babbling in the manual mode: Evidence for the ontogeny of language. *Science, 251,* 1493-1496.

Philip, M. (1990). The Learning Center for Deaf Children: The Transition from a Total Communication School. In *Bilingual, Bicultural Considerations in the Education of Deaf Students: ASL and English.,* pp. 46-47. Washington, DC: Gallaudet University College for Continuing Education.

Philip, M. (1994). *What is all the hoopla about first and second languages?* Keynote presentation at the "ASL and English: A Winning Team" Conference, Greensboro, North Carolina, August 7-9, 1994.

Preisler, G. (1983). *Deaf children in communication: A study of communicative strategies used by deaf children in social interactions.* Stockholm, Sweden: University of Stockholm Institute of Psychology.

Preisler, G. (1990). Development of communication in deaf infants. *Augmentative and Alternative Communication, 6*(2), 122-123.

Quigley, S., & Paul, P. (1984). ASL and ESL? *Topics in Early Childhood Special Education, 3,* 17-26.

Raimondo, B. (1994a). *A hearing parents' perspective on raising a deaf child.* Presentation at the French-American Conference on Bilingual Education, Kendall Demonstration Elementary School, Washington, DC., April 20.

Raimondo, B.(1994b). *The American Society for Deaf Children Testimony on the reauthorization of the Individuals with Disabilities Education Act.* Submitted to the U.S. House Subcommittee on Select Education and Civil Rights, April 28, Washington, DC.

Ramsey, C. (1993). *A Description of Classroom Discourse and Literacy Learning among Deaf Elementary Students in a Mainstreaming Program.* Unpublished doctoral dissertation. Universtiy of California, Berkeley, CA.

Ramsey, C. & Canty, M. (1994). *Inclusion meets education: Can deaf children learn in any classroom?* Presentation at "Inclusion? Defining Quality Education for Deaf and Hard of Hearing Students." Gallaudet University, Washington, DC, October 26-28.

Rawlings. B., & Jensema, C. (1977). *Two studies of the families of hearing impaired children.* Office of Demographic Studies, Series R., No. 5. Washington, DC: Gallaudet College.

Risberg, A. (1968). Visual aids for speech correction, *The American Annals of the Deaf 113,*2, 178-194.

Risberg, A., Algefors, E., & Boberg, G. (1975). *Measurement of frequency-discrimination ability of severely and profoundly hearing-impaired children.* STL-QPSR 2-3. Stockholm: Royal Institute of Technology, pp. 40-48.

Risberg, A., Felicetti, A., Plant, G., & Spens, K-E. (Eds.) (1992) *Proceedings of the second international conference on tactile aids, hearing aids, and cochlear implants.* Stockholm, Sweden: KTH Department of Speech Communication and Music Acoustics.

Robert, M. & Weiss, A. (1988). *The Innovation Formula: How Organizations Turn Change into Opportunity.* New York: Harper and Row.

Rodda, M. & Grove, C. (1987). *Language, cognition, and deafness.* Hillsdale, NJ: Lawrence Erlbaum.

Salander, S., & Svedenfors, B. (1993). Standardprov i svenska ht 92, åk 10 Östervångsskolan. ('Standardized achievement test in Swedish, fall semester, 92, grade 10, Ostervang School'). Nordisk Tidskrift för Dövundervishengen ('Nordic journal for the Education of the Deaf'), N. 1, pp. 41-41.

Saylor, P. (1992). A Hearing Teacher's Changing Role in Deaf Education. *Harvard Educational Review, 62, (4),* 519-534.

Schildroth, A. (1994). The Annual Survey of Hearing Impaired Children and Youth. Unpublished figures. Washington, DC: Gallaudet Research Institute.

Schildroth, A. & Karchmer, M. (1986). *Deaf Children in America.* Boston: Little, Brown, & Co. Inc.

Schiff-Myers, N., Djukic, J., McGovern-Lawler, J., & Perez, D. (1993). Assessment considerations in the evaluation of second-language learners: A case study. *Exceptional Children, 60,* (3), pp. 237-248.

Schleper, D. (1992). *PreReading Strategies.* Washington, DC: Gallaudet University.

Serna, I. (1994). *Mentoring and recording bilingual children's languages and literacy development.* Panel presentation at the 1994 Conference of Teachers of English to Speakers of Other Languages, March 8-12, Baltimore, MD.

Serna, I., & Hudelson, S. (1993). Becoming a writer of Spanish and English. *The quarterly of the National Writing Project & the Center for the Study of Writing and Literacy, 15,* (1), 1-5.

Singleton, J., & Newport, E. (1987). *When learners surpass their models: The acquisition of American Sign Language from impoverished input.* Paper presented at the conference of the Society for Research in Child Development, New Orleans, LA.

Skutnabb-Kangas, T. (1994). Linguistic human rights: A prerequisite for bilingualism. In I. Ahlgren & Hyltenstam, K. (Eds.), *Bilingualism in Deaf Education: Proceedings of the International Conference on Bilingualism in Deaf Education, Stockholm, Sweden.* International Studies on Sign Language and Communication of the Deaf. Vol. 27. Hamburg, Germany: Signum Press.

Sörensen, R. Kjær. (1975). Indications of regular syntax in deaf school children's sign language. *Sign Language Studies, 8,* 257-263.

Sörensen, R. Kjær, & Hansen, B. (1976). *The sign language of deaf children.* Copenhagen, Denmark: The Center for Total Communication.

Sörensen, R. Kjær, Lewis, W., Lutz, H., & Sonnichsen, J. (1983). *To-sproget döveundervisning* [Bilingual teaching of the deaf]. Copenhagen: Kobenhavns Kommunale skolevaesen.

Sörensen, R. Kjær, Lewis, W., Lutz, H., & Ravn, T. (1984). *Tø-sproget döveundervisning, 2* [Bilingual teaching of the deaf, 2]. Copenhagen: Kobenhavns Kommunale skolevaesen. Forsogsafdelingen.

Sörensen, R. Kjaer, Lewis, W., Lutz, H., & Ravn, T. (1988). *To-sproget döveundervisning, 3* [Bilingual teaching of the deaf, 3]. Copenhagen: Skolen pa Kastelsvej, Kobenhavns.

Spencer, E., Bodner-Johnson, B., & Gutfreund, M. (1992). Interacting with infants with a hearing loss: What can we learn from mothers who are deaf? *Journal of Early Intervention, 16*(1), 64-78.

Stevens, R. (1976). Children's Language Should be Learned and not Taught. *Sign Language Studies, 11,* 97-108.

Stevens, R. (1980). Education in Schools for Deaf Children. In: C. Baker and R. Battison (eds.). *Sign Language and the Deaf Community.* Silver Spring, MD: National Association of the Deaf, 177-191.

Stokoe, W. (1960). *The calculus of structure.* Washington, DC: Gallaudet Press.

Stokoe, W. (Ed.). (1978). *Proceedings of the National Symposium on Sign Language Research and Teaching.* Silver Spring, Md: National Association of the Deaf.

Stokoe, W., Casterline, C., & Croneberg, D. (1965). *A dictionary of American Sign Language on linguistic principles.* Silver Spring: Linstok Press.

Strong, M. (1988). A bilingual approach to the education of young deaf children: ASL and English. In M. Strong (Ed.), *Language Learning and Deafness* (pp. 113-129). Cambridge: Cambridge University Press.

Strong, M. (In press). A review of bilingual/bicultural programs for deaf children. *American Annals of the Deaf*, (forthcoming in the April, 1995, Issue).

Stuckless, E. & Birch, J. (1966). The Influence of Early Manual Communication on the Linguistic Development of Deaf Children. *American Annals of the Deaf, 111*, 425-460, 499-504.

Supalla, S. (1986). Manually coded English: The modality question in signed language development. Unpublished masters thesis. University of Illinois, Urbana-Champaign.

Supplement to the General Section of the Swedish Compulsory School Curriculum. (1983). Stockholm, Sweden: Swedish National Board of Education.

Svartholm, K. (1990) Dövas Två Språklära, Svenska för Döva ("The Two Languages of the Deaf"). Stockholm: National Board of Education.

Svartholm, K. (1993, Winter). Bilingual Education for the Deaf in Sweden. Sign Language Studies, 81, pp. 291-332.

Svartholm, K. (1994). Second language learning in the deaf. In I. Ahlgren & Hyltenstam, K. (Eds.), *Bilingualism in Deaf Education: Proceedings of the International Conference on Bilingualism in Deaf Education, Stockholm, Sweden*. International Studies on Sign Language and Communication of the Deaf. Vol. 27. Hamburg, Germany: Signum Press.

Swedish Ministry of Education, Government Bill 1980/81:100, Supplement 12, p. 297.

Swisher, M.V. (1984). Signed input of hearing mothers to deaf children. Language Learning, 34, 69-86.

Thomas, R. (1989, October). *The role of parents in transition*. Paper presented at the Southeast Regional Conference, Southeast Regional Institute on Deafness, Clearwater, Fl.

Thompson, M. & Thompson, G. (1981). Mainstreaming: A closer look. *American Annals of the Deaf, 111*, 425-460, 499-504.

Titus, A. (In press). *Bilingual/Bicultural education for Deaf students: Managing the change through transition workshops*. Indianapolis, IN: Indiana School for the Deaf.

Titus, A. (In press). *Communication issues on campus*. Indianapolis, IN: Indiana School for the Deaf.

Toby, E. & Hasenstab, S. (1991). Effects of a nucleus multi-channel cochlear implant upon speech production in children. *Ear and Hearing, 12, (4)* supplement.

Educating Deaf Children Bilingually

Treesberg, J. (1988). Let the Deaf be Deaf (A hearing mother within the Deaf revolution). *Washington Post Health Section*, April 5.

Treesberg, J. (1991). Death of a strong Deaf. *The Nation*, vol. 252, no. 5, pp. 154-158.

Trybus, R. (1980). What the Stanford Achievement Test has to say about the reading abilities of deaf children. In H. Reynolds & C. Williams (Eds.). *Proceedings of the Gallaudet Conference on reading in relation to deafness.* Washington, DC: Gallaudet College.

Trybus, R., & Jensema, C. (1978). *Communication patterns and education achievement of hearing impaired students.* Office of Demographic Studies, series T, No. 2. Washington, DC: Gallaudet College.

Trybus, R., & Karchmer, M. (1977). School achievement levels of hearing impaired children: 1977 national data on achievement status and growth patterns. *American Annals of the Deaf, 122,* 62-69.

Tucker, J. (1994). *Recent developments at Maryland School for the Deaf.* Presentation at the French-American Conference on Bilingual Education. Kendall Demonstration Elementary School, Washington, DC. February 28.

Tvingstedt, A. (1985). *Hard of hearing pupils in the regular school system.* Paper presented at the Symposium on Education of Handicapped Children and Youth, Brioni, Yugoslavia, 1985. Reprinted by the Swedish National Board of Education (Stockholm).

Tvingstedt, A. & Hartman, K. (1989). The hard of hearing pupil in the classroom. In H. Hartmann & K. Hartmann (Eds.) *Hard of Hearing Pupils in Regular Schools.* (Published Proceedings of International Conference on Hard of Hearing Pupils in Regular Schools, Berlin, 1988).

Valli, C., & Lucas, C. (1992). *Linguistics of American Sign Language: A resource text for ASL users.* Washington, DC: Gallaudet University Press.

Van Cleve, J. (Ed.). (1986). *Encyclopedia of Deaf People & Deafness.* NY: McGraw-Hill.

Vestberg-Rasmussen, P. (1973). Evaluation of reading achievement of deaf children. In E. Kampp (Ed.). *Evaluation of hearing handicapped children.* Proceedings of the Fifth Danavox Symposium, Ebeltoft, Denmark.

Vorih, L. & Rosier, P. 1978). Rock Point Community School: An example of a Navajo-English bilingual elementary school program. *TESOL Quarterly, 12,* 263-269.

Vygotsky, L. (1962). *Thought and language.* Cambridge, MA: MIT Press.

Wallin, L. (1988) *Deaf People and Bilingualism. In R. Ojala (ed.), Proceedings, X World Congress of the World Federation of the Deaf.* Espoo, Finland: The Finnish Association of the Deaf.

Weaver, C. (1990). *Understanding whole language: From principles to practice.* Portsmouth, NH: Heinemann.

Wedenberg, E. (1951). Auditory training of deaf and hard of hearing children. *Acta Otolayngol. Suppl.,* 94.

Weinstock, J., & Erting, L. (1994). *Facilitating ASL and English literacy development in preschool.* A presentation at the "ASL and English: A Winning Team" Conference, Greensboro, North Carolina, August 7-9, 1994.

Wilbur, R. (1987). *American Sign Language: Linguistic & applied dimensions.* San Diego: College Hill Press.

Wilding-Daez, Minnie Mae. (1994). Deaf characters in children's books: How are they perceived? In *Post-Milan: ASL and English Literacy: Issues, Trends, and Research.* Washington, D.C.:Gallaudet University College for Continuing Education.

Wischmeyer, L. (1994). *Supporting the young bilingual child: Strategies for hearing parents and professionals.* A presentation at the "ASL and English: A Winning Team" Conference, Greensboro, North Carolina, August 7-9, 1994.

Woodward, J. (1978). Some Sociolinguistic Problems in the Implementation of Bilingual Education for Deaf Students. In Stokoe, W. (Ed.). *Proceedings of the National Symposium on Sign Language Research and Teaching.* Silver Spring, Md: National Association of the Deaf.

Woodward, J., Allen, T., & Schildroth, A. (1988) In M. Strong (Ed.) *Language, Learning, and Deafness.* Cambridge: Cambridge University Press.

Woodward, M. (1957, December). Linguistic methodology in lipreading research. *John Tracy Clinic Research Papers,* IV.